NORTHCLIFFE

Viscount Northcliffe

From a Painting by Tablo

Northcliffe

NORTHCLIFFE

BRITAIN'S MAN
OF POWER

By WILLIAM E. CARSON
Former American Correspondent
of the Northcliffe Newspapers

NEW YORK
DODGE PUBLISHING CO.
33d St. — EIGHTH AVENUE — 34th St.

92
N P136

Copyright, 1918, by Dodge Publishing Company

CONTENTS

LIST OF ILLUSTRATIONS

* These illustrations are used through the courtesy of *Everybody's Magazine.*

FOREWORD

An ancient saying, " The hand that wields
the pen holds the scepter of government,"
has been strikingly illustrated in the career
of Lord Northcliffe. Essentially a product
of this age, he represents that vast development of modern times which controls governments and sways nations,—the power of
the press.

A genius in business-building, world-
famous as a journalist and newspaper
owner, Lord Northcliffe has become the
most forceful and dominating figure in
British public life. He was, above all else,
the first man to arouse the English people
to the importance of strenuous and efficient
methods in conducting war. Defying a tem-
pest of execration, he has exposed abuses,
smashed cabinets, unmade and made prime
ministers, dethroned popular idols, and re-
lentlessly pursued and attacked the national
tolerance of muddling—at once the Englishman's habit and, strangely enough, his

boast. In short, anything that threatened
or interfered with an efficient prosecution of
the war has been a target for Lord Northcliffe's deadly journalistic lance. Through
his great newspapers, especially *The Times*
and the *Daily Mail,* he has kept Britain
alert to all that menaces the nation's safety
and prestige.

When the real story of the war is written,
historians will probably call it a war of
highly organized armies, machine guns, and
artillery; but the men who have had to do
with the business of it will always know
that the leaders of the people who maintained efficiency behind the armies filled a
rôle as important as that of the ablest generals. For a leader to arouse public opinion, and even oppose it, for the country's
good, has often needed a higher degree of
courage than to lead a regiment where
shells were falling. Such has been the mission of Lord Northcliffe, who, by his fearless efforts in promoting national efficiency,
has revolutionized the whole system of government in Great Britain, with far-reaching
effect on the destinies of the British Empire. Through the power of his press he

convinced the nation that it was necessary to discard old ideas and to adopt a new system in which the business man would take the place of the politician. The fact that such a system was born amidst the musty traditions of British statesmanship makes it seem almost miraculous.

In this eventful revolution of war time Lord Northcliffe has taken the foremost part. No other man has had so much to do with the commercialization of government and in bringing about a general recognition of the theory that good government is simply good business. Even while the war is raging he has foreseen that a special preparation is needed for the colossal adjustments of peace. He has also warned the world that unprecedented social changes are impending, and that the spread of Socialism is certain to cause vast upheavals in which existing institutions will undergo many alterations.

The achievements of Lord Northcliffe in war time form only a part of his story. No other man who has scaled the heights of fame in this age has made the ascent so quickly as he, and none has had such a marvelous career. Indeed, the story of his rise from obscurity to eminence is so full of strange experiences and amazing events that it reads almost like fiction. From its beginning to the present time it is a dramatic blending of romance and hard facts.

Owing to his frequent visits to this country and the consequent publicity that he has received, the name of this enterprising journalist, publisher, and public man has become familiar to large numbers of Americans who admire his versatility, originality, brilliant achievements, and efficient methods. He is unique among Englishmen in having a thorough knowledge of our national aims and problems, his outlook being far more American than English, although he remains as British as ever and is the most ardent of patriots.

As the head of the British War Mission to the United States, Lord Northcliffe, in 1917, became even more widely known by reason of the magnitude of his work. The enormous expenditures that he supervised totaled eighty million dollars a week, and covered all commodities needed by Great Britain for war purposes. Under his control were ten thousand men, engaged in buying war supplies. His efficient methods made his work such a pronounced success that on his return to England he was thanked by the king and received the higher title of viscount.

Such is the man whose services to his country have been recognized the world over and who is undoubtedly the most interesting figure in public life at the present time. His strenuous personality and stirring deeds have incidentally created a widespread demand for a complete account of his eventful career.

While it is true that in recent years many newspaper and magazine articles describing this remarkable genius have appeared, yet none has presented a correct picture of him. The reason is that he is far too big to be compressed into a single article, for volumes could be devoted to his achievements.

In England the real Northcliffe is as little known as in America, which probably accounts for the conflicting views of him that exist there. By his own countrymen he has been called the most dangerous of men and the sanest of men, an unselfish patriot and a self-seeking egotist. He is to-day the most admired and the most vilified man in Great Britain.

The only way in which his true character can be revealed is by relating what he has accomplished and summing up the results. When that is done, the real Northcliffe emerges to replace the Northcliffe of imagination. Such is the object of the present volume, which tells the complete story of Lord Northcliffe's career and enables him to be seen as he actually is.

The author, it may be added, was associated with the great journalist for many years, and belonged to the staff of his newspaper organization. Before and behind the scenes, the writer had an opportunity to study this masterful man, and to observe, at close range, his achievements in the business, social, and political realms. The resulting story reveals the true Lord Northcliffe, portrays his life of endeavor, and shows him to be animated by patriotic motives and high ideals in his public enterprises. The career of Lord Northcliffe, in short, supplies the best answer to all questions as to his place in the world to-day.

I

WHEN ENGLAND AWOKE

" You shall not tell the people the truth," the British censor had, in effect, declared. The British press was muzzled.

Incompetency's idea was to lie smugly behind a wall of secrecy. To tell the truth to the people who were paying the price of war with blood and treasure would be treason.

It was England's darkest hour.

At that fateful time, in the spring of 1915, when the war outlook was serious and the safety of the Allies trembled in the balance, one man in England had the courage to speak out. But for this single fearless, unselfish patriot, England's doom would have been sealed because she would have awakened too late from her torpor and complacency.

While the British censor was suppressing the facts and incompetency rejoiced, this

man was preparing to attack the mighty
fortress of official incapacity, to scale its
walls, and to plant the standard of efficiency
on its highest tower.

The man who displayed this unflinching
courage was Lord Northcliffe, unquestionably Britain's strongest man and a power
in the British Empire. As the owner of
The Times,—the famous " Thunderer,"—the
Daily Mail, and other great English newspapers, he represents the mightiest force of
the press. As a leader he represents the
great mass of the British people.

Undaunted by threats and unintimidated
by warnings from high officials, Lord Northcliffe prepared to launch a swift attack and
reveal the truth about the war to the British public, which remained blissfully igno-
rant in regard to what was taking place at
the front.

On May 20, 1915, Lord Northcliffe called
his editors together at the *Daily Mail* office
in London, to discuss this momentous question.

As they assembled in the council room,
he entered briskly and took his seat at the
head of the table. A determined-looking

man of middle age, heavy shouldered and strongly built, with massive head pushed forward aggressively, his keen eyes took in every one at a glance. His greeting was terse. Even a stranger would have instantly perceived that this forceful man whose magnetic personality filled the room was a leader of men.

In his hand Lord Northcliffe held a dispatch that contained alarming news from the front. Before him was spread an editorial based on this dispatch. When he had read both to his editors, it was necessary to decide whether the news should be published. To submit it to the censor would mean its suppression. To publish it without the censor's permission would be a serious offense, as Lord Northcliffe very well knew. Anything, in short, that might tend to unsettle public confidence and give comfort to the enemy, would be practically equivalent to treason.

It was a tense and dramatic moment. While consternation reigned among his staff, Lord Northcliffe rose and paced the room, swiftly reviewing the situation. The risk, he knew, was great. Could he face a possible accusation of treason by publishing the truth, and at the same time withstand the consequences of daring to attack the idol of the British public—Kitchener of Khartoum? Northcliffe, who looked grave and felt even more grave than he looked, realized that it would be taking desperate chances, but his sense of patriotism outweighed all other considerations.

Somewhat brusquely he asked his experienced colleagues for their opinions and listened to what they had to say. It was a daring move that he had in mind, and as they expressed their views, they watched his face anxiously to see which way he would decide. Was Northcliffe strong enough to make the great decision which might lead to the most brilliant achievement in his career? Was he willing to risk going down himself that Britain might be saved?

Lord Northcliffe paced the length of the table and back once. His mind was made up. He wasted no words in argument.

Turning to his editors, he said firmly and decisively: " That news must go into the paper. We have got to save England; the people must know the truth."

One of his editors, a veteran journalist whom he esteemed highly, ventured to suggest that a delay might be advisable, that there was great personal risk attached to this action.

" There is no other alternative," reiterated Northcliffe, " the people must have the facts."

Addressing his managing editor, he gave his final instructions. " The editorial is right," he said. " Send the paper to press."

The next day, May 21, the British public was astounded when the *Daily Mail* published an editorial entitled: " The Tragedy of the Shells; Kitchener's Grave Error," in which were embodied the main facts contained in the news dispatch. It was fearlessly declared that Lord Kitchener, the idol of the nation, then absolute czar of the War Department, was sacrificing thousands of British soldiers by supplying the army with shells which were almost useless in fighting the Germans. Despite repeated warnings, he had persisted in sending out shrapnel when what was vitally needed was high-explosive shells that would blast a passage through the German trenches and entanglements and enable the British troops to advance.

The editorial declared, moreover, that while huge explosive shells fired from the German "Big Berthas" and wide-mouthed howitzers plowed their way through the British defenses, causing frightful slaughter, the British were compelled to reply with shrapnel, which was almost as ineffective as blowing peas against a concrete wall.

All England was in an uproar when the *Daily Mail* editorial appeared. Rival newspapers attacked Lord Northcliffe with great bitterness, declaring that the statements concerning Kitchener were maliciously false. The government was urged to suppress the offending newspaper and arrest its editors, who were declared to be guilty of treason. So great was the nation's faith in its idol, Kitchener, that the general public refused to believe the charges, and Northcliffe found himself, for the time being, the most detested and execrated man in England.

A mob in a London street howled at the *Daily Mail* and shouted for vengeance; members of the London Stock Exchange, to show their indignation, ceremoniously burned copies of the "scurrilous sheet," as they termed the newspaper. Meetings were held all over England, at which people solemnly pledged themselves never again to read any of the Northcliffe journals. Feeling rose to such a pitch, that threats were made against the newspaper owner's life, and an armed guard was found necessary for his protection.

Through all this commotion, however, Lord Northcliffe did not lose his head, but remained cool and undaunted, because he knew that his statements were based on facts. He was also sustained by a high sense of duty and patriotism; for if there is one dominating impulse in the character of this man, it is his intense love for England. With him it masters every other consideration. That is why he had determined to speak out when he discovered that Kitchener's policy was bringing his beloved country to the verge of defeat, regardless of the attacks which he knew would follow.

At that critical time, when an avalanche of censure and abuse was sweeping down on the *Daily Mail* and its owner, Will Irwin, the American correspondent, called

on Northcliffe and found him grave but
resolute. "How is the circulation of the
Daily Mail?" asked Irwin. "It's increasing," replied Northcliffe; and he added ironically: "I suppose they're buying copies to
burn them."

But the situation was serious. Advertisers began to drop off, rival newspapers
increased their attacks, and Northcliffe was
urged to retract his statements. Instead of
doing so he caused the charges made by the
Daily Mail to be repeated in *The Times.*
Replying to his critics, he declared in the
Daily Mail: "All that we have hitherto
written will be justified in the near future."
Meanwhile, the government, realizing that
what the *Daily Mail* had said was perfectly
true, took no action toward punishing its
fearless owner for having published the
truth.

To understand the precise state of affairs,
it is necessary to get an idea of the war
situation in May, 1915. At that time the
Allies were in a serious predicament. The
French had been forced back at several
points, and a break followed by another and
possibly a successful drive on Paris seemed

inevitable. All hopes of holding Gallipoli were being abandoned by the British, the Turks, under German leadership, having rendered the campaign there abortive. On the eastern front the Russians were in retreat at some important points, their forces badly disorganized. Modern strategy, as carried out by the Germans, had thus challenged the highest skill of the generals who led the armies of France and Russia.

But to the British public this disheartening array of facts seemed of minor importance, because the London newspapers were continually filled with reports of British victories in Belgium. "British Forces Advance"; "Huns in Retreat"—so read their headlines from day to day. The French might retire, likewise the Russians, but what mattered that as long as one British soldier was a match for three Germans and the enemy shrank from facing British bayonets?

It was such stuff as this that was fed to the British public in the spring of 1915, when the censor made everybody in England happy by putting his blue pencil through almost anything in the shape of bad news. Thus the impression became gen-

eral that the war would soon be over, that
the Kaiser, like Napoleon, would be shipped
to St. Helena, and that British " Tommies "
would be seen parading victoriously in the
streets of Berlin.

That was what the man in the street believed. But there were some people in England who shook their heads and silently
doubted all these glowing stories. Men who
had returned from the front whispered that
all was not well. That there was some foundation for this pessimism the sequel will
show.

In April, 1915, Lord Northcliffe received
a dispatch from a military expert, who represented his newspapers at the front, in
which it was stated that the British army
was endangered by an alarming shortage of
high-explosive shells. How this dispatch
managed to pass the French and British
lines has never been told.

A practical newspaperman and well qualified to fill the position of " star reporter,"
Lord Northcliffe sometimes investigates important matters himself instead of relying
on some one else for his information. On
this occasion the situation was so critical

that he decided, with his characteristic thoroughness, to ascertain the facts by acting as his own reporter. With this object, he secretly crossed the English Channel and visited the British headquarters, where he learned that the statements contained in the dispatch were substantially correct. Having secured this information he returned to London, where he immediately held a council at the *Daily Mail* office. Then followed the publication of the news, with all the sensational developments already described.

It was a daring feat to print the news and to defy the censorship. It was even more serious to defy British public opinion by attacking Lord Kitchener, the grim, taciturn hero of the nation, who allowed no interference with the War Department which he governed with absolute power. And yet, much as he admired Kitchener, Northcliffe had taken the right course.

The truth is that while Lord Kitchener had done some magnificent work in raising a great British army at the beginning of the war and getting it over to France, yet he was not a military expert versed in the science of modern warfare. He was undoubtedly a good business man and a wonderful organizer, but he had gained most of his experience in India and Egypt, and his long absences from Europe had kept him out of touch with the latest developments in arms and ammunition.

As time went on a realization of these facts began to dawn in England. Protests from the front regarding the deficiency of high-explosive shells began to reach the heads of the British government in such volume that the truth could no longer be suppressed, and the censorship was lifted. It was then discovered that Lord Northcliffe had been right after all. Rival newspapers at once learned the facts from their own correspondents, and instead of continuing to denounce the fearless journalist as a traitor they repeated what the *Daily Mail* and *The Times* had already said.

Whatever satisfaction Northcliffe might have derived from this vindication did not obscure his original purpose in making his charges. While the British troops, as the result of the outcry that was raised, were promptly supplied with suitable munitions, there still remained the difficulty that they were not getting enough. Northcliffe at once seized the opportunity to make himself heard again.

The war, he declared, was being mismanaged because the War Department was conducted on inefficient lines. That department, he insisted, should be restricted to its proper military business of raising and training soldiers, while the purely industrial business of producing munitions should be ·kept distinctly apart. And so it came to pass. Stirred by the arguments of the Northcliffe press, the British government created a new cabinet post, Minister of Munitions, and David Lloyd George, a man of the people and admired by the masses, a practical man as well as a statesman, was selected to fill the position.

Here again was seen how dominating is Northcliffe's sense of patriotism. He had ruthlessly attacked Kitchener, whom his newspapers had once lauded as a national hero, because the head of the War Department had proved inefficient. He now gave his utmost support to Lloyd George, the Welsh radical, whose political ideas he had bitterly opposed. As Chancellor of the Exchequer Lloyd George had done good work, and Northcliffe was ready to admit that he was the right man to head the munitions department.

Raising the slogan, " Shells and More Shells! " Lloyd George, backed by the Northcliffe press, speedily aroused the people of England to the importance of supplying what was needed, and in an inconceivably short time Great Britain was covered with a network of arsenals and munition factories. Northcliffe had correctly interpreted the spirit of the English people. They were ready to make any sacrifice that would lead to victory, but they required direction.

Hundreds of thousands of girls and women, drawn from all classes, including school-teachers, stenographers, domestic servants, and salesgirls, and even the daughters of the well-to-do, all anxious to " do their bit," were soon engaged in munition manufacturing. They had to be taught the use of deadly explosives. It meant the establishment of a new school of labor. To accommodate these workers new towns of temporary houses, similar to our military camps, were put up in the country districts. Huge government factories were built in the important industrial centers, and correlated industries were enlisted in the work of supplying munitions. In many ways the whole face of England became entirely changed. Efficient organization replaced haphazard effort, enthusiasm supplanted indifference, and for the first time the people of Great Britain set themselves, with heart and soul, to the big task of winning the war.

Northcliffe had at last won his fight for high-explosive shells. The factories, indeed, were turning them out rapidly and in such vast quantities that Britain was able not only to supply her own army and heap up reserves for any imaginable contingency, but also to supply her allies.

This, in brief, is the story of the momentous decision made by Northcliffe on the twentieth of May, 1915, which undoubtedly saved England from defeat. When properly equipped the British army, instead of remaining supinely on the defensive, made a general advance, scattering the German shock battalions and giving the cause

of the Allies a new impetus. The French,
taking heart again, drove back the Germans
at several points, while the Russians, catching the same spirit, cleared the enemy out
of the territories on the eastern front and
kept them out until the débâcle of German
intrigue made chaos of Russia.

Momentous as Northcliffe's decision had
been to the Allied cause, it was of equal
importance to himself. His stand against
official incompetency had been the supreme
test of his power. If he had failed he
would not only have met his Waterloo, but
would probably have sunk in influence and
reputation to the level of a common scold.
With success, however, there came the realization that this man, fearless of consequences, had struck only because his country was in danger and that by his action he
had saved England. Northcliffe's power
was thus confirmed, and he came to the
front again as the unofficial spokesman of
the British people and the mandate of their
will.

How far-reaching Northcliffe's influence
ultimately became was strikingly shown in
the autumn of 1916, when he brought about

the most effective political revolution ever wrought through a group of newspapers —the overthrow of the Asquith government. The story can be told in a few words.

The Liberal party, which had been in power under Mr. Asquith when war was declared, and the coalition government which succeeded it, under the same leadership, were both found to be wanting in the strength and energy required to pilot Great Britain safely in a time of grave national peril. A scholarly politician of the old school, Mr. Asquith was clearly not an ideal leader, and therefore when it became evident that the government was mismanaging the war, Northcliffe, thundering with Jovian authority, demanded the appointment of an efficient, compact war cabinet that could get things done. So great was the force of public sentiment aroused by his newspapers that Mr. Asquith was at last compelled to retire, giving place to Lloyd George as prime minister.

In accordance with Northcliffe's advice, given editorially, the new premier at once formed a cabinet of practical, self-made

business men who were experts in their own
lines, such as Sir Joseph Maclay, the Shipping Controller, once captain of a tramp
steamer; Lord Devonport, Food Controller,
who started life as clerk in a grocery and
now owns a chain of retail stores; and Sir
Albert Stanley, once an American citizen,
who became a traction expert in the United
States before returning to England, the
land of his birth.

Even more interesting than these notable
men is Sir Eric Geddes, who was appointed
Deputy-General of Munitions. A self-made
man who had gained a variety of experiences in all parts of the world, from railroad builder to business manager, he took
over the production of rifles, small arms,
transport vehicles, machine guns, and salvage. He introduced a system by which
empty brass cartridge cases were used over
a dozen times. He reorganized and reconstructed the railway system in northern
France, which required the building of a
terminal as large as the Grand Central Terminal in New York City for the efficient
handling of trains.

Under Geddes' direction, lines were built

so expeditiously that when the Germans re-
treated on the Somme in 1917 the railway
followed right behind them. He also took
charge of the canals in northern France,
over which are moved each month hundreds of thousands of tons of freight and
thousands of wounded men. He gathered a corps of experts in all branches,
knowing that for an expert job it was requi-
site to get experts and leave them alone.
After the Battle of Jutland there was dis-
satisfaction with the management of the
British fleet and a demand for younger and
redder blood. Geddes was then made Controller of the Navy, and subsequently he
was appointed First Lord of the Admiralty.

The appointment of experts to manage
the various departments of the government
put an end to a system of compromise and
delay. Northcliffe himself regarded this innovation as the most sweeping change that
had taken place in British public life since
the passage of the Reform Bill in the reign
of William IV. Stripped of its glamour,
the whole episode was merely a translation
of efficient team work into terms of national
administration. In other words, it was the

case of a practical man applying practical methods during a national crisis. The result has been that to-day in no Allied country have business talents been so completely commandeered as in England. With the exception of the premier,—Lloyd George,—Mr. Balfour, and a few other seasoned office holders, the cabinet is practically a board of directors that can deal with any problem of cost and distribution that happens to come up.

The remarkable achievement of Northcliffe in saving England in the dark hours of 1915, and his subsequent triumph in forcing the retirement of a British prime minister who had proved to be inefficient, were only in keeping with the whole course of his journalistic career. For the last twenty years he has been at the forefront of every national movement, some of the most important of which he started himself. In looking backward no one can fail to be impressed by the almost prophetic insight that has characterized most of his agitations.

Probably the first of his important battles, and one which sounded the keynote of his subsequent career, was in the days of the

South African War, when the embattled
Boer farmers were out-fighting, out-maneu-
vering, and out-generaling the British forces.
At that time, when he was plain Alfred
Harmsworth, the enterprising journalist,
through his newspaper, the *Daily Mail,* ham-
mered the incompetents in the War Department and the incompetent generals in the
field until Lord Roberts, and then Lord
Kitchener, were sent out to South Africa to
bring victory.

With a broad vision of imperial unity
rivaling that of Cecil Rhodes, Northcliffe insisted that the Boers, though beaten, were
not disgraced and must be welcomed into
the British family. With other far-seeing
men, he urged that the South African states
should be consolidated into an autonomous
colony, and assisted materially in bringing
about that magnificent result. To-day, with
minor exceptions, the Boers have become the
staunchest supporters of the British cause,
and General Smuts, once a bitter foe of
England, now sits in the War Council in
London.

The same vision of unity in its relation
to other British colonies has for years been

a tenet of Northcliffe's faith. For the purpose of strengthening the bonds of Empire he has issued overseas editions of his newspapers, which have had an enormous circulation in all parts of the world. He has also organized overseas clubs, for the purpose of cultivating a spirit of fraternity among all men of British descent, and these have gained a vast membership. Whenever opportunity has been afforded, he has raised his voice in defense of the rights of the British colonies, and in his newspapers and periodicals has emphasized the wonderful progress that is being made in all the self-governing dominions. During the present war he has been unstinted in his praise of the heroism displayed by Britannia's sons from Canada, Australia, New Zealand, and other parts of the Empire that fly their own modifications of the Union Jack.

Northcliffe's prediction of the great war, in a widely published interview in 1909, would apparently endow him with seerlike qualities were it not for the fact that his prophecy was based upon information obtained from his correspondents and confidential agents. When he discovered that

Germany was preparing to strike more suddenly than in 1870, when France was drawn into a disastrous war, he urged England to get ready for the impending conflict. His warnings, however, fell on deaf ears, with the result that England, like America, was unprepared when the crisis arrived.

When the war began he saw at once what the British public did not realize, namely, that it would be a long war, and that the task of raising and equipping an adequate army was gigantic. He saw, too, that compulsory service must come, as he had insisted for several years. The British people, however, would have none of it, believing that conscription was undemocratic and that a volunteer army would suffice. In spite of opposition from a large element of the public and the attacks of some influential newspapers, the undaunted advocate of efficiency carried on his campaign for conscription, and eventually won the fight. The result has been that Great Britain to-day has an army of four millions on the fighting line, while men unfit for service in the field are engaged in some form of activity nationally beneficial.

Despite the pleas of pacifists for disarmament, Northcliffe fought successfully for the maintenance of the British navy at the standard of twice the strength of its most powerful rival. But for his continued pressure, the German navy would have been permitted to surpass that of Great Britain. After the war began, his broom swept the almost sacrosanct British admiralty clear of various incompetents and brought about the substitution of young and able efficients.

In the early days of the war, when stories of sacrifice and slaughter were partly concealed by the censorship, the Northcliffe newspapers presented the facts instead of attempting to evade them. When the direful retreat from Mons occurred, these papers were the first to relate how narrowly the Allied troops had escaped worse disaster. Instead of keeping quiet and pretending that each successive mistake that England made was another " strategic retreat," as decent Englishmen were expected to do, Northcliffe constantly pointed out the blunders and insisted upon their being remedied with all possible speed. Though not in the thick of the fighting, he was kept informed of

every important development, and was ready
at all times to expose incapacity in high
circles. The record of this power behind
the army is a narrative of unflinching bravery which has been a means of bringing
about a high state of military efficiency.

An embargo on exports to Holland and
the Scandinavian countries that were supplying Germany with food and other commodities—a plan which the United States
eventually adopted—was another policy for
which Northcliffe fought.

He has also been the greatest advocate
of the freedom of the British press. From
its inception the censorship in England was
his target, his assertion being that it was a
device to mask inefficiency and conceal the
truth. His barbed arrows at last compelled
the government to modify its restrictions.

The progress of this resourceful man,
however, has not been along a rose-strewn
path of public applause. In fact, no man in
England, in recent years, has been the target of more bitter abuse. His enemies are
legion, particularly among his newspaper
rivals and the official inefficients. But much
as he is hated, he is feared still more, be-

cause no one knows where his lightning will strike next. Hence, incompetency shudders, while competents in the war game are constantly kept up to the mark. Alone among English citizenry he has refused to permit his countrymen to maintain their complacent torpor of superiority and the hereditary belief that they are immaculate and unconquerable by virtue of being English. Such heresy could have but one result, an utter detestation of Northcliffe by a certain proportion of the English upper classes.

This may possibly serve to explain why he has been so persistently loaded with honors. It is an old formula with the governing classes in England that whenever a man becomes dangerous to the established order of things, the best way to keep him quiet is to give him a title. This plan, however, proved a wretched failure in Northcliffe's case.

In 1904, when he was Mr. Alfred Harmsworth, he was made a baronet—a sort of hereditary knight—and was transformed into Sir Alfred Harmsworth. When he became more persistent than ever in his attacks on

the old school of politicians, it probably occurred to the higher powers that perhaps
the title was not big enough. In 1906,
therefore, Sir Alfred was honored with a
peerage, receiving the title of baron and a
seat in the House of Lords. As Lord
Northcliffe the versatile journalist proved
to be even more energetic in stirring up
trouble for the clique of elderly politicians
in the official circle. Presumably as a last
resort, he has recently been created a viscount, but his enemies already opine that
even a dukedom would furnish no curb to
his activities.

From even this brief review it can be
readily understood why Northcliffe's appeals
to the public have assumed all the force and
meaning of a national message, and have
made him far more powerful than any British statesman of the present era. And what
is more, the people of England regard him
with confidence, because he invariably sees
dangers ahead and warns the government
how to avoid them. Amidst the perils of
war he has acted as Britain's national pilot,
and his advice has usually been followed
whenever it has become necessary, for the

safety of the ship of state, to jettison an incapable cabinet or to drop incompetent heads of departments.

In attempting to describe Lord Northcliffe most writers have found themselves at a loss for words to make his amazing personality known to the world. Searching for appropriate terms, they have called him " The Colossus of the Press," " The Napoleon of Journalism," " The Modern Warwick," and " The Goad of Empire." They have described him as the personal director of democratic Britain, the champion of war, and the dare-devil leader of British public opinion.

All these phrases, however, are too mildly insufficient to portray the self-made man who has risen from obscurity to giant eminence, whose magnificent achievements are written on history's pages, and who to-day is unquestionably the most commanding figure in the British Empire. Such is Lord Northcliffe, a public man who has no parallel in the United States or any other country.

Modern history contains no such character as this forceful man who holds no

public office, and yet is able to make or unmake governments by welding millions of
supporters together in carrying out his
great enterprises for his country's welfare.
Through his extraordinary genius and ability, as the facts have shown, he has unified
British democracy, which, under his guidance, has transformed Great Britain into a
single-minded, purposeful nation whose constant aim is efficiency.

The leader of the British press and undoubtedly the most influential journalist in
the world, Lord Northcliffe, through his
newspapers, especially *The Times* and the
Daily Mail, reaches every grade of Britain's
population from proletariat to prince, with
the result that he has built up a following
more permanent and powerful than that of
any statesman. Whenever he agitates for
a change in the government or launches any
other great movement, a large proportion
of the British public follows his leadership.
Thus he has become the unofficial spokesman of millions of British voters just as
surely as if he were their chosen prime
minister.

While he possesses all the power of a great

politician upheld by the votes of a nation, Northcliffe's power, unlike that of even the greatest politician, is continuous and untrammeled because it is derived from the newspapers that he owns and directs. No American newspaper owner has ever had such enormous power as this world-famous journalist possesses, nor has any group of American newspapers ever exerted a national influence comparable with that of the Northcliffe press. The main reason is to be found in the material differences between the social conditions of Great Britain and those of the United States.

While this country is a huge melting pot for many races fusing together to make a nation, the British public, on the other hand, is a coherent public with a common language, a common heritage, and common ideals. In other words, the people of Great Britain are all British and are influenced by whatever appeals to Britons.

There is still another point of difference. Because of the vastness of the United States, even an important newspaper can influence only a comparatively small part of the country. A New York newspaper, for example, has little or no influence on the public of San Francisco, Chicago, Boston, or even Philadelphia. In Great Britain, on the contrary, the great mass of its forty-six million people are concentrated within two small islands and the Northcliffe newspapers reach every corner of the United Kingdom on the day of publication. The people of Great Britain, moreover, take more seriously than we do the editorial utterances of important newspapers, and this explains why it is that a great newspaper, such as the London *Times,* commands a national following and when it calls for action can count on a substantial response.

Given these fundamentals, plus the gift of leadership, the well-nigh superhuman energy, and the almost psychic instinct for public needs which Lord Northcliffe possesses, it can be readily understood how he has been able to weld his newspapers into a national force that can make or unmake governments and formulate policies to an extent unknown in the United States. Through them he has become one of the most dominating figures that Great Britain has ever seen. At his command forces are arrayed

that sway elections and enhance or destroy
political reputations.

The policy of the Northcliffe press, it may
be added, has been wholly constructive, and,
as Lord Northcliffe has never sought a public office, whatever appeals he may make
are clearly not inspired by any desire for
political honors. His newspapers, which express his vivid ideas and reflect his remarkable personality, have in the face of abuse
and every accusation up to treason twice
undone and remade the high councils of
England at war.

To-day there is no man in Great Britain,
and certainly but few in the world, more
conspicuous than Lord Northcliffe or so
vitally interesting to the public. His career
has proved in many ways that the big things
of the world are always done by individuals
and that one-man power is the principal
thing that counts. That is why some of his
admirers have described him as the biggest
man in the world.

Perhaps one of the best summaries of
Northcliffe's personality, his marvelous combination of pluck, originality, endurance,
and perseverance, has been given by Isaac

F. Marcosson, an American writer, who has made a careful study of the Northcliffe press and its enterprising founder.

" Whether," says Marcosson, " Northcliffe is a crisis-monger or merchant of clamor, prophet of panic and depression (as his enemies make out), or whether he is the voice of democracy, the safeguard of public liberty, and the custodian of the nation's welfare (as his friends and supporters attest), one fact is certain: he is the liveliest and most vital entity in England, a man alternately praised and damned, who by the changes he has wrought must be regarded as the Warwick of the war. If he lived in America he would be a President maker."

To use American terms, Northcliffe is Britain's exponent of " the big stick," " the man with the punch," and " the apostle of efficiency." A still better epitome of his character is contained in the phrase of an English admirer, " The man who gets things done."

Northcliffe's value as a national asset to England has not been overlooked by the Germans. " Strafe Northcliffe!" has long been the cry of the subsidized German newspapers, some of which have declared that hanging is too good for Germany's most persistent enemy. Since the war began he has been a relentless foe of German propaganda, and has ceaselessly called attention to the importance of fighting this subtle influence which the Teutons employ to misinform neutrals and, if possible, to cause dissension among the Allies.

Realizing that while Northcliffe and his newspapers are on guard a powerful influence against Germany exists in England, the Kaiser, it is said, has actually offered the title of baron and the iron cross to any of his officers who succeeds in keeping the eminent newspaper owner quiet for all time. That some efforts have been made to earn this reward was evidenced some months ago when Northcliffe's country house on the coast of Kent was bombed by aeroplanes and shelled by a destroyer. On the latter occasion the famous editor narrowly escaped with his life.

The achievements of this man of destiny in recent years form a suitable climax to his past career. No man ever had a more eventful life; none has had a greater variety of experiences. That being the case, it follows that his life story is one that abounds with lights and shades, with humor and pathos. Let us now proceed to follow that story from the beginning to the present day, and to learn from it how Alfred Harmsworth, an obscure writer, became a celebrity with the title of Viscount Northcliffe.

II

GENIUS IN TRAINING

IT is an interesting fact that ancestry has much to do with the making of character, and that whatever is great in a man may be the result of certain inherited traits. All that is needed for their development is a suitable environment and a touch of inspiration.

Buffon, who took this view, has defined genius as patience which requires the electric spirit to arouse it into power. Those who agree with the theory and believe that talent is hereditary, will find that Lord Northcliffe's parentage affords convincing proof that his genius was, in a measure, due to happily balanced qualities inherited from his father and mother. He is, in short, that rare and perfect mixture of Irish and English which successfully combines the virtues of the two divergent races. He has all the vision, humor, initiative, aggressiveness, and electric spirit of the Celt, tempered with the patience, bulldog tenacity, persistence, courage, and practicability of the Anglo-Saxon.

The world-famous journalist was born July 15, 1865, at Chapelizod, County Dublin, Ireland, and received the name of Alfred Charles William Harmsworth. His father, Alfred Harmsworth, who belonged to a branch of the Harmsworth family long settled in Yorkshire, was a barrister of some distinction. In London, where he practiced, he was regarded not only as a brilliant lawyer, but as a man of rare judgment, quick perception, tact, and versatility. During his career he was counsel in a number of important cases, one of his greatest legal triumphs having been achieved in connection with a celebrated libel action.

The destined leader of the British press was equally fortunate in having a mother who possessed more than ordinary attainments and force of character. Mrs. Geraldine Mary Harmsworth was the daughter of William Maffett of County Dublin, and a member of an Irish family which has been distinguished for centuries. Many army officers and members of the British civil service have borne the name of Maffett.

With an Irish mother and an Irish birthplace, Great Britain's strong man is usually
regarded as more Irish than English.

Ireland, it has been said, is a good country to be born in, but a good country to get
out of, although at times it may be a good
country to go back to. However this may
be, the fates decreed that Alfred Harmsworth, the future genius, should be brought
up in England. When he was scarcely a
year old, his father, who had been engaged
in some important Irish litigation, returned
to London to resume his ordinary legal
practice. A home was established in Hampstead, a well-known suburb of north London. There the other members of the family
were born, three daughters and six sons.

No better place than Hampstead could
have been found in which to rear a future
editor and publisher. It is a quarter of
London which abounds in literary associations, having been frequented for two centuries or more by artists and men of letters. The reader who is familiar with the
careers of English novelists will recall that
Wilkie Collins was a resident of Hampstead, and it was there that George du

Maurier wrote his famous story " Trilby."
Rose Cottage, in which the Harmsworths
lived, had once been tenanted by Leigh
Hunt, the poet and essayist, friend of Keats
and Shelley, Charles Lamb and Lord
Byron.

As they grew up, the Harmsworth boys
developed into stalwart, athletic, typically
English lads, with a great liking for cricket
and other outdoor sports. Near their home
was Hampstead Heath, an open space of
two hundred and fifty acres, well wooded,
diversified with several sheets of water, and
to a great extent left in its natural state.
It was a fine playground, and also a suitable
place to arouse an interest in the picturesque
life of the past. In the early coaching days
the Heath was the haunt of such celebrated
highwaymen as Dick Turpin, Claude Duval,
and Jack Sheppard, who have figured in
many a novel. As may be surmised, such
an environment was well calculated to stir
a youthful imagination.

At an early age, Alfred Harmsworth was
sent to a private school in Hampstead.
From all accounts there was nothing of the
model boy in his behavior at that period,

nor anything from which highly moral lessons for the young might be derived. He was not particularly studious; he seems to have been quite as mischievous as any of his schoolmates, and to have gone through the usual boyhood experiences of playing and fighting, and the minimum amount of studying. Nevertheless, those who knew him as a boy assert that he was usually at the head of his class, and without any special effort on his part. He did not excel in arithmetic, but seemed to have a pronounced aptitude for English composition, history, and geography. Out of school he was a daring lad, full of high spirits, and much addicted to practical joking. He is described as having steel-grey, searching eyes, hair of the peculiar shade sometimes termed " mouse colored," a fair complexion, and striking features, the audacity which lurked within being concealed by a thoughtful expression.

According to his schoolfellows, Alfred Harmsworth was a " bear " for asking questions of all sorts and conditions of people on every conceivable subject. He was forever investigating the whys and wherefores, soaking up information as a sponge soaks up water; later in life he astonished people by his encyclopedic knowledge of the most out-of-the-way subjects.

It was at this interesting period that the Harmsworth family left Hampstead and settled in St. John's Wood, another London suburb, also famous as a literary and artistic center. Here the boys grew up and received part of their education, three of them having attended the Marylebone Grammar School, an excellent institution, corresponding in some respects to an American high school.

While living in St. John's Wood the future celebrity is said to have figured as the hero of a romance. The story, as related by an old resident of the district, is as follows: The Harmsworths lived in a detached house with a large garden, on one side of which there was an unoccupied house, while on the other side there was a select seminary for girls from twelve to sixteen. After school hours the Harmsworth boys were continually playing cricket, and the ball was often sent flying over one of the garden walls. In the case of the garden of the untenanted house it was easy enough to recover

the ball, but when it went into the school
garden the situation was different. Naturally
enough, the Harmsworth boys were a thorn
in the side of the prim old maid who conducted the seminary. If she took her young
charges out for a walk, going or coming
they were sure to meet the attractive Alfred or his younger brother, the burly
Harold, and discipline was much upset. If
two or three young ladies retired to a se-
cluded corner of the garden for a ladylike
game of croquet, before long the wretched
cricket ball would make its appearance,
causing them to flee in terror.

The irate school principal sent many
sharp notes on the subject to Mr. Harmsworth, who remonstrated with his boys
without effect, and sometimes even took a
hand in the game himself. Mrs. Harmsworth, like a good mother, was even more
lenient. She wanted the boys to have not
only the back garden to play in, but the
whole world. Napoleon, she argued, had
made the world his playground; why should
not Alfred do the same? Even in those
early days she perceived her son's capabili-
ties and placed no limitations on the possi-

bilities of his career. She sent polite notes to the school principal, but made no guarantees that the cricket should be stopped.

In these circumstances, the principal ordered the offending ball to be confiscated the next time that it made its appearance. It is said that when the ball was again sent flying over the wall, a graceful little girl of thirteen, with large, dark eyes, took possession of it. Harold was sent over to negotiate for its recovery and demanded the ball in rather a peremptory English manner. The little girl refused to give it up. Alfred made the next attempt, and by employing a skillful combination of tact and Irish blarney he not only succeeded in getting the ball, but made an ally of the little girl, who promised that thereafter she would throw it back herself. Tradition says that six years later the little girl with the dark eyes became Mrs. Alfred Harmsworth.

Some good Irish fairy must surely have substituted ink for water at the baptism of Alfred Harmsworth. His ambition to become a writer and publisher was clearly shown at the grammar school at Stamford, Lincolnshire, to which he was eventually sent. While there he started a printed magazine that dealt with happenings of interest to the boys and their teachers. It was brightly written and remarkably well edited. Even then, although he was only fifteen years old, the youthful genius displayed the courage and optimism which have been his guiding stars through life. The first number of his magazine contained the naïve announcement: " I have it on the best authority that this paper is to be a marked success." Thus early in life the boy publisher discovered for himself the blessed uses of advertisement and foreshadowed the policy that eventually made the name of Harmsworth a household word in England. In the second number he published this: " I am glad to say that my prediction as to the success of my magazine has proved correct."

This attraction to journalism, however, was not at all to the liking of Mr. Harmsworth, who wanted Alfred to become a lawyer. He decided to put a check on his youthful ambitions, and to this end arranged for a practical object lesson, calculated to work a cure by showing the dark side of newspaper life. A friend of the family was induced to take the aspiring youth to the offices of a London evening newspaper, one afternoon, to see the first edition printed. On the way this friend, who was himself in the newspaper business, dilated on the horrors, perils, temptations, evils, and poor earnings of newspaper folk.

Gloomy and depressing, this description of a journalist's life was a fitting introduction to the offices of the newspaper, which were in an old, dilapidated building that reeked with the combined odors of well-oiled machinery and newly printed paper. But the sight of the busy reporters and copy readers, the copy boys, running hither and thither, the mysterious offices of the editors, and the roar of the whirring presses, fairly entranced young Harmsworth. " Why, this is ripping! " he exclaimed enthusiastically, and added, " I should just like to work here." The next moment he was interviewing a printer's devil and discovering how the ink-smudged boy earned his living, afterwards picking up some information from a pressman as to how many copies an hour the big press could turn out. Before he left the place he had become infected with that subtle atmosphere of a printing plant which appeals to every born newspaperman and, once felt, is never overcome. From that moment Alfred Harmsworth resolved to make his way in the world as writer, editor, and newspaper owner.

It was in vain that his father took him to the law courts to witness the trial of some important cases, in the hope of curing his newspaper obsession. The dignified judges and counsel in their wigs and gowns appealed to the youth from a picturesque point of view, and he could see the possibilities of some good "magazine copy," but nothing could induce him to begin the study of "Blackstone's Commentaries" and "Chitty on Pleadings." When his father presented him with the two volumes nicely bound in calf, Alfred's publisher-like comment was: "They've got jolly fine covers." History, however, does not record that he ever looked into their pages.

So strong was his determination not to follow the law that at last parental objections were overcome, and on leaving school he was allowed to try his hand at writing. In 1881 young Harmsworth, then sixteen years old, was introduced to a shrewd old Scotchman, James Henderson of Red Lion House, Fleet Street, London, a man of no great literary capacity but of much perception. Among a number of weekly papers that he published was one called the *Young Folks' Budget*. As Alfred had edited a printed school journal, there were no mysteries of type or proof for him, and he could write interestingly. Much impressed by his ability, Henderson engaged the youthful aspirant to write short stories and articles for the *Budget*. His contributions soon made a hit, and what is more, they attracted the attention of Sir William Ingram, owner of the *Illustrated London News*, who published a boys' paper called *Youth*. He invited the young writer to send stories to that periodical, and Alfred was thus kept busy writing for Henderson and Ingram.

It was at this time that the future publisher first made the acquaintance of writing folk, some of whom afterwards became famous in the literary world. Several writers whom he met were visitors at Red Lion House, where Henderson served a luncheon at one o'clock every day, to which members of the staff and outside contributors were invited.

On one of these occasions Henderson introduced the youthful Harmsworth to another guest, a rather eccentric-looking young man, with a pale, oval face and wonderful eyes. Although the visitor wore a velvet coat, usually regarded as a sign of affectation, his manner was friendly and unassuming. After the introduction, while Alfred was trying to make up his mind as to what sort of man the wearer of the velvet coat might be, Henderson remarked admiringly, in an undertone, " Yon body can write." The " body " was Robert Louis Stevenson. It was Henderson, by the way, who suggested for Stevenson's great story the title " Treasure Island," used by the author in place of " The Sea Cook," which he had originally selected.

A year after Alfred entered the writing business, Sir William Ingram, impressed by his energy, industry, and versatility, engaged him as assistant editor of *Youth* at a salary of twenty-five dollars a week. It was in this way that he gained his first practical lessons in journalism.

While holding this position the youthful sub-editor was suddenly called upon to help his mother, who was left in rather straitened circumstances by the death of his father. There was a large family to provide for, and the younger children had to be reared and educated. The older boys were therefore obliged to give their assistance; two of them obtained employment in government offices. Young as he was, Alfred took the lead in directing the family affairs.

At the age of eighteen, young Harmsworth, eager to see more of the world, left home and shared a room with another youth who lived in Battersea, one of the working-class quarters of London. His experiences at this formative period were of great value in after years. A close observer, he began to find out what sort of reading matter was needed by the people among whom he lived. He soon discovered that their demands were not being met by the publishers of that time.

Those were the early days of the wood-pulp industry, which enabled paper to be produced at a remarkably low cost. Photo-

engraving had also been introduced, and
this cheaper process was supplanting hand
work to a great extent. The observant
Harmsworth, who was well informed on
these subjects, was quick to perceive that
cheap paper and cheap illustrations would
mean a new era of cheap periodicals in
which large fortunes would be made, and
he foresaw that he might make a fortune
himself.

The youthful editor's appetite for anything novel in the shape of literature was
then insatiable. At the *Illustrated London
News* office he could see papers from all
parts of the world; nothing worth noticing
escaped his attention. He devoted his
evenings to studying the publications of
various English towns and cities, to reading
the magazines of continental Europe, and
especially to watching the development of
publications in America, ever the leader in
the publishing industry. The more he
worked and studied the more he became convinced that England, as far as journalism
was concerned, was much behind the times.
In other words, the English people were
getting not only what they did not want,

but what they had to take because there was nothing else.

English journalism in 1883 was of the same dull, lifeless, old-fashioned type that had existed in England in the 'fifties, but the English people had moved far ahead. Not only had the educated classes increased enormously, but a sort of public school system had been established throughout the United Kingdom. For years the public schools, attended by the children of the lower middle class and the working people, had been turning out bright boys and girls with eager, receptive minds. They were developing an appetite for something new in the shape of reading matter.

In spite of this, most of the English newspapers were edited for what might be termed the "high-brow" classes and were not interesting to the masses. The periodicals were in much the same position. With few exceptions the monthly magazines were old-fashioned in appearance and contents, most of them appealing to only the high literary classes. The cheap weeklies, such as story papers and humorous sheets, were far behind the times, and for that reason had com-

paratively small circulations. In the matter
of popular reading matter the requirements
of the great mass of the English people, as
Alfred Harmsworth perceived, were ignored.

With a desire to get a still wider experience, as well as a chance to earn more
money, the restless genius left the Ingram
firm at this stage of his career and found
work elsewhere. After filling some minor
editorial positions, he obtained employment
as private secretary to a wealthy business
man, with whom he traveled extensively on
the Continent, and thus gained some valuable knowledge of foreign conditions. Later
on he joined the editorial staff of Iliffe &
Sons in the old city of Coventry.

At that time Coventry was the center of
the English cycle trade, and Iliffe & Sons'
business was mainly connected with that industry. Besides printing nearly all the
catalogues and other advertising matter for
the bicycle manufacturers in Coventry, the
firm published the *Cyclist* and *Bicycling
News,* both weeklies, and the *Cyclist Touring
Gazette,* a monthly magazine and organ of
the Cyclist Touring Club, an international

organization. At that time the big-wheel bicycles were in use; the modern " safeties " had not been invented.

Thorough in everything that he undertook, Alfred Harmsworth not only became an expert bicycle rider, but also familiarized himself with bicycle construction. Having read everything on the subject that he could find, he visited the factories and saw bicycles made. This gave him a wide knowledge of the cycle industry. Incidentally he formed an extensive acquaintance among professional bicyclists. With this training he was not only able to discuss bicycling matters from the standpoint of an expert, but he scored many a " beat " for *Bicycling News,* the paper which he edited, and increased its circulation.

While thus employed he did a good deal of free-lance work, contributing articles on sport and other topics to newspapers and magazines. He also became a writer for *Tid-Bits.* This paper, it should be explained, was really the pioneer of modern English popular journalism. The way in which it came into existence forms an interesting story.

In the early 'eighties a Manchester man named George Newnes made clippings from newspapers and magazines—short stories, jokes, and other things—which he pasted in scrapbooks. A large part of his collection was clipped from American Sunday newspapers. He was the proprietor of an eating house largely patronized by cab drivers. The scrapbooks were put on the tables, to entertain customers, and they proved to be immensely popular.

Newnes was not slow to notice that his clippings had made a great hit, and this gave him the idea of starting a weekly paper composed of similar scraps. In 1884 he published the paper, which he called *Tid-Bits*. To push its sale, he tried various guessing competitions and awarded liberal prizes. The paper also carried a standing notice that a thousand pounds ($5000) would be paid to the heirs of any reader who happened to be killed in a railway accident, providing that the victim had a copy of the current issue in his possession.

At first *Tid-Bits* was published in Manchester, but it proved so successful that Newnes soon moved to London. The enterprising publisher had a knack of getting clever young men to write for his paper, for he eventually abandoned the idea of having it made up entirely of clippings and, instead, printed original matter such as bright, snappy articles, and stories of a column or more. He was quick to notice the genius and versatility of young Harmsworth, who became a regular contributor of articles, always gladly accepted, which made an instantaneous hit.

In course of time Newnes started other weekly and monthly periodicals, including the *Strand Magazine,* the circulation of which reached over a quarter of a million in 1888, owing to the publication of the Conan Doyle detective stories, in which Sherlock Holmes, the scientific unraveler of mysterious crimes, figured so prominently. Later on the business was organized as a stock company, Newnes became a baronet, and when he died in 1910, at the age of fifty-nine, he was a millionaire, the pioneer fortune maker in this new field of literature.

Young Harmsworth's work as a free-lance proved so remunerative that eventually he resigned the editorship of *Bicycling News* and returned to London, to be nearer the publishers. In those early days he lived at Hampstead with Max Pemberton, the novelist, who had recently left college and had married a member of the Tussaud family, proprietors of the well-known London waxworks exhibition. Max was free-lancing himself at that time, and the two young men often walked to Fleet Street together to sell their articles and stories.

In 1887, at the age of twenty-two, Alfred Harmsworth entered into partnership with an Irish journalist named Carr, and a business was started under the firm title of Carr & Co. The young men arranged to publish an English edition of *Outing,* the American sporting magazine; they also published an educational paper of small circulation, the *Private Schoolmaster,* and a weekly cycling paper. They had taken two small offices in an old-fashioned three-story building in Paternoster Square, the center of the London book-publishing district.

To add to his income, the industrious Harmsworth continued his free-lance work, including his contributions to *Tid-Bits.* He was greatly interested in the progress of

Alfred Harmsworth, 1891

The youthful publisher at Elmwood

that publication, which in many ways embodied ideas that had been latent in his own
mind about papers for the masses. Newnes'
success, in fact, had stimulated his own ambition. What Newnes had accomplished he
believed that he could accomplish himself,
and he resolved to start a paper of his own,
an undertaking for which he was thoroughly
well equipped.

It was at this interesting stage that an
American newspaperman had the good fortune to become acquainted with the youthful writer and publisher and to gather some
impressions which are now recorded for the
first time. They are of peculiar interest,
because they give an accurate pen picture
of Lord Northcliffe in the days when, as
Alfred Harmsworth, he was preparing to
launch his first weekly publication. Since
he became famous, the great journalist has
figured prominently in newspaper and magazine articles, and some of the misstatements
concerning his early life, which have been
made by highly imaginative writers, must
certainly have astonished him, if brought to
his attention. Therefore, the following
story, compiled from notes that were made

over twenty years ago, form a notable addition to this chapter.

* * *

To those who look backward, London in the 'eighties of the last century seems to have been rather a depressing, unprogressive city. Electric lighting was not general, modern hotels had only just been started, and the various improvements that have transformed the English metropolis were then unknown. Although it is only thirty years ago, it is difficult to imagine London without modern buildings, elevators, automobiles, taxis, motor busses, rapid-transit subways, electric traction, moving-picture theatres, telephones, gramophones, and suffragettes. Even the London fogs of the "pea soup" variety seemed to be darker, thicker, and more sulphurous than they are to-day.

It was on one of those depressing, foggy days in February, 1888, that I first met Alfred Harmsworth. Although a mere youth at the time, I had gone from New York to London as the representative of some trade journals, with the object of sending them news and special articles. Like

Harmsworth, I had worked my way upward as cub reporter and editorial assistant and had set out to see the world.

Some weeks after my arrival in London, the manager of a typewriter company, with whom I had become acquainted, suggested that I might increase my slender income by writing articles on American topics for some of the English weeklies. Forthwith he gave me a letter of introduction addressed to " Mr. Alfred Harmsworth," who, he assured me, was the English equivalent of an American " live wire." " What Harmsworth doesn't know about the writing business isn't worth knowing," remarked the typewriter man. " He can tell you what to do."

With the letter in my pocket, I groped my way through the fog to the office of Carr & Co. in Paternoster Square. Mounting one flight of stairs in an old building, I entered a diminutive office, where I handed my letter to the sole occupant, a handsome, tall, broad-shouldered, smooth-faced young man with " mouse-colored " hair combed in a long lock over the right side of his forehead. He wore a suit of light-grey English tweed, made extremely loose after the fashion of the time. Somehow he reminded me of portraits of Napoleon in early youth —striking, keen-eyed, and evidently full of enthusiasm. When I inquired for Mr. Harmsworth, he admitted that he was the man for whom I was looking.

On reading the letter of introduction and learning that I had recently come from New York, he gave me a hearty shake of the hand and told me to take a seat by the fireside. There was an open-grate fire in the office, and the warmth was acceptable after a walk through the cold, penetrating fog. Harmsworth seemed to radiate cheer-fulness. When I mentioned the weather, he remarked humorously, " Why, this is only a mild specimen. Wait till you see one of our black fogs; that's where we hold the world's championship."

Then we settled down to talk. Without any ceremony, he asked me what had brought me to London, what papers I was representing, what the publishers paid me, and how much they made themselves. " What sort of pay do their editors get? " he asked. When I told him that some of the editors were paid five thousand dollars a year, which was considered a good salary in New York, he remarked: " Some of our head clerks over here get more than that. A thousand pounds ($5000) a year is not a great salary." He added: " From what I have heard, I am convinced there are better chances to make money in England than in America. We have the money here, more of it than America has, and if a man has brains enough he can get his share of it. I have never had any inclination to emigrate. In fact, I believe with Tennyson that if you would have money you must go where money is. When we have plenty of it here, what's the use of running away from it? "

After we had talked for a while, I could see plainly that although Harmsworth had an English accent and appearance, his temperament was decidedly American. He had none of the reserve of the average Englishman, but was ready to talk with any man who had anything worth saying. He fired a volley of questions at me regarding myself and what my experience had been, asked how much I earned and how much I wanted to earn, and what I expected to do with myself. Sometimes, during our conversation, I dropped a remark that attracted his attention to a marked degree. "That's a good idea for an article," he would observe as he made notes on a pad, or "That's something we ought to adopt over here."

We discussed the American newspapers and magazines, their circulation and rates of payment to writers. "How do you think English magazines compare with American?" he asked, and without waiting for a reply, he added, "Very badly, of course." Then he proceeded, "Have you seen *Tid-Bits?*" I said that I had. "Is there any paper like that in the United States?" he inquired. I told him there was not, because the Sunday newspapers published articles, stories, and jokes such as appeared in *Tid-Bits.* "That's true," observed Harmsworth. "Our papers have been deadly dull, but the English people are demanding something better and they will have to get it before long."

Our conversation took place in the larger of the two offices, but even there space was limited, and one had to dodge piles of *Out-ings* and *Private Schoolmasters* in moving

about. I happened to stumble over a stack
of cycling papers. "I know it's a bad
paper," remarked Harmsworth ironically,
"but you needn't kick it so viciously." In
one corner of the room there was a Remington typewriter. "You see," he observed,
"we can't get along without American inventions. We also have a mimeograph for
duplicating, and if our people were sufficiently advanced we might have a telephone." In those days telephones were comparatively scarce in London, and were seldom seen excepting in large business establishments.

We talked about papers and circulations,
free-lancing and schemes for money making,
for over an hour, and at last I rose to go,
fearing to outstay my welcome, but Harmsworth stopped me. "You can't escape just
yet," he exclaimed. "I've got to pump
some more out of you." Then he invited
me to lunch, telling me that he had his mid-
day meal brought in from a restaurant a
few doors away. We lunched together in
a little private office, a third as big as the
outer office, our talk going on meanwhile.
Harmsworth was extremely frank. He told

me that he was making about $2500 a year from his interest in the business and his free-lance work. In addition to Carr, a barrister named Markwick had an interest in the publishing enterprise.

For an Englishman who had never been in the United States I found Harmsworth to be remarkably well informed. He had gathered a mass of ideas about the United States from Americans whom he had met and also from his extensive reading, and while some of his notions were remarkably accurate, others were just as erroneous, which of course is not surprising. He thought, for example, that New York at that time was far behind London in many ways, although he admitted that in the matter of telephones and other labor-saving devices, as well as modern office buildings, New York might be ahead. From a social point of view, however, he imagined New York in 1888 to be at about the same stage of development as London had been in 1850—a dull, depressing sort of place. From what he said, he evidently considered American men, as a rule, to be far behind Englishmen in the matter of general education, while American women, he thought, were superior in this respect to the average Englishwomen.

American newspapers and magazines, Harmsworth admitted, were wonderful, and were far ahead of anything that Europe had ever produced. He asked me about American boys' papers and their circulations. I mentioned the Munro papers, the *Fireside Companion* and *Family Story Paper;* the Street & Smith publications; Frank Tousey's *Boys of New York;* and Frank Munsey's *Golden Argosy.* He had seen some of these, and was anxious for information about their circulation and profits. Even after lunch I was not allowed to escape, for as he was going out, he asked me to take a walk with him, and we strolled along for about half an hour discussing the subjects uppermost in his mind—newspapers and magazines.

Some days later I happened to call at the office again, and was introduced by Harmsworth to his partner, Carr, a genial Irishman, who had just a trace of a cultivated Irish accent. I also met Markwick, the barrister, who was what might be termed an

outside partner. On this occasion, Harmsworth, who had already told me about his
work for *Tid-Bits,* mentioned that he had
written a small book on English railways
for Newnes, which was sold for a shilling.
" I am now writing another book," he
added, " and I should like to have you come
in every day and give me a hand with it.
The book will be called, ' A Thousand Ways
to Earn a Living,' and as you have been
in a good many lines in the United States,
and have kept your eyes open, you can undoubtedly tell me a few things that I don't
know. What do you say?" I replied that
I would accept his offer.

The next day we met at the office and
went to work on the book. I operated the
typewriter and made suggestions, while
Harmsworth planned and dictated. I found
him to be a wonderfully fluent and ready
writer, quick in perception and remarkably
witty, always seeing the humorous side of
things and the bright side as well. In fact,
he was a pronounced optimist. As we
worked together, however, I could see that
in many ways his mind had a decidedly
practical bent, and that beneath his out-

ward gaiety there was a solid substratum of keen business shrewdness and editorial ability.

The little book which we produced was eventually published in Newnes' Popular Shilling Series. It was full of information about various trades and professions, alphabetically arranged from " Accounting " to " Yacht Building." It told the reader how to enter these callings, the salaries received, and the general prospects. Here is what young Harmsworth had to say about journalism:

" It is impossible to hide successful newspaper work under a bushel. Rival newspaper proprietors are ever on the lookout for smart men, and are loath to lose a valuable assistant, for it is a well-known fact in the newspaper world that the majority of new ventures are promoted by newspapermen who have been underpaid or harshly dealt with by their employers. A good man has therefore excellent prospects of advancement."

In the course of our talks at this time, Harmsworth confided to me that he intended to start a weekly paper to be called *Answers to Correspondents.* He explained that it would be full of interesting questions and equally interesting replies. " If the paper pays," he explained, " and I know it will, I shall rent several rooms in some building, and will have experts there to answer questions. On payment of a shilling, anybody will be entitled to ask a question and get a reply. I believe that such a place would be packed all day with people in need of information. What do you think of these ideas? " he asked.

I replied that I was unable to pass judgment on the idea of a question bureau, but as to the paper I did not think it would succeed. I pointed out that there already existed in London a weekly paper, which was made up entirely of questions and answers, but it had only a small circulation. " Yes," he answered, " that is true, but it's a dull publication, consisting of fossilized information for the benefit of old fossils. My paper will be a live weekly like one of the American papers. I have noticed that the questions sent to *Tid-Bits* are always interesting, and people like to read the answers. I won't publish dull questions or answers, and if our supply of questions runs

short I'll manufacture them myself." I remarked that in England, as well as in
America, many newspapers had questions
and answers columns which were hardly
noticed by readers excepting those who had
put the questions. He insisted, however,
that the reason was that the questions and
answers were not interesting. Our argument left me with plenty of faith in Harmsworth's ability but not much faith in his
idea.

His optimism and belief in himself at this
time were unbounded. For example, one
evening as we were passing the Houses of
Parliament, I called his attention to the
Clock Tower, where an illuminated device
above the dial indicated that the House of
Commons was in session. " I expect to be
in there some day," he replied thoughtfully.
" I haven't quite made up my mind whether
it will be the Commons or the Lords. I
rather think I shall go into the House of
Lords, because there would be more scope
there."

Another prophetic remark that I recall
was made by him one day as we were passing the *Times* building. The older part, a

quaint, red-brick structure built in the form of a square, dates from the middle of the last century. "Isn't it a funny-looking old building for a newspaper?" observed Harmsworth. "That is one of our great British institutions, and the building is typical of John Bull's conservatism. I shall probably own a daily newspaper some day, and may even get *The Times,* but if I do I shall never transform it into a yellow journal. That would be sacrilege, and the British public wouldn't stand it."

On a public holiday—Easter Monday, I think it was—we went out to Hampstead Heath to see the historic houses, including Rose Cottage, the former home of the Harmsworths. We saw the holiday crowds from the East End amusing themselves on the Heath, and afterwards had lunch at an old inn, Jack Straw's Castle, a popular bohemian resort in those days. Some writers and artists were lunching there, and among them was Seymour Lucas, a well-known portrait painter. "I mean to have Lucas paint my portrait some day," said Harmsworth, which I thought rather an astonishing remark to be made by a young man earning about fifty dollars a week. Some years later, however, Lucas did paint his portrait, and it was exhibited at the Royal Academy.

Near proximity to the great, or even to the future great, is said to be infectious in some cases. That Alfred Harmsworth's ambition did much to inspire others one incident will serve to show. The only employees that the struggling firm of Carr & Co. could afford were an advertising canvasser and an office boy. One day, when I called at the office, I found the latter, a youth named Norton, executing some fancy steps. He told me that he had a great desire to go on the variety stage and make a name for himself. A few years later Norton and his brother made their début as professional dancers, appearing as the " McNaughton Brothers." They met with great success at the English music halls and have occasionally toured in this country.

Harmsworth was preparing to start his new paper when I left England in the spring of 1888. Eventually I returned to New York, and did not revisit London for three years. What happened in the mean-

time forms another story, and one so unparalleled that it reads almost like a romance.

* * *

With this chapter the account of Alfred
Harmsworth's early training comes to an
end. Although he was only twenty-three
years old, he had laid the foundations of
future success by careful study, persistent
hard work, and ceaseless observation, which,
added to genius and ambition, supplied
qualities that invariably win. He was thus
well prepared to start upon the great venture that was destined to bring him fortune
and fame.

III

SUCCESS AT TWENTY-FOUR

MAKING a start in any business is usually a hazardous proceeding when capital is limited and much competition has to be faced. This is especially true of starting a new paper. There is, in fact, probably no line of endeavor in which money can be lost so quickly in case of failure, and without any return for hard work and the capital invested.

Alfred Harmsworth knew this to be true when he started his first paper, for brief as his career had been, he had seen many a wreck in the London publishing world. He knew, moreover, that not only would he be obliged to compete with Newnes, the successful publisher of *Tid-Bits,* but that several imitators of Newnes, reinforced by a large amount of capital, were already publishing weeklies. To any one less determined than the ambitious young man who originated brilliant ideas in a small office in Paternoster Square the outlook would have seemed hopeless, but his determination to succeed was overwhelming.

Heedless of all warnings from well-meaning friends who feared disaster, Alfred Harmsworth completed his plans, made up his paper, and sent it to press. It was issued on June 2, 1888, a weekly periodical of twenty-four pages, printed on cheap paper, without illustrations and without a cover. On the first page was its title: *Answers to Correspondents*. It was sold for one penny (two cents).

In addition to a variety of interesting paragraphs, written in the editorial office, the new paper contained a selection of short articles, supplied by the editor and some of his free-lance friends. The rest of the pages were filled with bits of humor, some really good short stories, and three columns of brightly written editorial chat, in which the youthful publisher discussed his new enterprise and asked for public support.

Here are the titles of some of the articles that appeared in the first number: " A Liv-

ANSWERS TO CORRESPONDENTS

☞ ON EVERY SUBJECT UNDER THE SUN. ☜

No 1   [Entered at Stationers' Hall.]   **JUNE 2ND, 1888.**   [European Postage. ½d.]   Price 1d.

"ANSWERS" IS PUBLISHED EVERY WEDNESDAY MORNING

The trade can obtain "Answers" from all wholesale agents and from the office,

26, Paternoster Square,

A LIVING CLOCK.

Dr. WILLIS mentions an idiot, who was accustomed to repeat the strokes of a clock near which he lived, with a loud voice. Afterwards having been removed into a parish where there was no church clock, he continued as before to call the hours successively; and this with so great accuracy, both as to the number of tolls, which be pretended to count, and as to the length of the intervening hours, that the family where he boarded conducted all their business by his proclamation of time.

ASS DRAWING WATER.

SOME years ago an ass was employed at Carisbrooke Castle, in the Isle of Wight, in drawing water by a large wheel from a very deep well, supposed to have been sunk by the Romans. When his keeper wanted water, he would say to the ass, "Tom, my boy, I want water; get into the wheel, my good lad," which Thomas immediately performed with an alacrity and sagacity that would have done credit to a nobler animal; and no doubt he knew the precise number of times necessary for the wheel to revolve upon its axis to complete his labour, because every time he brought the bucket to the surface of the well, he constantly stopped and turned round his head to observe the moment when his master laid hold of the bucket to draw it towards him, because he had then a nice evolution to make, either to recede or advance a little.

SILK STOCKINGS.

MEZERAY, the French historian, acquaints us that in 1559 Henry II. of France was the first who wore silk stockings in that country, at the marriage of his sister with the Duke of Savoy

They are nevertheless said to have been worn in this country earlier, both by Henry VIII. and Edward VI. The latter was presented with a pair of long Spanish silk stockings by Sir Thomas Gresham

Howell relates in his "History of the World" that Queen Elizabeth, in the third year of her reign, 1561, was presented with a pair of black knit silk stockings by her silk-woman, Mrs. Montague, and thenceforth she never wore cloth ones any more.

CONTENTS

Interesting answers are inserted in the paper; others go by post.

ORIGIN OF GROG.

THE British sailors had always been accustomed to drink their allowance of brandy or rum clear, till Admiral Vernon ordered those under his command to mix it with water. The innovation gave great offence to the sailors, and, for a time, rendered the commander very unpopular among them. The Admiral, at that time, wore a grogram coat, for which reason they nicknamed him "Old Grog," etc., hence, by degrees, the mixed liquor be constrained them to, universally obtained among them the name of 'Grog.'

HAIR POWDER.

HAIR powder was introduced by some ballad singers at the fair of St. Germains, in 1614. In the beginning of the reign of George I. only two ladies wore powder in their hair, and they were pointed a for their singularity And at the coronation of George II. there were only two hairdressers in London. But in 1795, it was calculated that there were in the kingdom of Great Britain fifty thousand hairdressers; and supposing each of them to use one pound of flour in a day, this upon an average amounted to 18,250,000 pounds in a year, sufficient to make 5,314,280 quartern loaves.

ECCENTRIC CHARACTER.

The R. v. Mr. Hagamore, of Catshoge, Leicestershire, was a very singular character. He died the 1st of January, 1776, possessed of the following effects, viz.—£700 per annum, and £1,000 in money, which (he dying intestate) fell to a ticket-porter in London. He kept one servant of each sex, whom he locked up every night. His last employment of an evening was to go round his premises, let loose his dogs, and fire his gun. He lost his life as follows: Going one morning to let out his servants, the dogs fawned upon him suddenly, and threw him into a pond, where he was found breast high. His servants heard his call for assistance, but being locked up could not lend him any. He had 50 gowns and cassocks, 100 pairs of breeches, 100 pair of boots, 400 pair of shoes, 80 wigs (yet always wore his own hair), 58 dogs, 80 waggons and carts, 80 ploughs (and used none), 50 saddles, and furniture for the ménage, 30 wheelbarrows, so many walking-sticks that a layman in Leicester Fields offered £8 for them, 80 horses and mares, 200 pickaxes, 200 spades and shovels, 74 ladders, and 249 razors.

Front page of the first Harmsworth paper

ing Clock," " Hair Powder," " An Eccentric Character," " Silk Stockings," " Ancient London," " Fossil Bacon," " Right and Left Boots," " George the Third at Home," " Death from Imagination," " Forests under the Sea," " Artificial Memory," " Living on Nothing a Year," " A Terrible Time with a Tiger."

The new paper failed to make an immediate hit, the sale of the first issue amounting to only 13,000 copies. Contrary to the expectations of its promoter, readers failed to send interesting questions to be answered, so that the original idea had to be abandoned. Realizing that he had been mistaken in his opinion concerning the British public's thirst for information, Harmsworth soon dropped the words " to Correspondents " from the title of his paper, leaving the word " Answers." Then he decided to use matter similar to that which appeared in *Tid-Bits,* while introducing some new features.

To save expenses the hard-working editor wrote most of the articles himself, and used matter from American newspapers to fill some of the pages. He also acted as his own circulation manager and personally visited the principal news dealers to call their attention to his paper. Still it moved very slowly, the monetary returns barely covering the cost of printing.

Although he was an optimist from the start, there were times when Alfred Harmsworth must have had some gloomy moments. In spite of all his efforts, the circulation of the paper remained small, and advertising was difficult to get. All things considered, the chances of success were not encouraging. A young man with less faith, less patience, and less enthusiasm would have given up the task.

During all those critical months, however, his mother never wavered in her belief in her son's genius. When nearly all his friends had lost confidence, she encouraged and inspired him, urging him to keep on and win success. Her judgment was excellent, and the young publisher relied upon her counsel. Abraham Lincoln once said: " All that I am, all that I ever hope to be, I owe to my mother." When he had conquered failure and achieved success, Alfred Harmsworth could say the same.

But even while he was passing through

this crisis, he never once lost his undaunted
self-confidence and belief in the future. So
great was his conviction that he would eventually win out, that he married his fiancée,
Miss Mary Elizabeth Milner. She was a
typical English beauty of nineteen, highly
talented and broadly educated. Her father,
who lived at Kidlington in Oxfordshire, had
business interests in the West Indies. After
marriage, the youthful couple lived in a
small, old-fashioned house in Hampstead.

Young Mrs. Harmsworth, herself an optimist, was delighted at the courage with
which her husband was making his fight
for success, and her encouragement was at
that time vitally important to him. She
took an active part in his work and shared
the struggles of the first year, going to the
office every day to assist in reading manuscript, clipping newspapers, and typing the
correspondence. Having unusually good
powers of observation and possessing excellent judgment in literary matters, she was
a great help, especially in giving hints concerning stories and articles that would interest women readers.

In spite of much hard work and constant

inspiration, however, Harmsworth was unable to effect much increase in his paper's circulation. For this he was not to blame, because the best paper in the world cannot succeed without capital with which to advertise it, and capital was needed to make *Answers* a success. As it was not forthcoming, the ingenious editor did what he could to advertise the paper himself. Among other plans that he devised, a letter in facsimile handwriting was printed by thousands for distribution. It had the appearance of having been written by a young woman to a friend, and described the wonderful stories appearing in *Answers*. Men were hired to drop these letters in the letter boxes of private houses, mostly in London. The scheme had some success, and gained many readers.

Just at this critical stage, when capital was so urgently required, an old family friend, a retired army officer, came to the rescue like the good genie in the " Arabian Nights." Having faith in Harmsworth's ability, he decided to back *Answers* to the extent of twenty-five thousand dollars.

With this help the young publisher was

Mrs. Alfred Harmsworth
(In 1897)

able to improve his paper by starting competitions and offering prizes as Newnes had done, while traveling readers were given the benefit of $5000 insurance. Among the first prizes were free trips to Paris. In spite of this, and the fact that the paper was well advertised, success was not achieved, and in June, 1889, one year after its first appearance, the weekly circulation was only 48,000.

But the skill, judgment, and tenacity which have distinguished Lord Northcliffe in recent times were just as pronounced in the days when he was Alfred Harmsworth and was struggling to make his first success. He would not give up the fight; and fortune, which ever favors the brave, at last bestowed her rewards. The story is soon told.

In October, 1889, when the outlook seemed discouraging, the resolute editor evolved a brilliant idea which was destined to make *Answers* a success. He lost no time in putting it into operation. At the beginning of November all England was astonished by the appearance of huge posters in lurid colors, displayed on walls and fences, bearing the magic words: " £1 a Week for

Life!" Harmsworth had offered the unprecedented prize of £1 a week for life to any person who made the nearest guess to the amount of money in the Bank of England on a certain date. He staked everything on the enterprise.

At that time the buying power of £1 ($5) in England almost equaled that of $10 in the United States. It was therefore a tempting offer. Each competitor was obliged to cut a coupon from *Answers*, and have it attested with the names and addresses of four friends. The coupons were then forwarded to *Answers'* office for registration. News of the competiton spread like wildfire, and its success was instantaneous. At last the number of competitors reached the amazing total of 718,000, so that the paper, through the names on the coupons, was brought to the attention of between three and four million people. When seen, it was taken regularly by thousands. So great was the interest aroused that, day after day, the newspaper reports of the Bank of England's balances were discussed on every side, while men in all ranks of life were caught in the excitement.

The circulation of *Answers* now mounted upward at a rapid pace, and before long it had reached 200,000 a week. Advertising at high rates was thus easily obtained, and money literally poured into the publishing office. From barely paying expenses the paper, in a few months, was showing a profit at the rate of over $50,000 a year. Six years later the annual profits had leaped to $300,000. Alfred Harmsworth now realized that his dreams had come true, and that at last he was on the road to fortune. As to the competition, that was won by a soldier in the British army, who guessed within £2 of the actual balance in the Bank of England.

Answers had been started in the diminutive office of Carr & Co. in Paternoster Square, rented for $3 a week. As the paper became a big success through the competition, it was necessary to rent offices in the next building to accommodate the clerks employed in checking coupons and otherwise coping with the large circulation. As soon as prosperity was assured, the enterprising publisher was joined by three of his brothers, Harold, Cecil, and Leicester, the first acting as business manager and the others assisting editorially. As head of the business department Harold Harmsworth showed remarkable ability, and helped to make the paper a still greater success. In fact, the rapid growth of the business was entirely due to Alfred Harmsworth's genius as an editor and an originator of ideas, coupled with his brother's business skill. The importance of the latter quality may be understood from a brief explanation, which is essential at this point.

In the United States, as is generally known, the subscription system is in common use among magazines, and the bulk of their circulation is obtained by this method. A yearly subscription is sent to the publisher and the magazine is mailed regularly. In towns and cities, of course, there are news dealers who sell the standard magazines, but even with that assistance, most of the circulation is obtained through readers who subscribe direct. The minor periodicals are entirely dependent on the subscription system.

The subscription department of an important magazine is a highly organized and expensive part of the business. It requires much bookkeeping and correspondence, while the wrapping and mailing necessitates the employment of a large staff of girls—hundreds in some cases. Then comes the cost of postage, which is a heavy item.

In Great Britain the system is entirely different. Owing to the small area of the United Kingdom, as explained in the first chapter, the people are all gathered compactly within a radius of a few hundred miles. Even in a village of any size there is usually a news dealer, while Smith & Sons have a news stand at every important railway station. The English people have thus become accustomed to buying their papers from a news dealer or ordering them through a news dealer instead of subscribing by the year. This does away almost completely with the subscription business, so that a magazine with a big circulation needs only a comparatively small staff. From this it can be understood why *Answers* could be published from a small office.

A point of equal interest is that in England a periodical or newspaper can be made to pay on its circulation alone, regardless of advertising, while in this country advertising is essential. This is because of the lower cost of production and a cheap method of distribution. It may be added that while, in this country, the American News Company has almost a monopoly as a distributing agent, in England there are a large number of wholesale dealers, all of whom are naturally interested in pushing the circulation of periodicals in order to increase their own profits as middlemen. This, of course, helps the publishers.

It did not take Alfred Harmsworth long to grasp the fact that the future success of his business depended on buying cheap paper and keeping down the cost of production to the lowest point. In other words, he was to be in the position of a manufacturer of periodicals. He bought a certain quantity of white paper at 2½ cents a pound, and by editing and printing turned it into 200,000 copies of *Answers* which retailed for two cents each. Eight copies of *Answers* weighed a pound, and while the white paper had cost only 2½ cents these copies could be sold for sixteen cents. Even after the cost of production and the discount to wholesale dealers was deducted, a big profit was left. This principle eventually enabled the Harmsworth business to become the largest publishing business in the world. The whole fabric rested on the system of buying white paper cheaply and transforming it into copies of a periodical, the retail price of which yielded a large profit. Advertising was simply an additional bonus, and was not primarily essential.

It was here that Harold Harmsworth's ability was displayed. He bought paper at the lowest market price, and superintended the cost of production so carefully that no waste occurred. As the business grew, his skill as the financial head became increasingly important.

The success of *Answers* had become so great by the beginning of 1890 that larger quarters were needed for the editorial staff. Accordingly two floors were leased in a Fleet Street building. Soon after this move occurred, Harmsworth issued two comic papers for the masses, *Chips* and *Comic Cuts,* which had some resemblance to the comic supplements of American Sunday newspapers, excepting that they were printed solely in black

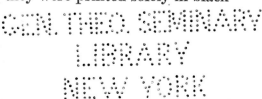

and white, and in addition to comic matter they contained exciting serial stories and some editorial chat. These papers sold for a halfpenny (one cent) each, and both were pushed by means of competitions.

There was this essential difference, however, about the Harmsworth comics, that whereas the American comic supplement leaves something to the intelligence of the reader, the Harmsworth papers did not. For instance, in a series of pictures conveying an obvious joke which, in America, would have required nothing more than an exclamation mark and an interrogation point, the same pictures in the English joke sheets would be accompanied by elaborate analytical explanations. For instance, some comic pictures representing the adventures of a man and a bull would probably have required such an elementary diagnosis as the following:

" The bull sees the man. What ho! He chases him. Eh, what? Will he catch him? Just wait. Ah, the tourist prudently sprints for the nearest tree and shins up it like a streak of greased lightning, while the baffled bull paws viciously below.

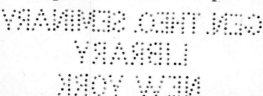

Ha, ha! The man has the laugh this time. But how is he going to get out of the field? " etc., etc.

Harmsworth was determined to drive the point of his illustrated jokes into the heads of his English readers with a hammer, if necessary. The plan was thoroughly successful, for the comics eventually gained huge circulations, the weekly issue of *Comic Cuts* exceeding half a million. Each paper helped to advertise the others, *Answers* calling attention to the comics, while the latter urged readers to buy *Answers*. This plan was adopted from the start and was continued as the papers increased in number. At the end of 1890, *Answers*, which had been much improved, appeared in an orange-colored cover, and in this form it is still published. From the tint of its cover the paper was popularly termed " the golden one." It certainly proved to be golden for the Harmsworths.

Among various competitions which were employed at this time, the "Answers Puzzle " was introduced, and this alone netted a fortune. It consisted of a box about the size of a match box, containing small balls of different colors. The object of the puzzle was achieved by shaking these in such a way that they would divide into appropriate colors and spell the word " Answers." This puzzle made as big a hit in England as the " 15 Puzzle " or the " Pigs in Clover Puzzle " did in this country. Nearly a million were sold in a few weeks. There was a competition to see who could get the balls into position in the shortest space of time, and at least two hundred persons came from all parts of the United Kingdom to try for the handsome prizes offered.

In the early days of *Answers* its enterprising founder had paid almost the equivalent of a year's profits for a serial story by a famous author, and Fleet Street critics then declared that he was headed straight for ruin. Now that *Answers* was prosperous he caused further astonishment by paying the highest prices for articles and other contributions. This not only enabled the paper to obtain the best material, but the circulation of the report did much to increase its popularity.

The success of the young publisher, his ability as an editor, and his ingenuity in bringing his papers to the attention of the public soon caused the name of Harmsworth to become well known. People of importance began to take an interest in this brilliant young man who was already amassing a large fortune, a fact which was not overlooked by the editors of London society journals.

When his papers were well established, Alfred Harmsworth decided to become the owner of a home in the country where he could work and rest far removed from excitement. With this object, in 1891 he purchased an estate named Elmwood on the coast of Kent, about seventy miles from London, and not far from Broadstairs, a popular seaside resort. The house, a typical English mansion, over a century old, had been called Elmwood from a grove of ancient elms that surrounded it. The grounds were extensive and had been attractively laid out. That the new owner of Elmwood was to be included among the local celebrities was attested by the county guide book, which in its next edition added the following passage in its ponderous, highly respectable style:

"A notable feature of the village of St. Peter's is Elmwood, the seat of Alfred Harmsworth, Esq., who has done so much to improve the tone of our cheaper periodical literature."

In September, 1891, the American newspaperman whose early impressions of Alfred Harmsworth were recorded in the preceding chapter, visited London after an interval of three years. In the meantime he had himself risen in the world, having become the editor of a New York magazine. A month's vacation enabled him to cross the Atlantic again. Naturally he had a strong desire to learn how fortune had treated the optimistic projector of *Answers to Correspondents* and its proposed adjunct, the inquiry bureau. Once more the newspaperman will tell his own story.

* * *

The day after I arrived in London I happened to walk along Fleet Street, where I noticed a number of street hawkers selling a paper with an orange-colored cover bearing the significant title *Answers*. Although I had heard nothing from Harmsworth, I decided at once that this must be his paper,

Elmwood

Alfred Harmsworth's country house on the coast of Kent

Courtesy of Macmillan Co.

and that judging by the way it was selling it had made a hit. In fact, a news dealer from whom I bought a copy told me that it was not only one of the best sellers among the penny papers but that its publisher had already cleared a fortune. The *Answers* offices were not far off, so I decided to call there.

Alfred Harmsworth was in when I called, and I was given a cordial greeting. The three years that had passed since our last meeting had not made any appreciable change in his appearance. He was then twenty-six years old, looked as youthful as ever, and was as full of enthusiasm as in the days when we had discussed money-making schemes in the little office in Paternoster Square.

Although *Answers* was going to press when I called, Harmsworth was perfectly cool and smiling; for while he was a born hustler, yet he never seemed to hustle. When I made a remark to that effect, he replied: " The reason is that I direct everything and leave the carrying out to others. The secret of success, I have already discovered, is to originate, direct, and scrutinize, but to do nothing which can be done just as well by assistants."

From the start he had been a believer in young men, and even then it was noticeable that some of his sub-editors were scarcely more than boys. "Yes," he said, when I mentioned this, " they are young; but young people know best what young people want, and a large number of the readers of our comic papers are young folks."

Even on my first examination of *Answers* and the other papers which he showed to me, I could see that their success was largely due to the fact that he put his personality into them. He wrote a good deal of editorial chat, and each paper, from beginning to end, had a personal touch that made it different from rival publications.

During my stay in England I accepted an invitation to spend a week at Elmwood. The old mansion had been furnished with rare taste, and it was in an ideal spot for a vacation. In a corner of the grounds, at some distance from the house, a frame bungalow, consisting of one large room, had been erected, which served as an editorial sanctum and working place.

From the day of my arrival I was pressed into service, Harmsworth's secretary having gone away for a two weeks' vacation. Consequently there was a lot of manuscript to read, proof to revise, and letters to answer. " You'll have to work for your board," remarked my host, in his usual breezy style. " As we haven't got a woodpile, you can read some proof."

Most newspapermen, in spite of what they may say to the contrary, really enjoy talking shop, so I was glad to lend a hand as editorial assistant. Once more we worked together and discussed publishing schemes. Again I was subjected to a volley of questions regarding the progress of American magazines and newspapers. Incidentally, I was told the story of *Answers'* success and what had taken place subsequently.

Harmsworth's former partner, Carr, it appeared, had retired from the business in London, and had gone to live in Dublin, where he became the Irish agent for the Harmsworth publications. As the business increased this position yielded a large revenue. The army officer who had helped to back *Answers* at the start had sold out, receiving

several times over the amount he had originally invested.

The success of *Answers* and the comic papers, which were constantly increasing in
circulation and yielding larger profits, only
served to whet the ambition of their energetic founder. Harmsworth, in fact, had
just begun to lay the foundations of what
was destined to become the biggest publishing business in the world. His three brothers who assisted him were already deriving
substantial returns from their interests. Incidentally, I learned that several bright
young men were being trained to take
charge of new periodicals which were
planned. So optimistic was Harmsworth in
regard to the future, that on my return to
New York I was appointed literary agent,
for the purpose of keeping him closely in
touch with American publishing developments.

* * *

The progress of the Harmsworth business
from 1891 onward was remarkable. It was
in 1891 that its tireless promoter hit upon
the idea of issuing two papers for young
women, on entirely new lines. He called

them *Forget-Me-Not* and *Home-Sweet-Home*. These papers, attractively designed and illustrated, were made up of interesting stories, fashion hints, answers to correspondents, advice to the lovelorn, etc., and were sold for a penny each. Some young women assisted in the editing and were trained in Harmsworth methods. So successful were these papers that they soon had circulations of over 200,000 weekly. They were followed by *Home Chat,* a pretty little magazine for women, costing a penny, which repeated the success of the other papers and reached over 250,000 readers. In this country such a publication as *Home Chat* could not have been sold for two cents, owing to the higher cost of production.

In those days the " penny dreadfuls "— the English equivalent of the American dime novel—sold largely among boys and undoubtedly did much harm. Preachers denounced them in vain. Wouldn't it be possible, Harmsworth thought, to destroy the popularity of the " dreadful " by providing something that would be as popular with boys, and yet would be without its unhealthful features? As the result of this idea, he started a weekly series of halfpenny stories for boys, tales of adventure, etc., which were issued under the title of the "Union Jack Library." These met with instant success. A hundred thousand English boys were soon reading them regularly.

Other boys' papers, which sold for a penny, were next brought out, and these also became immensely popular. From the start these journals aimed at the encouragement of physical culture and patriotism, interest in travel and exploration, and pride in the British Empire. An outgrowth of this department was the establishment of the Union Jack Club, which has a large membership in Great Britain and the British colonies.

The success of the Harmsworths inevitably brought a number of additional rivals into the cheap-periodical field. Imitations of *Answers* continually appeared, the majority of which were started by men with little or no experience and did not last long. Alfred Harmsworth, on the other hand, had behind him several years of hard, practical work in every branch of the periodical-publishing business. Hardly one of the imitation papers survived more than a few months, in spite of insurance schemes, prize competitions, and other devices which were used to gain circulation.

Among these new ventures, however, there was one success, the promoter of which was Cyril Arthur Pearson, a plodding, ambitious young man, who had been a free-lance writer and had afterwards held an important position in the office of George Newnes, the publisher of *Tid-Bits.* Pearson wanted to start a paper of his own, and enlisted the support of Sir William Ingram, proprietor of the *Illustrated London News,* in whose office Harmsworth had gained his first magazine experience.

In 1890, with the backing of Ingram, Pearson started *Pearson's Weekly.* His paper was on the same general lines as *Answers,* and to push it he employed various competitions and offered large prizes. Backed by ample capital, and well advertised, the paper soon gained a big circulation. Pearson adopted Harmsworth methods from the start. When *Answers* was clothed with an orange-tinted cover, Pearson immediately arrayed his paper in a crimson cover. When the Harmsworths started comic papers, boys' papers, and women's papers, Pearson followed suit.

Eventually he built up a large business and brought out some publications of a higher class, including the *Royal Magazine* and *Pearson's Magazine*. Although he cleared a fortune from his interest in the stock company which he organized, he was never a serious rival of the Harmsworths.

In 1894 three firms practically controlled the cheap-periodical field in England—the Harmsworths, Newnes, and Pearson, and the Harmsworths were already in the lead.

IV

DEALING IN MILLIONS

THE youthful prophetic instincts of Alfred Harmsworth did not prove false. " I mean to have the largest publishing business in the world some day," he had remarked to a friend in the first years of *Answers'* success, and now his ambition was in a fair way to be realized.

The reward of all good work is not rest, but more work and harder work. At least, that was the case with Alfred Harmsworth. He had kept his mind fixed on the splendid things that he intended to do, and as the days slipped by he found himself either consciously or unconsciously seizing upon opportunities that led to the fulfillment of his desires, just as the coral insect takes from the running tide the elements needed for its building.

Success, indeed, seemed to be in the youthful publisher's blood. He was apparently

one of those men who are determined to
march cheerfully forward, alert and alive to
whatever opportunities are encountered, and
thus able to turn them to profitable account.

In 1894 the Harmsworth business had increased so rapidly that it was necessary to
find larger quarters.   Accordingly, an old-
fashioned four-story building (24 Tudor
Street) was purchased.   The new home of
the Harmsworth publications was just off
Fleet Street—London's "newspaper row"
—and therefore on historic ground.   Within
a stone's throw, in Gough Square, Dr. Johnson compiled his famous dictionary and, subsequently, was often interviewed by the talk-
ative Boswell.   Interviewing by modern
Boswells, however, was never tolerated by
Alfred Harmsworth, who persistently
avoided time wasters whose ability to talk
exceeded their ability to work.

Under its new owner, the old building
was soon transformed into a modern-looking
structure.   It was renovated from top to
bottom, painted a dazzling white, and sur-
mounted with a huge sign, "Answers," in
gilt letters.   At the same time the Harmsworths decided to do their own printing.

An adjacent building was leased, presses were installed, and in order to cope with the large circulation of the various papers it became necessary to employ day and night forces. The presses were constantly at work.

Alfred Harmsworth's office on the first floor, a small, artistically furnished sanctum, was at that time a favorite resort for writers and magazine artists who had contributions to offer. Among the former were several producers of fiction who afterwards became well known as novelists. Even then the energetic publisher was a conspicuous figure in London journalistic circles, and among the rank and file in Fleet Street he was familiarly referred to as " Alfred," or sometimes admiringly as " Alfred the Great."

With the growth of the business the staff constantly increased, and at the same time Harmsworth began to rear a brood of under-studies to carry on his work. All his assistants were young men and women—the younger the better—capable of receiving impressions and at the same time ambitious and full of initiative. They were trained in what might be termed the "Harmsworth School of Journalism," and they gradually imbibed the style and spirit of their preceptor. They also became specialists. For instance, a young man would concentrate all his attention on supplying matter for a boys' paper, another would edit a comic sheet, while still another would devote all his thoughts and energies to keeping *Answers* to the front.

Young women were trained to write entertainingly for *Home-Sweet-Home* and other papers that appealed to feminine readers. Some of them became editors. They were encouraged, by means of attractive rewards, to originate new ideas for making the papers more popular and to invent schemes for increasing circulation.

Thus, in course of time, Alfred Harmsworth gathered about him a staff of highly specialized young editors and writers who gave such a distinct and personal tone to his publications that whenever a new paper was issued from 24 Tudor Street his increasing thousands of readers knew at once that it would have what they liked—the Harmsworth touch.

From the start, the young publisher be-

lieved in paying liberal wages to the members
of his staff. Cheap men, he often declared,
could take care of only cheap jobs, and he
wanted no cheap men around him. Long
before Henry Ford introduced the high-
wage system in Detroit, Alfred Harmsworth
had it in full operation in his London offices.
He also adopted a system of profit sharing
which is still unexampled in the publishing
business in England or in any other country.

Whenever he selected a man to take
charge of one of his papers he agreed to
pay him, in addition to a good salary, a
liberal percentage on the circulation above
a certain figure. If the circulation increased
under his management, he made money for
himself and the firm; if he failed, he was
soon replaced by a more capable man.

The result was that the young men who
conducted the Harmsworth papers took as
much interest in the business as if it had
been their own. In fact, the chief difficulty
was to prevent them from overworking themselves in their eagerness to become rich.
There were no " clock watchers " in the
Harmsworth offices, everybody was well satisfied, and even the sub-editors had monetary

inducements to exert their energies and
originate ideas. By this method of profit
sharing Harmsworth transformed an able
employee into a master, while the fact that
the man had an interest in the business made
it impossible for a rival publisher to get him
away by offering a larger salary. This plan
was continued and extended as the business
grew, and it had much to do with the ulti-
mate success of the firm.

The rapidity with which new papers were
originated and developed in the early days
is strikingly shown in the case of the Harmsworth religious publications. The story of
how this branch of the business was established is interesting in many ways. It serves
to show that Alfred Harmsworth was a thorough expert in the art of advertising.

The first Harmsworth religious weekly, a
paper of an entirely new type, called the
Sunday Companion, appeared in 1894.
Heralded by all the profuse and sensational
publicity methods that had been used successfully in pushing the other papers, it attracted widespread notice and made a
decided hit. The truth is that its ingenious
promoter had discovered—long before Billy

Sunday made the same discovery on this side of the Atlantic—that religion stands in as much need of advertising as any secular commodity. That is why illustrated posters of an unusually startling description were used in boosting the new weekly. One in particular, inscribed " In that Great and Terrible Day," depicted the dome of St. Paul's Cathedral surrounded by aircraft which were dropping bombs, while fire and devastation reigned below.

This picture might have served as an illustration of what happened during the first year of the war, when Zeppelins actually dropped bombs within a few hundred yards of the Cathedral square. It was, moreover, intentionally prophetic, as it used to advertise the fact that the *Sunday Companion* was making a feature of a blood-curdling story based on the Book of Daniel and Revelation, in which the horrors foreshadowing the end of the world were vividly described.

Harmsworth's wonderful insight into the psychology of the masses was shown in starting this publication at a time when English religious papers were mostly uninteresting,

their contents being made up of religious
news, heavy sermons, and dreary articles.
From his own investigation the sagacious
publisher was convinced that thousands of
English families were literally pining for
some bright Sunday reading matter, and his
new paper was designed to supply this want.
The *Sunday Companion* was unsectarian,
and it consisted of cleverly written illustrated articles, short stories, and thrilling
serials. The heroes of the serials were as a
rule exponents of muscular Christianity.

Like every master business man, Alfred
Harmsworth had a positive genius in selecting men, and this was plainly shown in his
choice of a religious editor. The man selected for the position knew nothing whatever of religious journalism, but he had
shown great ability in conducting a popular
weekly paper for Newnes, the publisher of
Tid-Bits. He displayed equal talent as a
producer of religious papers, and soon made
a success of the *Sunday Companion*.

Prize competitions with a decidedly religious flavor were lavishly employed in advertising and increasing the circulation of the
new weekly, large cash prizes being offered.

In addition, the enterprising editor started an organization, somewhat on the lines of the Christian Endeavor Society, which was called the Bible Band of Britain. Every member wore a celluloid badge with the initials " B. B. B.," and was pledged to fight pernicious literature, spread Bible truths, and incidentally make known the merits of the *Sunday Companion*. In course of time this organization gained nearly 100,000 members. With the assistance of the Bible Band and various other methods of publicity, the *Sunday Companion's* circulation increased rapidly. Three years after it was started it had over 350,000 readers, and the profits were fully $100,000 a year. Five other religious weeklies, consisting of home papers and story magazines, were ultimately started and pushed in the same way, and all of them attained circulations of over 200,000 weekly.

Aside from supplying the masses with wholesome reading matter for the home, the Harmsworth religious weeklies accomplished a great deal of good in other directions. Atheistic attacks on religion that were flourishing in England at the time, were vigorously answered, and these answers were read and digested in the homes of the masses, many of whom had previously been unreached by religious publications. By means of prize competitions Sunday schools were helped, church-building funds were raised, and large numbers of religious workers were given free vacations in the summer time.

The terrible condition of poor boys and girls in the slums of London, who were obliged to go barefooted and insufficiently clad in the bitter winter months, gave these papers another opportunity for charitable work. Appeals were made for clothing, boots, and stockings, and these poured into the *Sunday Companion* receiving station in such large quantities that the staff was unable to cope with the details of checking and distribution. Eventually this department was transferred to the London City Missions, which has since carried on the work.

The skill of the versatile religious editor in devising circulation schemes attracted much attention in those days. On one occasion he obtained several tanks of water from the river Jordan, the fact that it came from the sacred river being certified by a British consul and some Turkish officials. A cut-glass flask filled with this water was presented to any reader who bought a certain number of copies of the religious weekly which was being pushed, and who otherwise helped the paper. "Christen your Babies with Jordan Water" suggested the astute editor as the coupons poured in. "Earth from Bethlehem," "Gold, Frankincense, and Myrrh," and a weird musical instrument called the "Harp of David" were also used as premiums.

Several children's magazines next made their appearance—illustrated penny papers, some of them containing colored pictures, and all of them so well adapted to the needs of English children that they were at once successful. Later on the Harmsworths entered the magazine field and issued the *London Magazine,* an English adaptation of the American ten-cent magazine, which was so popular from the start that it soon had a circulation of 50,000 a month. It was sold for sixpence (twelve cents).

Another profitable branch of the business, subsequently started, was the educational department, which issued educational works for home instruction in bi-monthly parts, at

sixpence a copy. At the end of the year
cloth covers for binding were supplied.
Among the works issued in this manner was
the "Harmsworth Self-Educator," which
gave instruction in a large variety of arts,
crafts, sciences, and languages. Then followed "Popular Science," a "History of the
World," a "Natural History," the "Harmsworth Encyclopedia," and the "Children's
Encyclopedia." The work last named, which
was lavishly illustrated, contained interesting
answers to hundreds of questions that a child
would be likely to ask, covering a wide range
of subjects. It had an unusually large sale
in Great Britain and was afterwards revised
and published in book form by a New York
firm. The "part" system, it may be added,
while successful in England, has never been
popular in this country, the subscription
book plan being preferred by the reading
public.

This brings us to another stage in the
career of Alfred Harmsworth. In 1895, although scarcely seven years had passed since
he had started his first paper in the small
office in Paternoster Square, his business
had reached such large proportions that it

already held the front rank in the English publishing world and defied all competition. At the age of thirty he had become a millionaire, his wealth having continued to pile up so rapidly that it must have been a source of astonishment e͏en to himself.

The business, however, had not grown of its own accord. It had to be built up from the foundation and demanded foresight, enterprise, energy, diplomacy, patience, perseverance, and the most scrupulous fair dealing. At each stage of its development the editorial ability and originality of Alfred Harmsworth were strikingly displayed, together with the skill of his brother Harold, who proved to be an ideal executive. In editorial matters Alfred listened, weighed, sifted, sorted, and then decided, and whenever his decision was made the case was closed.

The rapid growth of the business had been largely brought about through the adoption of novel ideas, which members of the staff and others were encouraged to present. Whenever a scheme was submitted, with the declaration that it would make millions for the firm, the schemer was referred to Harold

Harmsworth, who, with pencil and pad, soon found out whether it was a money maker. If there were possibilities of its yielding a good profit, a liberal price was paid for it.

A constant succession of new ideas put into practical operation by a highly organized and efficient staff enabled the business to expand until the Harmsworth papers were taken by practically every member of the average British household, from mother, father, son, and daughter, down to the youngest reading child. Alfred Harmsworth became, in fact the universal periodical provider. His publications catered to every taste. There were magazines that highly educated people could enjoy, and there were halfpenny comic sheets that would interest the most illiterate reader.

In 1897 the firm of Harmsworth was recognized as one of the wealthiest and most successful publishing houses in England. In that year the business was organized as a stock company with a capital of £1,300,000 (about $6,500,000). Alfred Harmsworth and his brothers retained a controlling interest in the new company, which was incorporated as Harmsworth Brothers, Ltd. Some years later the company, with increased capital, was re-incorporated as the Amalgamated Press, Ltd., and under this title the business is conducted at the present time.

When the company was originally incorporated, the preferred and ordinary (common) shares were offered at £1 ($5) each, and thousands of people, largely readers of the Harmsworth papers, became stockholders. Since then, the ordinary shares have risen as high as $40 a share, and at the present time are selling somewhere near $25. Many of the original shareholders made fortunes through the advance. Forty per cent annually has been regularly paid on the ordinary shares, and five per cent on the preferred.

The continuous growth of this great publishing enterprise has been evidenced by a corresponding increase in the size of the company's business quarters. In 1898 the editorial offices were moved to a large new building in Carmelite Street, near the Thames Embankment, now known as Carmelite House. In 1912 this was replaced by a still larger building, Fleetway House, in Farringdon Street, which was erected at a cost of $675,000, and is said to be the finest editorial building in Europe. Since then it has been found necessary to lease offices in other buildings to accommodate the various offshoots of the business.

The plant of the Amalgamated Press has developed into one of the largest printing establishments in the world, the small quarters in Tudor Street having been replaced, many years ago, by extensive works in Lavington Street, South London. Here are printed the fifty publications owned by the company. Some years since, it was found that economy could be effected by making ink, and the company started an ink factory.

A still more important development occurred in 1902, when the far-sighted founders of the business decided to make their own paper. At that time the Amalgamated Press was buying more paper than any other publishing house in the world, and it was not considered a good policy to allow the supply of raw material to be controlled by outside sources. Although the initial expense was great, future requirements made it essential for the company to control a supply of wood pulp, and thus insure a constant stock of

Fleetway House

Editorial and business offices of the Amalgamated Press

Courtesy of Macmillan Co.

cheap paper, by establishing a paper mill. With this object a thorough investigation of timber properties in Canada was made, and after expert advice on the subject had been received, a tract of pine timber land, embracing about 3400 square miles, was purchased in Newfoundland, the oldest of the British colonies. Here, in 1906, one of the largest pulp and paper making plants in the world was completed, at a cost of over $6,000,000.

The plant includes two private railways, steamers which carry the stock to England, and trunk telephone lines of over 100 miles in length. In the course of a year 1,500,-000 trees are felled and 4,500,000 logs are driven down the river. Running full time, the paper-making machines can turn out 200 tons of paper every day. They are among the largest paper-making machines in existence. Sixty thousand tons of paper are made every year, besides 25,000 tons of pulp. More than 2500 tons of paper and between 1000 and 2000 tons of pulp are shipped to England every three weeks.

The power for the mill is supplied by the great falls of the Exploits River, which flow for nearly half a mile over a series of declivities. The fall is 120 feet. At the highest point a solid concrete dam, 882 feet long, has been built, making possible the generation of 2500 horse power. The paper business has been incorporated as a separate company, the Newfoundland Development Company, Ltd., with a capital stock of $7,000,000 in $5 shares. The Amalgamated Press, Ltd., and the Associated Newspapers, Ltd.—the latter an associated company——are heavily interested.

At Botwoodville, in northern Newfoundland, the paper company has a port, whence the paper is shipped to England. The company employs nearly 2000 workmen, and three communities peopled by them and their families have sprung up in what was recently a primeval forest. Of these the principal one, Grand Falls, with a population of 3000, has become the second town of importance in Newfoundland. A flourishing, up-to-date place, it is supplied with well-paved streets, electric lights, churches, schools, a public library, a bank, a theatre, "movies," and all the other adjuncts of civilized life. No expense has been spared in making the dwellings of the workers as comfortable as possible, and well-designed houses have also been erected for members of the staff.

Only newspaper stock is manufactured in Newfoundland; the finer grades of paper are made at Gravesend, about thirty miles from London. There the companies interested have erected the Imperial Paper Mills, covering seventeen acres and constituting one of the largest paper mills in the world. Pulp from Newfoundland is transferred from the steamer to the mill, which faces the Thames. Large motor trucks, capable of hauling several tons, convey the paper from the mill to the printing works.

It may be added that the Newfoundland company has proved a highly profitable enterprise. A year or so before the war, when business was normal, the Amalgamated Press received about $250,000 as its share of the annual profits. At that time the yearly profits of the Amalgamated Press amounted to £263,283 (about $1,315,000), dividends of forty per cent were paid on the common stock, while £25,000 ($125,000) additional was added to the reserve fund.

In spite of the war, which caused a shortage of print paper and thus had a deterrent effect on the publishing business, the progress of the Amalgamated Press has been highly satisfactory. New magazines, appealing to a great variety of readers, have been brought out from time to time, and all have proved to be money makers. As in former times, no expense has been spared in keeping all the papers to the front by means of prize competitions and other devices. Circulation experts are constantly traveling about the United Kingdom, investigating conditions and ascertaining demands in the shape of reading matter. On the mechanical side, every novelty of merit is carefully scrutinized. Men travel in all progressive countries to obtain fresh ideas for the company. While it is gratifying to have built up the greatest periodical business in the world, those responsible for the welfare of the Amalgamated Press fully realize that even the greatest success can be maintained only by constant watchfulness.

Some idea of the work entailed in printing the fifty publications of the Amalgamated Press may be gathered from the following facts extracted from the company's souvenir book:

Fifteen million words are checked in the course of a year by the reading department.

The number of letters cast by the linotype and monotype machines in the course of a year is 700,000,000.

If all the pages of the publications printed during a year were placed side by side to make a continuous strip, the length of the strip would be nearly a million miles.

Twelve million inches of cuts are made by the photo-engraving department in the course of a year.

The paper bill amounts to $5000 a day.

At the present time at least 50,000 news dealers handle the fifty publications of the Amalgamated Press, which have grown out of the little weekly paper, *Answers,* which Alfred Harmsworth started so unpretentiously less than thirty years ago. The weekly publications alone have a circulation of eight millions, while the monthly magazines have large and increasing circulations.

In recent years the name Harmsworth

has been almost entirely dropped in connection with the business, while the Amalgamated Press has become increasingly prominent as the publisher of what were formerly called the Harmsworth publications. It should be stated, however, that the founder of this great periodical company, who became Lord Northcliffe in 1906, has continued to take a deep interest in its progress.

The circulation of the publications of the Amalgamated Press is not confined to Great Britain, but extends to Australia, Canada, South Africa, India, and other parts of the British Empire. As in the early days, Lord Northcliffe still uses his influence in keeping these periodicals intensely British in tone, appearance, and make-up, and this largely contributes to their success.

Here it may be remarked that in spite of the close relationship that exists between the United States and Great Britain and the fact that the two countries speak the same language, their taste in reading matter is widely different. Lord Northcliffe knows that his papers would not succeed in the United States, and he also knows that American papers would have no success in

England. With few exceptions American publications have failed when introduced there. Even American advertising matter cannot be used in England without considerable revision. British and American national temperaments, in short, are so diverse that what makes an instantaneous hit in one country falls flat in the other. This may be a cause of surprise when it is remembered that the works of such American writers as Mark Twain and Bret Harte are as firmly enthroned in England as in this country; but the explanation undoubtedly is that their appeal is not merely national but international.

The Amalgamated Press still adheres to the plan adopted in the days of Harmsworth Brothers, of employing young men and women—almost youths and girls, in some cases—to edit certain papers. In this way is carried out the original idea of the founder, that young people know best what young people want. The directors, it may be added, are all employees of the company, and are thus able to conduct the business in a practical and thoroughly efficient manner.

The profit-sharing plan, which produced

such excellent results in the early days, is still continued, and the head of each department profits as his department grows. A system of pensions has also been established, so that old or ailing employees who retire from the business, after faithful service, may be suitably provided for. At the present time the pension fund amounts to over $300,-000, and it is constantly growing larger.

A believer in high wages and the principle that the efficient laborer is worthy of his hire, Lord Northcliffe has caused the workers in many departments of the Amalgamated Press to be paid much above the market price. This enables the company to obtain the highest skill. Not long ago a London printing firm complained that the Amalgamated Press had secured the pick of the printing trade by means of " extravagant " wages paid to compositors and pressmen.

To get the best work out of people Lord Northcliffe believes that rest and recreation are essential. With this object in view, the offices of the Amalgamated Press are closed at six o'clock every Friday evening and are not opened until business hours on Monday morning. At present nearly 3000 persons are employed in the editorial, business, and printing departments. Prior to the war the employees had formed a militia regiment. They had also two bands, and cricket, football, and golf clubs, as well as various social organizations.

Although an ardent believer in hard work, Lord Northcliffe is a strong advocate of vacations. The heads of departments are therefore obliged to take an occasional holiday, preferably out of England, in order to get a change of scene and interest. Northcliffe himself plays the game of business for all that is in it, but while he exacts the same toll from his employees he also realizes that the best results are obtained from men in good condition, and it is his constant endeavor to keep all his workers mentally and physically fit.

Unique among millionaire publishers, Lord Northcliffe has raised a goodly brood of wealthy men among his helpers, and has followed the example of Andrew Carnegie by sharing a part of his riches with those who assisted him in building up his great business. His brother Harold, the financial genius, whose skill as a business manager largely contributed toward the transformation of a small enterprise into what has become the gigantic Amalgamated Press, is now a multi-millionaire himself. A few years ago he was raised to the peerage with the title of Lord Rothermere. Two other brothers, Cecil and Leicester, ceased to take an active part in the business some years before the incorporation of the Amalgamated Press, but have derived large fortunes from their interests in the company. Both are now Members of Parliament, and are prominently identified with English political life. Three younger brothers who were also extensive shareholders, were placed in possession of big incomes.

Some of the young men who became connected with the business in the early days and grew up with it earned from ten to twenty thousand dollars a year in editorial positions. Several left the firm with a hundred thousand dollars or more. One member of the staff, who entered the business in 1895 at a salary of $15 a week, was eventually promoted until he became editor-in-chief of *Answers* and other papers, his salary and commissions amounting to $50,000 a year. Some years ago, when a change was made in the management, he accepted half a million dollars to cancel his contract. The only member of the original staff still connected with the company is George A. Sutton, who began his career as a stenographer, afterwards became secretary to Lord Northcliffe, and is now general manager of the Amalgamated Press. He is said to receive a larger salary than that of the President of the United States.

Thus ends the story of the periodical business of Alfred Harmsworth, started in so small a way and transformed, through his genius, into a vast industry. Even the wildest dreams of his youth were more than realized when he became the head of the greatest publishing business in the world, founder of one of the largest paper-making companies, and a Crœsus in point of wealth.

V

A WONDERFUL NEWSPAPER

In presenting the story of Lord Northcliffe the facts concerning his periodical business and his newspapers have been kept apart, for the reason that his activities in these fields of endeavor form distinct phases of his career. The two departments, moreover, have always been kept separate, and are managed by different companies. Therefore, an account of how he became the world's foremost newspaper owner has been given in the three following chapters, each of which forms a special narrative.

From the time that he started out as a journalist, Alfred Harmsworth had been inspired with the ambition to own and edit an important London newspaper. He had kept that goal in view, and was determined not to be satisfied until he had reached it. Visionary as this idea might have seemed when he was struggling to earn his living as a free-lance writer, nevertheless his ambition was destined to be realized while he was still youthful.

The career of Alfred Harmsworth had proved, even then, that to the man with seeing eyes and well-trained mind opportunity comes, not once, but many times in a lifetime. Therefore, when the goddess of opportunity sought for a purchaser for the London *Evening News* she went straight to the door of the young publisher at 24 Tudor Street.

In October, 1894, when he was twenty-nine years of age and had established his periodical business so successfully that it had already brought him a fortune, Alfred Harmsworth astonished London by announcing that he had bought the *Evening News*. The manner in which he became owner of this newspaper formed another remarkable incident in his eventful life, and it also contained certain elements of the picturesque which, it has been said, should form the background of every great business.

The *Evening News* had been started in London in 1881 to support the Conservative party, but had never been a success. Although money had been lavished on the paper, and the Conservatives had dug into their pockets to the extent of over two million dollars in their efforts to bolster it up, the unfortunate sheet had gone from bad to worse. It was badly edited, changes of management were frequent, and in 1894 the circulation was racing toward the zero point. Facing a big deficit, the directors of the stock company which owned the paper became thoroughly dissatisfied, and at last decided to sell out.

Just at that time there happened to be a shrewd young Scotchman named Kennedy Jones employed as a reporter on the London *Evening Sun,* then owned by T. P. O'Connor, M.P. Opportunity knocked at his door also, as the sequel will show.

A native of Glasgow, Jones was a husky, alert, clean-shaven young man with a slight Scottish accent, who had gained his first newspaper experience in Edinburgh and Manchester. Later on, with a wife and an increasing family, he had migrated to London, where he soon made a name as a reporter, particularly in the line of sporting news. " K.J.," as he was popularly termed, knew everybody about town, especially at the music halls and race tracks. He was a born hustler for news, and his beats were innumerable. Although his salary on the *Sun* was only twenty-five dollars a week, he had started life with an abnormal supply of energy, ambition, and grit, the qualities which enable a man to overcome all difficulties and even to rise above an unfavorable environment in achieving success.

In his youthful days Jones had bought groceries from an enterprising storekeeper in Glasgow named Lipton, who was strangely ambitious. This man, Lipton, continually surprised the lad by declaring that he meant to become a millionaire, which inspired him to become ambitious also. Eventually, when the ambitious grocer developed into a multimillionaire and became Sir Thomas Lipton, head of one of the greatest businesses in the world, Jones was convinced, more than ever, that there was something in ambition.

When, therefore, Jones the reporter happened to hear one day that the ill-fated *Evening News* was for sale, and recalled that it was Alfred Harmsworth's ambition to become a newspaper owner, he realized that he was facing the great opportunity of his life. What followed would be impossible to-day in either London or New York, but it happened in London in 1894.

With nothing but an astonishing amount of self-assurance, Jones called on the directors of the *Evening News* and told them that if they would give him an option on the paper for one week he would find a purchaser for it. His manner was so convincing that the directors, ready to clutch at any hope of even a partial salvage, actually came to terms, and Jones walked away with his option. Here is the rest of the story, as it was related some years later by Jones himself to an intimate friend:

"When I had obtained the option, the next thing was to interview Alfred Harmsworth. At that time I was a hard-working, hustling reporter, and was not particularly well dressed or impressive in appearance. Accordingly, I decided to send a deputy to 24 Tudor Street, and for this purpose selected my friend, Louis Tracy, the novelist, who was then writing stories for the *Evening Sun*. Unlike myself, Tracy always looked impressive, and wore the conventional

frock coat and silk hat which then distinguished the solid citizen of London. When
I broached the subject to him and promised
him a share in the enterprise, he agreed to
assist me in putting through the deal. With
this object he went round to *Answers'* office
at once, and submitted the offer to Alfred
Harmsworth, who was favorably impressed,
although he seemed to suspect that Tracy
had not originated the idea.

" ' Is this your own scheme, Mr. Tracy? '
he asked. Tracy explained that it was I
that had obtained the option. ' Then,' replied Alfred Harmsworth, ' Jones is the man
I want to see.' The result was that I called
at 24 Tudor Street myself, and after some
consultation with Alfred and Harold
Harmsworth, a meeting was arranged with
the directors of the *Evening News*. The
books were examined, the plant was inspected, and ultimately the paper was bought
by the Harmsworths for £25,000 ($125,-
000)."

Having acquired the paper, Alfred
Harmsworth saw that Jones, who not only
was a journalist of wide experience but had
proved that he was original and enterpris-

ing, was just the sort of man to edit and manage it. So, from twenty-five dollars a week as a reporter, Jones stepped into the position of managing editor of the *Evening News* at a salary of five thousand dollars a year, with an eighth interest in the paper as well. Mr. Tracy also received liberal compensation for his assistance in arranging the affair.

At first sight, the *Evening News,* as a property, looked far from promising. The offices were in an antiquated building in Whitefriars Street, the presses were old and worn, and about the whole establishment there was that atmosphere of decay which pervades decrepit businesses as well as senile human beings. When, therefore, it became known in Fleet Street that Alfred Harmsworth had bought this unlucky paper, men shook their heads and declared that he had been " buncoed." In fact, Harold Harmsworth, who accompanied his brother and Kennedy Jones on their first visit to their new property, laughingly remarked to an acquaintance they met: "We are on our way to see our gold brick, and," indicating Jones, " there is the man who planted it on us."

In building up and transforming the *Evening News,* however, Alfred Harmsworth displayed the same tireless energy that he had shown in making a fortune out of his periodicals. He went to the office every day and worked there until late at night, suggesting new features and introducing novelties, his intensely practical and businesslike mind sifting every detail and intuitively separating the relative from the inconsequential.

Jones, with his wide experience in every branch of newspaper work, now proved to be invaluable. He knew what the masses wanted, and also the weak spots of the old-fashioned evening newspapers. He employed the best men for the sporting department, with the result that the racing, football, and cricket reports, which make or mar an evening paper in London, soon put the *Evening News* in the lead.

Within a few weeks, by effectively administering his own brand of the elixir of life to the tottering paper, Harmsworth revitalized it and made it a money maker. With its smart headlines, snappy news stories, bright special articles, women's column, joke column, serial fiction, and other features, the modernized *Evening News* became the talk of the town, and by the end of the first year it had not only repaid the original investment, but was in a position to pay six per cent on its shares. At the present time the circulation is over a million daily.

With all its brilliant success, however, the *Evening News* was, for Alfred Harmsworth, merely in the nature of a trial horse in daily journalism. It was an experiment or, as a miner would term it, a prospect in the domain of newspaperdom. There was still the same craving of the masses for a bright morning newspaper to be satisfied. Convinced by the success of the *Evening News,* in a single year, that he had struck a mine of virgin gold, the far-seeing young publisher decided to start what had long been in his mind, a morning paper conducted on entirely new lines.

In America we have come into an era when the afternoon newspaper is the swift, rapid-fire distributer of news, with a following that constantly increases, but in England the morning paper still remains the heavy gun. Alfred Harmsworth was well aware of the latter fact when, in the spring of 1896, he prepared to launch his new daily, and invested over two and a half million dollars in the enterprise.

With his characteristic thoroughness, he made sure that the machinery of organization would be in working order on the day of publication by having the paper issued daily, for private examination, during a period of three months. Although not a single copy of the paper was circulated, every issue was subjected to the same rigorous criticism that it would have received had it already been placed in the hands of the public. In those three months Alfred Harmsworth was appraising material, sounding tendencies, examining, changing, improving, criticizing, and gathering a staff of the ablest and most progressive newspaper men that he could find.

When at last, one morning in May, 1896, the new morning paper, the *Daily Mail,* was presented to the British public, it had a real individuality which could be summed up only in that comprehensive phrase, the Harmsworth touch. It was, moreover, the first morning paper to be issued in Great Britain for a halfpenny, or one cent. The price was a radical departure, but one which made an instant appeal to the masses, as its founder had expected. Not only was the style and appearance of the new daily entirely different from that of the other morning papers, but the whole spirit of the newcomer was thoroughly in accordance with modern ideas. Widely advertised, as it had been, through the Harmsworth weekly periodicals, the *Daily Mail* proved an immediate success. It started on its wonderful career with a circulation of over a quarter of a million.

The lines on which the new daily was managed, as well as the novelty of its appearance, caused much astonishment among the editors of the old-fashioned London dailies, the majority of whom lived in antiquated seclusion, their intercourse with members of their staffs being usually conducted by letter. In some cases, if a reporter did not receive an assignment by the first mail in the morning he was not expected to go to the office.

To these editors of the old school the mere suggestion of liveliness in a newspaper was anathema. From the normal, everyday interests of average men and women they stood far apart. Enterprise was considered by them the deadliest of sins. They ignored the entire change in the educational system of England that had taken place with the establishment of a public school system, and the development of a new generation of thinking masses, while they also failed to notice the progress that had been made in the industrial and economic life of the nation. Not only were the venerable and highly respectable newspapers which they edited ponderous in tone, but they contained, day after day, profound essays on foreign topics, scientific papers which nobody but a scientific man could understand, and editorials of four thousand words or more on high politics. Therefore it is not surprising that their aggregate circulation was small.

Into this antiquated, easy-going, complacent journalistic world, the *Daily Mail* suddenly burst with all the force of a high-explosive shell. In marked contrast with the conventional English newspaper methods, Alfred Harmsworth and his editors kept themselves in personal touch with the members of the staff, watched their work, and drilled them into a high degree of efficiency. The system adopted was, in fact, much the same as that which is followed in any well-regulated American newspaper office.

Compact in size—a pigmy compared with the blanket sheets of the other London dailies, and smaller than any of the New York papers—the *Daily Mail* consisted of eight pages, the news being condensed into the smallest space so that it could be read quickly. The fourth page was devoted to short editorials and special articles. On the sixth page were magazine features and a serial story.

The British public liked the new paper. It was a success from the start, and in less than a year its circulation was over three hundred thousand. By the end of the second year this had increased to half a million, and during the Boer War, in 1900, it reached the million mark. At present the normal circulation is somewhere about 1,500,000.

An examination of the early numbers of the *Daily Mail* shows, curiously enough, that the paper, from an American point of view, was quite conventional in almost everything except its condensed news and the introduc-

Alfred Harmsworth in 1897

Reading his newspaper, the Daily Mail

tion of some new features. The truth is that Alfred Harmsworth, above all else, was afraid of alarming the British public, which, as he knew, objected to being Americanized. Suspicions were allayed by the conventional appearance of the new paper. Once sure of a steadily increasing circulation, however, the discerning publisher began to brighten his paper. Additional novelties were introduced, headlines were given more " punch," editorials were cut down, and signed articles on popular subjects appeared on the fourth page. For breadth of interest nothing has ever equaled these articles, which cover a wide variety of topics and from the start have constantly maintained a high standard of authority and distinction.

From the outset the motto for *Daily Mail* representatives was: " Get the news and get it first." No effort or expense was spared in living up to this commandment. Eminent writers and correspondents, at high salaries, were sent to all parts of the world in which events of importance were occurring. Shortly after the paper was started, for example, the late George W. Steevens was sent with General Kitchener's army to Khar-

toum, where Gordon was avenged and the
Khalifa's power in the Sudan was shattered.

When the South African War broke out
in 1889, the magnificent organization which
Harmsworth had established enabled the
Daily Mail to get ahead of the British government in respect to news from the front,
and the War Department was often obliged
to acknowledge the receipt of information
supplied by the enterprising paper.

It was during the Boer War that the
Daily Mail proved itself to be unrivaled as
a money raiser. Upon the purchase by the
paper of " The Absent-Minded Beggar " by
Rudyard Kipling, this famous poem was
published in pamphlet form and also set to
music. The proceeds of copyright fees and
incidental contributions, which eventually
amounted to five hundred thousand dollars,
were expended in providing ambulances and
comforts for soldiers, while the surplus that
remained was large enough to cover the cost
of building a hospital for wounded veterans.

Possessing a remarkable news sense, Alfred Harmsworth always grasped the possibilities of a big story with the quickness
that characterizes the born newspaperman,

and like a " star " reporter he delighted in going after an important story himself.

In the early days of the *Daily Mail* he added greatly to the reputation of the paper by two important beats. One was an interview that he obtained with the late Cecil Rhodes regarding the situation in South Africa preceding the Boer War. The " Colossus of South Africa," as Rhodes was popularly termed, had persistently refused to be interviewed, but the enterprising owner of the *Daily Mail* managed to see him and laid the case frankly before him. " I have just started a morning paper, Mr. Rhodes," he said, " and to present your own story to the public, fully and correctly, would be a great advantage to you and would be a great achievement for me." Rhodes was so much impressed by the grit of the youthful publisher that he forthwith gave him a full and exclusive story which made a great sensation in England and was published throughout the world.

Later on, when the Conservative government was getting shaky and all sorts of rumors were afloat, Alfred Harmsworth again acted as a reporter, and scored another

beat through interviewing Arthur James
Balfour, then British prime minister, and
obtaining from that statesman the first news
of his resignation, the downfall of the Conservative government, and the plans for a
general election.

Even in these days, as Lord Northcliffe,
the famous journalist still preserves the
reportorial habit, and in situations of great
importance he has occasionally acted as his
own reporter. For instance, during the
Home Rule agitation in Ireland in 1914 he
made a first-hand study of the problem in
Ulster and interviewed the leaders on both
sides. Since the present war began he has
on several occasions visited the front.

From the beginning American news was
featured conspicuously in the *Daily Mail*.
An office was opened in New York, with an
experienced correspondent in charge, and
direct cable communication with the London
office was established. Before that time the
London newspapers had seldom printed
more than an occasional paragraph of American news, usually obtained from Reuter's
Agency and headed " American Intelligence." The *Daily Mail* began to publish

items of popular interest cabled from New York and sometimes devoted a column or more to accounts of sensational murder trials, fashionable weddings, new inventions, and social movements of a novel character.

During the McKinley-Bryan campaign in 1896 two or three columns daily were cabled to the paper, and at that time George W. Steevens wrote a series of articles entitled " The Land of the Dollar." This established a precedent for American election news, which, since then, has been allotted a large amount of space in the *Daily Mail*. A special news service was maintained during the Spanish-American war in 1898, when Charles E. Hands was sent to Cuba with the American army. In recent years the paper has made a feature of direct Washington news.

Aroused by the competition of the *Daily Mail,* the managements of the other London dailies began to change their business methods. A more up-to-date appearance was given to these older papers, and their presentation of news was improved. Some of them opened New York offices and competed

with American news, so that in course of
time the British public was made more familiar with American affairs, to the manifest
advantage of Great Britain and the United
States.

Although the *Daily Mail* had at first a
clear field, a rival paper soon appeared.
Within a year Harmsworth's persistent
competitor, Pearson, started a morning
paper called the *Daily Express,* which re-
sembled the *Daily Mail* in make-up and contents. Pearson even went a step further
than the *Daily Mail* by presenting the news
on the first page of his paper, while Harmsworth had followed the English custom of
devoting the outside page to advertising.
Eventually the *Daily Express* became a
good property, and at the present time it
has a large circulation, although its success
was never so pronounced as that of the
Daily Mail.

In building up the enormous circulation
of his paper Harmsworth displayed his
genius as a publisher in a striking way.
Among other things, he solved the problem
of placing the *Daily Mail* so promptly in the
hands of readers throughout Great Britain

that it became a national organ and not merely a local newspaper. At Manchester, two hundred miles north of London, he opened a branch office with a printing department, and there an exact duplicate of the London edition is produced every morning, the entire contents of the paper being telegraphed every night over private wires. By means of special trains the Manchester edition is able to reach Edinburgh, Glasgow, Aberdeen, and other distant places in time to be placed on the breakfast table with the local newspapers. The London edition has its radius to the south, covering the country as far as Cornwall. It is therefore correct to say that the *Daily Mail* is obtainable every morning from Land's End to John o' Groat's House.

In order that English people traveling or residing on the Continent may be kept in touch with home and world affairs, a smaller yet satisfactory edition of the *Daily Mail* is published in Paris and is distributed in most parts of Europe. Until the outbreak of the war a Riviera edition was printed at Nice during the winter season, thus supplying the needs of thousands of English read-

ers at Monte Carlo and other resorts on the
Mediterranean coast.

In recent years the headquarters of the
Daily Mail have been at Carmelite House,
near Fleet Street, formerly the home of the
Amalgamated Press, where the *Evening
News* also is published. The building is full
of mechanical wonders, including the Hoe
presses, the largest in England. In the editorial department an instrument called the
" electrophone " is occasionally employed
when important speeches are delivered at
some distance from London, which enables
them to be instantly recorded by stenographers in the *Daily Mail* office, and to be set
up in type without delay. Late news is telephoned direct to the Paris office. In the
foreign department a tape machine de-
livers news direct from New York. The
circulation department has a great array
of motor wagons, trucks, and bicycles to
facilitate delivery of the paper to local
dealers.

Through the enterprise of its management,
the *Daily Mail* has entered intimately into
the social and business life of Great Britain,
a fact which can be demonstrated by a re-

cital of just a few of its achievements in recent years.

This paper was the first English daily to realize that the automobile was not merely a toy or a luxurious convenience but foreshadowed a complete transformation in methods of land transportation. The publicity and encouragement it gave to the industry did much to stimulate English automobile manufacturers in catching up with their French rivals.

Realizing from the start the possibilities of aviation, the *Daily Mail* has offered, in all, the sum of two hundred thousand dollars in cash prizes to encourage flying contests. It has done more than any other single agency to popularize the sport and to equip the British army and navy with what the present war has proved to be an indispensable weapon.

Among the interesting events of early days was the award of a prize of five thousand dollars to Blériot, who first succeeded in crossing the English Channel on a trip from Paris to London. Another long-distance prize was awarded for a flight from London to Manchester—about the same dis-

tance as from New York to Boston. A
prize was offered, later on, for a flight from
London to Scotland and back, a distance of
one thousand miles. The *Daily Mail* now
has a standing offer of fifty thousand dollars to the first aviator who succeeds in
crossing the Atlantic, the prize being open
to aviators of all nations.

A few years ago this enterprising journal
was the promoter of a movement to check
the alarming decline in British agriculture.
As an object lesson a small farm was stocked
and equipped and a tenant selected, for the
purpose of proving that any person of intelligence, by adopting the right methods, could
make a small farm yield a good profit. The
entire country became interested in the experiment, which was remarkably successful.

Another useful project was the evolution
of the *Daily Mail* loaf. The idea was to
show that modern systems of milling were
producing a flour which lacked the nutritious
elements of wheat. Accordingly, three thousand dollars was spent in an effort to produce a standardized loaf for the British public, containing at least eighty per cent of
the wheat. As the result of this agitation a

distinct and permanent improvement in the bread of the nation was brought about.

In recent years the English love of gardening was stimulated by prizes offered by the *Daily Mail,* amounting to five thousand dollars, for the finest bunches of sweet peas raised in home gardens, while another large sum was offered for a new variety of rose.

Among other things, the *Daily Mail* has carried on a campaign for pure milk; it has awarded prizes for the best designs of cottages and other small houses; and it has paid out thousands of pounds in conducting a plan of insurance by which readers of the paper are indemnified for accidents occurring in public vehicles. A brokerage exchange, which has been established, enables readers to buy or sell stocks without the red tape and heavy charges that usually characterize stock-exchange transactions in London.

When taxi cabs were introduced in London and horse cabmen were thrown out of employment in large numbers, the *Daily Mail* raised nearly forty thousand dollars in a few days for their relief. At the same time a pension scheme for the older men was arranged, and over five hundred cabmen were trained as motor drivers.

Impressed by the difficulties of the blind in keeping in touch with passing events, a weekly edition of the *Daily Mail* in Braille type was started a few years ago.

In recent times the power of this live daily as a money raiser has frequently been evidenced. In 1912, for instance, over three hundred thousand dollars was raised for the relief of the *Titanic* victims, the money being contributed exclusively by women readers of the paper. During the war eighty thousand dollars was raised in four days for the purpose of establishing a Union Jack Club for soldiers and sailors.

Viewed from a strictly commercial point of view, the various enterprises and achievements of the *Daily Mail* have proved a source of great profit, by indirectly increasing circulation. This, in turn, has made possible the securing of an abundance of advertising, at rates that range from fifteen hundred to twenty-five hundred dollars a page. The outside page, which is naturally the preferred position, has been at times in such demand that advertisers desiring it have been put on a waiting list. From a broader standpoint the Northcliffe policy of anticipating the demands of the British people has given the *Daily Mail* national prestige, and has made the paper an almost inspired chronicler of Great Britain's political, social, and commercial needs.

As Alfred Harmsworth, and to-day as Lord Northcliffe, the guiding spirit of the *Daily Mail* has proved himself to be the most influential newspaper proprietor in the British Empire. Much of his success has been attained by keeping abreast of popular movements, and never being afraid to change his policy in order to be in harmony with the spirit of the masses. Whenever he has seen the waves rising from the level of the populace, he has preferred to go with the current rather than be overwhelmed by it. His success has often been due to his cutting away from old moorings. Through his ability to look into the future and anticipate coming events, which has sometimes been remarkable, he has surprised the public by his knowledge of affairs, and this has done much to increase his following.

So deeply has his popular newspaper be-

come interwoven with the fabric of British
social life that when it agitates for any reform the public response that follows is usually too great to be ignored. Holding itself
clear outside the humdrum game of politics
as played by other papers, and viewing issues from a non-partisan standpoint, Lord
Northcliffe's *Daily Mail* has become a medium by which its owner's piercing insight
into the heart of things, and his courage to
express himself regardless of the views of
others, have made his pen the lash that has
driven muddlers and incompetents from
office and enabled him to dethrone popular
but inefficient idols, even when they were in
the form of prime ministers and governments.

VI

WOMEN AND PICTURES

" CHERCHEZ la femme " is the advice given by the French whenever an explanation of most human mishaps is demanded. And, strange as it may seem, woman, who brought our first parent so much disaster, was destined to cause the first halt in Lord Northcliffe's successful career.

Until that time the versatile publisher's judgment of the British public's needs and desires, as far as newspapers were concerned, had been almost infallible; but when he endeavored to gauge correctly the mysteries of the feminine mind he failed, as some of the greatest figures in history failed, thus proving that even the most brilliant of men has his limitations. How it all happened forms a most interesting story.

Following the success of the *Evening News* and the *Daily Mail,* Northcliffe, or Alfred Harmsworth as he was then, became

169

imbued with the idea that women did not
read ordinary daily papers with deep interest because the reading matter appealed
chiefly to men. Thus he reached the conclusion that there was a distinct need for
a women's newspaper, written and edited by
women, and giving news that would interest
women exclusively. As the result of this
decision, he started such a paper in October,
1903, having chosen the attractive title, *The
Daily Mirror.*

Summed up in a few words, this enterprise proved to be an utter failure. And
yet, by abandoning his original idea and
bringing into play his undaunted genius,
Harmsworth actually turned the paper into
a gigantic success. When he had overcome
failure he made a clean breast of his first
defeat.

In an article entitled, "How I Lost a
Hundred Thousand Pounds" ($500,000),
he said: "Having for many years fostered a
theory that a daily newspaper for women
was in urgent request, I started one. This
belief cost me one hundred thousand pounds.
I found out that I was beaten, that women
did not want a paper of their own. It was

simply another instance of failure made by mere man in diagnosing woman's needs. Some people say that a woman never really knows what she wants. It is certain that she knew what she did not want. She did not want the *Daily Mirror* as it first appeared."

As a woman's paper the *Daily Mirror* was about the size of *Collier's Weekly*. It was unillustrated, it gave a condensed summary of the world's news, and devoted a large amount of space to social gossip, fashions, home chats, and other topics supposed to be of foremost interest to women readers.

The employment of a staff composed entirely of women led to some of the most amusing incidents in the whole range of modern journalism. In addition to the ladies of the staff—editors, copy readers, and reporters—two or three men were stationed in the office in an advisory capacity. The latter soon discovered that the *Mirror* was a " live " paper in more ways than one.

The truth is that, at that time, the woman journalist was comparatively new in England, and the ladies of the *Mirror* seemed unable to separate their social life from their

business duties.   In this country, of course,
the newspaper woman is a recognized institution, and the women of the press have
proved themselves to be fully as capable as
the men.   But in England, when the *Daily
Mirror* was started, the situation was different.

A member of the original staff, who is
now engaged in American newspaper work,
has given an amusing account of what was
witnessed in the *Mirror* office in the early
days.   In relating his story, he says: "When
the paper was first started, the editorial department was the scene of much comedy,
with an occasional touch of tragedy.   Every
moment there was wrangling between the
lady reporters and editresses, who bounced in
and out of the rooms like the funny charac-
ters in an English pantomime, more intent
on squabbling than on working.   Amidst the
banging of doors would be heard such epithets as ' creature,' ' impossible person,' or
' cat,' intermingled with angry commands,
such as, ' I say you shall,' followed by the
defiant retort, ' I say I won't.'

" That wasn't the worst of it, however.
The poor males about the place were turned

into messenger boys and were kept running errands. One thoroughly disciplined and subdued married man was actually enlisted to do shopping, even to the extent of matching ribbons. All the ladies stopped work to have their tea at five o'clock every afternoon, no matter how exciting the news might be. Sometimes one of the men would be sent out to buy them cakes and other eatables. Then the ladies divided themselves into little cliques and one set wouldn't speak to another set.

"One afternoon, at tea time, the city editress rushed into the reporters' room and announced that there was a big fire near the Mansion House (the official residence of London's Lord Mayor). 'One of you ladies will have to cover the story,' she said. The lady reporters took no notice of the interruption beyond remarking that the editress was 'a most extraordinary person,' and went on discussing their social affairs. When, at last, the editress returned and raised a rumpus, each reporter declared that she couldn't possibly go to the fire because she had an important engagement elsewhere. One of the men had to cover the assignment. That was

a typical incident. The lady reporters had
absolutely no news sense. All they could
talk about was dress, social functions, and
women's wrongs."

Among the men who kept an eye on the
Mirror was an able journalist named Bolton,
who usually had charge of the paper at night
when it went to press. Among other duties,
he was authorized to settle disputes among
the women and preserve order. To have
filled such a position satisfactorily would
have required the cunning of Machiavelli,
the grace of Don Juan, and the wisdom of
Socrates, a combination of qualities which, of
course, no man on earth ever possessed.
The result was that purgatory itself would
have been a paradise in comparison with
what Bolton had to endure. There were,
for instance, frequent disputes among the
ladies as to assignments, and the space that
stories should fill. Rows on these subjects
were constantly in progress. One evening a
friend of Bolton's, who happened to call at
the *Mirror* office, found him surrounded by a
phalanx of angry women.

"Do you realize, Mr. Bolton," exclaimed
one of them, "that I have been working for

hours on this story, and it ought to fill at
least two columns; but that indescribable
person over there (indicating the city editress) has actually cut it down to two
inches?"

"My dear madam," replied Bolton, "I
have been a reporter myself, and sometimes
when I had worked a whole day on a story
it never appeared at all."

"That may be true," retorted the lady
reporter icily, "but my story is a *good*
story."

Several other ladies, holding proof sheets,
then broke into the discussion with various
complaints, all talking at once. In the midst
of the altercation the managing editress burst
through the group like a human cyclone, remarking excitedly: "Now, Mr. Bolton,
you'll have to decide what to do."

Here was a highly modernized version of
that classic fiction, the judgment of Paris,
but poor Bolton was hard pressed in attempting to follow the precedent. "I shall
have to refer these matters," he groaned eva-
sively, as he rubbed his aching head. He
knew only too well that there was no one to
whom he could refer the disputes. When

his friend left he was still arguing, and there seemed to be no end to the discussion.

It is not surprising that, some months later, Bolton, a complete nervous wreck, retired to a farm to raise poultry and follow other restful pursuits. His experience on the women's paper had been too much for him. He never returned to journalism, and in his household the *Daily Mirror* is a subject tabooed.

The wrangling of the women editors and reporters was not occasional but continuous; harmonious coöperation was found to be impossible, and personal animosities and petty rivalries held sway. In fact, the *Mirror* office was distinguished by much the same lack of a definite policy as distinguished the Bandarlog in Kipling's " Jungle Book."

The box office receipts furnish the best evidence of a theatre's prosperity; in the newspaper world circulation is the test of popularity. Judged from this standpoint, the outlook for the *Daily Mirror* was far from encouraging. The paper had started with a circulation of nearly half a million, but each day witnessed a greater falling off, until the profits were swept away like leaves in a wintry blast. This was serious. For while a successful newspaper can soon build up a fortune for its owner, a failure has a prodigious faculty of devouring money, and can gobble down thousands of golden coin with the same ease that a Broadway spendthrift gets rid of a ten-dollar bill.

It was undoubtedly a unique and disagreeable experience for Alfred Harmsworth to be dipping into his exchequer in response to the unceasing cry from the *Daily Mirror* for money and still more money. It was, however, a demand that continued for only a short time, for the shrewd publisher speedily came to the conclusion that, for the first time, he was beaten.

"How is the patient?" Harold Harmsworth was asked, one day, by a friend who thus jokingly referred to the *Mirror*.

"Very low, indeed," he replied, adapting his answer to fitting similes. "Her circulation is very bad, it's constantly getting worse, and I'm afraid she's going to die."

"She won't die," Alfred Harmsworth broke in, pugnaciously. "There must be some cure, and we shall find it yet," he

added, showing in a phrase his great qualities, optimism and determination.

Then again there came to his rescue that
sixth sense,—if so it may be termed,—the
instinct that had been his since he started his
first paper. He put to himself the question
he had so often asked and answered: What
do the people want in the way of newspapers? The *Daily Mail* supplies the morning news, and the *Evening News* covers the
later happenings. A morning or evening
newspaper would naturally compete and thus
divide the field and profits. Now, what is
there that we haven't already got?

As he surveyed the situation closely, the
big idea suddenly occurred to him, that people like pictures!

Beyond an occasional portrait, the London
dailies seldom contained any illustrations.
The *Daily Mail* had owed part of its success to having illustrated some of its articles.
The continuous success of the *Illustrated
London News* and the *Graphic* had shown
that a big demand existed for weekly illustrated papers. There was also, at that time,
an illustrated daily paper, the *Daily
Graphic,* which had been running for several

years with moderate success. That paper, however, used line drawings instead of reproductions of photographs, so that its novelty was slight. Elaborating this idea, Harmsworth decided, at last, that he would change the *Daily Mirror* into an illustrated paper, using halftone reproductions of photographs, and in supplying its contents would make use of the cameras of photographers instead of the pencils of reporters.

His next idea was to use halftone illustrations on almost every page, and to condense the reading matter—the ordinary news of the day—into the smallest possible limits. The policy of getting the first news, which had been followed with such success in the case of the *Daily Mail,* would be adopted in obtaining *Daily Mirror* illustrations. The editorial staff would be ordered to get the first photographs illustrating important events.

When these ideas had been worked out, Harmsworth reorganized the *Daily Mirror* office. The lady editresses and reporters departed, and their places were taken by a staff of live young men. At the same time, photographic and photo-engraving departments were started, and presses of a special type were installed to print the new illustrated paper. Instead of employing a number of writers and reporters, the energetic publisher organized a corps of photographers to cover events in Great Britain, while in place of correspondents, photographic representatives were appointed in all parts of the world. Thus it was impossible for an important event to occur anywhere without the *Mirror* being in a position to obtain the first and best pictures.

The illustrated *Mirror,* somewhat reduced in size, but with more pages, was issued at the end of 1903. It proved an immediate success. When the change was made the circulation had dropped to 20,000, but the new paper started off with a circulation of 60,000, which was soon increased to 100,000. As a woman's paper the *Mirror* had cost a penny (two cents). As a picture paper the price was reduced to a halfpenny.

Once the paper was started and meeting with encouragement, no expense was spared in making it a success. For the first time in British journalism, or in the journalism of the world for that matter, photographic

beats became as important as news beats.
Nothing was thought of hiring special trains
to get a handful of pictures to the *Daily
Mirror* office in time to illustrate some important news story.   Photographers were
dispatched to all parts of the world on special missions, just as newspaper correspondents are sent to write descriptive articles.
When, for example, the situation in China
seemed to be precipitating trouble, a few
years ago, a *Daily Mirror* photographer was
sent there to snap everything of interest and
await results, so that the *Mirror* was not
only supplied with a complete set of photographs of Chinese scenes and notables, but a
man was on hand with his camera, ready for
action if anything important happened.

When Colonel Roosevelt went on his African hunting trip, a *Daily Mirror* photographer accompanied his expedition, and the
American newspapers were dependent on the
enterprise of the London paper for their pictures of the mighty hunter in the depths of
the jungle.

The first bulletin of the Messina earthquake had no sooner reached the *Mirror*
office than a staff photographer was rushed

to the scene of the disaster. So quick was the action of the *Mirror* that it not only printed the first photographs showing the effects of the earthquake, but it actually cleared eight thousand dollars by selling duplicate sets to continental newspapers, even including some of the Italian journals.

During the Turkish-Italian War, a *Daily Mirror* photographer chartered an ocean steamer, the only vessel obtainable in Italian waters, to take him to Tripoli. He was the first to arrive there, and established a historic precedent by leaping ashore, hiring a cab, and giving the order: "Drive me to the battlefield."

When King George went to India to hold a durbar and assume the crown as Emperor of India, a *Mirror* photographer was sent ahead to make arrangements for getting a complete set of pictures illustrating this important ceremony.

During the present war the photographic beats of the *Mirror* have been innumerable, the camera men having been stationed on all parts of the fighting line. Some of them have taken photographs at the risk of their lives, and have outrivaled newspaper correspondents in their efforts to record important events.

When the *Mirror* was first changed into an illustrated paper, various ingenious devices were employed to increase its circulation. Here again Alfred Harmsworth showed that his skill in promoting novel " boosting " schemes was as great as ever. Among other things, a special performance was given at the Crystal Palace, a huge amusement building on the outskirts of London, to which free admission was obtained by presenting coupons clipped from the *Daily Mirror.* To carry out this idea cost less than five hundred dollars, but the effect on circulation was incalculable. Widespread interest was also aroused by the first non-stop automobile test of two thousand miles on a course around Great Britain, which was conducted by the paper. This lifted the circulation still higher.

A year after the paper was reorganized, it was announced that *Mirror* photographers would appear at various seaside resorts and at each place a group of people on the beach would be photographed. To every person whose face appeared in the published photographs the *Mirror* would present five shillings ($1.25) and a silver-mounted fountain pen. The result was that the photographers were literally mobbed by people anxious to be photographed, and in some instances were badly bruised. At Ramsgate, on one occasion, the camera man was pushed into the sea, washed away with his camera, and almost drowned.

Beauty contests, with big money prizes, which gave opportunities for theatrical preferment, were also introduced with great success.

Like the clever diagnostician that he was, Harmsworth had discerned just what the public wanted. Promoted by a corps of expert circulation men, who traveled all over Great Britain, the *Daily Mirror* was at last made a tremendous success. Within a year the paper which, in a few months, had cost its founder five hundred thousand dollars, and had once been at the point of death, was showing a profit of over seven thousand dollars a week and increasing daily in popularity.

It is a curious and interesting psychological reflection that the women who had shown so plainly that they would not have the original woman-made and woman-conducted *Daily Mirror* now formed the bulk of the supporters of the picture paper. At the present day any observer who travels in the London subway trains or on the motor busses during the morning hours will invariably notice that half the women passengers carry copies of the *Mirror,* and while most of them pay little attention to the reading matter every one of them takes an obvious delight in the pictures.

In the case of the *Daily Mirror* Harmsworth's strong common sense was shown by his realization that, figuratively speaking, the way to get past a stone wall is not by attempting to break through it but by finding a way over or around it. He displayed the same good judgment in his method of dealing with a Sunday edition of the *Daily Mail.*

At that time the English Sunday newspapers, although prosperous enough and having fairly large circulations, were mostly wretched affairs, consisting chiefly of a rehash of the week's news, while special features were provided by stories of crime and reports of unsavory divorce cases. Alfred Harmsworth decided to present something better by issuing a Sunday edition of his popular daily. As soon as this appeared, however, a great outcry was made against it by religious people all over the country, largely abetted by rival newspapers. "The *Daily Mail* is desecrating the Sabbath," it was declared. Furthermore, it was shown that while the Harmsworth periodicals included certain religious publications that advocated the observance of a Christian Sabbath, a Harmsworth newspaper was actually breaking the Sabbath.

It was in vain that the publisher pointed out that the existing Sunday papers were printed on Saturday night, and that the *Daily Mail* was merely following the same course. Opposition increased, and the controversy became so embittered that, acceding to the public's verdict, Harmsworth stopped the publication of the Sunday edition.

Some time later, he succeeded in his purpose of issuing a modernized Sunday edition when he purchased and transformed the *Weekly Dispatch,* a Sunday newspaper that had been founded in 1803. Like the *Evening News* before its revitalization under

Harmsworth management, the *Weekly Dispatch* had experienced frequent changes of ownership and its circulation had been decreasing for several years. As soon as Harmsworth took it in hand it was changed into a live, successful paper, while all objectionable features were eliminated. Thus it found its way into the homes of people who had hitherto objected to reading a Sunday edition.

In this way Harmsworth gained his point, and not only obtained his Sunday newspaper, but at the same time overcame the bitter antagonism which had been aroused by his endeavor to publish a Sunday edition of the *Daily Mail*. Furthermore, his wide vision had foreseen the difficulties of Sunday distribution and he had prepared to meet them. On week days special newspaper trains carry the London newspapers to all parts of the United Kingdom, but on Sundays the rigorous blue laws, framed long ago by the preservers of the sanctity of the British Sabbath, prevent the running of such trains. To overcome this obstacle, Harmsworth immediately organized a system of distribution by means of swift motor trucks, which covered a wide radius in supplying the *Weekly Dispatch* to news dealers.

This attention to important matters on the part of Alfred Harmsworth had always been typical of his working methods, his habit being to concentrate his mind on the big things while leaving the minor details to subordinates. To-day, as Lord Northcliffe, he has been enabled to retain his energy and capacity for work even with the increasing demands upon his business hours. Each new child of his creation has in turn received his parental care as if it had been his only offspring, and yet, at the same time, he has never neglected any member of his brood, no matter how thriving it might be. Neglect, as he knows, might cause one of his charges to drift into bad habits, and bad habits naturally result in deterioration in periodicals and newspapers just as they cause the downfall of human beings. Northcliffe, therefore, has given his closest attention to all his important publications, with that cosmic grasp of the essential which distinguishes the man who is really great.

In the case of the *Daily Mirror* he was a stern censor of the photographs that were presented for publication, and insisted on the highest standard of morality being observed. The idea of gaining circulation by appeals to the morbid or abnormal was, therefore, strictly condemned by him. How closely he kept watch on any tendency in this direction one instance will suffice to show.

The editor of the *Daily Mirror* had arranged, at great expense, to get by special messenger photographs of the championship fight between Jeffries and Johnson at Carson City, Nevada. In the meantime the British news dealers, having been informed of this impending feature, ordered over 1,250,000 copies of the prize-fight edition. Just as the paper was going to press Lord Northcliffe sent for the proof sheets and examined them carefully. Then he reached an unexpected decision. "Don't print one of those fight photographs," he told the editor. "I don't think it is wise to glorify the victory of a negro over a white man, and besides the pictures themselves are likely to prove offensive to our decent women readers."

At the last moment the whole paper was changed, and it appeared the next day without a single fight picture. The disappointment to news dealers, the temporary loss of circulation, and the futile expense incurred in obtaining the photographs were, however, minor incidentals to the owner of the *Daily Mirror*. Whether Northcliffe's prophetic intuition discerned the wretched career of Johnson in after years, his escape from this country to avoid prosecution, and his flight from England since the war, under threats of deportation, it is impossible to say, but in this case the great journalist's editorial judgment proved to be remarkably sound.

As explained in a previous chapter, Lord Northcliffe, from the start, arranged for the complete separation of his periodical and newspaper interests. The former, it will be recalled, was incorporated as a limited company known as the Amalgamated Press. The *Daily Mail,* the *Evening News,* and the *Weekly Dispatch* (which are popularly termed the "Northcliffe press") are also controlled by a stock company entitled the Associated Newspapers, Limited, while the *Daily Mirror* forms a separate organization called the Pictorial Newspaper Company. After the newspaper companies were organized, members of the staffs were given an opportunity to buy shares at attractive prices on the installment plan.

In this connection it is of interest to add that the system of profit sharing which Northcliffe, as Alfred Harmsworth, had introduced so successfully into his periodical business, was continued with equal success in the direction of his newspapers. Among the instances of men who became wealthy as the result of this system the following may be mentioned:

Lord Rothermere, as Harold Harmsworth, was associated with his brother's newspaper business from the start. To-day he is reputed to be the wealthiest member of the Harmsworth family. Some years ago he became a newspaper owner on his own account, and he now owns several important provincial journals, such as the Sheffield *Mercury* and the Glasgow *Record*.

Kennedy Jones, or " K. J.," as he is still popularly known in London newspaper circles, was also favored by fortune. After obtaining his interest in the *Evening News* and the editorship of that paper, as related in the preceding chapter, he became associated with Alfred Harmsworth's other ventures in the newspaper world, and thus acquired interests in the *Daily Mail,* the *Daily Mirror,* and the *Weekly Dispatch.* A few years ago he retired from newspaper life after disposing of his various interests. Today he is a man of millions.

Thomas Marlowe, editor of the *Daily Mail,* who has directed the paper for many years, is said to enjoy an income, through his salary and bonuses, in comparison with which the much-discussed salary of Arthur Brisbane would appear small.

Alec Kenealy, who was appointed editor of the *Daily Mirror* when the paper was changed from a woman's daily into a picture paper, displayed great ability as a journalist, having been trained in American newspaper methods. When he died a few years ago he had accumulated a large fortune.

Pomeroy Burton, another American newspaperman, who took charge of the business department of the *Daily Mail* in recent years, also became a millionaire.

As a sequel to the incidents recorded in this chapter it may be added that the *Weekly*

Lord Rothermere
(Harold Harmsworth)
A power in the financial world, brother of
Lord Northcliffe

Dispatch is published at Carmelite House, the headquarters of the *Daily Mail* and *Evening News*. By a strange coincidence, the *Daily Mirror,* although a great success, has its offices in a building which was associated with a journalistic failure. The Mirror Building in Bouverie Street, a few doors from Fleet Street, was erected about ten years ago by the promoters of a new morning paper, the *Daily Tribune,* which proved to be a losing venture. The owners of this paper unwisely failed to profit by the experience of the *Daily Mail* and, instead of issuing a paper of compact size, adopted the blanket-sheet style and antiquated make-up that distinguished the old-fashioned London dailies. As might have been expected the paper failed to make a hit, and after a brief and unprofitable career it ceased publication.

The fact that the *Daily Mirror* is published in what was once the home of the ill-fated *Tribune* has had no evil effect on its fortunes. Its popularity has steadily increased, while its circulation, at times, has exceeded a million. In recent years the paper has experienced a change of owner-

ship, which occurred when Harold Harmsworth desired to become a peer, an honor
that had already been conferred upon his
brother. Harold Harmsworth had long been
known as an enthusiastic Liberal, while Lord
Northcliffe is an equally staunch Conservative. There was consequently some difficulty
over the bestowal of a peerage on Harold
Harmsworth by the Liberal government, as
long as he held a large interest in the *Daily
Mail,* which is nominally Conservative in
tone. To overcome this objection, so the
story goes, Harold Harmsworth disposed of
his interests in the *Daily Mail* and purchased
the *Daily Mirror* from his brother, possibly
with the idea of making it a Liberal
organ.

Under its new ownership, the paper has
maintained its popularity as well as the high
standard of its contents. Since the beginning of the war a Sunday edition has been
issued, entitled the *Sunday Pictorial,* and so
eager is the British public to get war news
and war pictures that no objection to its
publication has been raised. The same is
true, however, of most of the London newspapers, which, owing to the demand for war

news, have issued Sunday editions regularly during the last three years. It seems quite possible that when the war is over the Sunday newspaper will have been established in England as a permanent institution.

VII

"THE THUNDERER"

When Alfred Harmsworth as a youth of twenty-three had confidently predicted that some day he would be at the head of a large periodical business and own a daily newspaper, besides having a seat in the House of Lords, he could scarcely have imagined that in less than nineteen years his ambitions would be realized. And yet, in 1906, he had become Lord Northcliffe, he was at the head of the largest publishing business in the world, and he owned some highly successful newspapers. Nevertheless, he still lacked the crowning realization of his early dreams, the ownership of the London *Times*.

At that time it would have seemed impossible for Northcliffe to gain control of the world-famous newspaper. In spite of his wealth and success, he appeared to the conservative classes in England to be identified with yellow journalism, and for that reason

the possibility of his becoming the owner of
The Times would have been regarded by
them as nothing less than a national calamity. For over a hundred years *The Times*
had remained in the possession of the Walter
family, descendants of the founder, and the
mere suggestion of changing its ownership
would have appeared hardly less startling
than a proposal to change the reigning house
of Britain.

Great was the astonishment, therefore,
when the newspapers one day, toward the
end of 1906, announced that Lord Northcliffe had purchased *The Times* and was
preparing to take an active part in its management. The manner in which the enterprising publisher obtained control of the
paper which Abraham Lincoln once declared
to be " the most powerful thing in the world
excepting the Mississippi " furnishes a striking illustration of the relentless persistency,
shrewdness, and subtlety which have enabled him to achieve most of his aims.

Probably no man in England had realized
more thoroughly than Northcliffe himself
the antagonism with which he was regarded
by the so-called conservative classes, and that

the mere rumor that he was planning to get
control of *The Times* would have been sufficient to array powerful influences against
him and render the feat impossible.

It was known in 1906 that members of the
Walter family, who headed a private syndi-
cate which controlled *The Times,* were de-
sirous of finding a suitable purchaser.
Shortly afterwards the announcement was
made that Cyril Arthur Pearson, Northcliffe's plodding rival, had obtained control
of the paper. Here it may be explained that
although Pearson also was regarded as a yellow journalist by the ultra-conservatives, he
was admitted to be of a milder type than
Northcliffe, and therefore, while the elect
regretted exceedingly that *The Times* should
have fallen upon such evil days, yet their
regret was tempered with the satisfaction
that Pearson's acquisition of the paper had,
at least, prevented Northcliffe from becoming its owner.

How did it happen, then, that Northcliffe was able to emerge triumphantly after
all? The answer is that unknown to Pearson, or even to the owners of *The Times*
themselves, he had quietly purchased, through

a confidential agent, a majority of the *Times* stock, which was in the hands of sixty-eight holders. Pearson had obtained a certain amount of stock and supposed that the remainder was practically in his hands. At the last moment, however, he was checkmated by the wily Northcliffe.

During his negotiations for the purchase of the stock Northcliffe, apparently to conceal his moves, let it be announced that he had left for the Continent. He went, in fact, to Boulogne, where he met Moberly Bell, the general manager of *The Times,* who was assisting him to get control of the paper. The scene of the conference was the Hotel Christol. In referring to the incident in recent times, Northcliffe said: " I am attached to the old hotel because of the fact that it was there, far from the madding crowd and the observant eyes of Fleet Street, that Mr. Bell and I concluded negotiations by which I became associated with *The Times.*"

It may be added that Pearson's attempt to get possession of *The Times,* and his subsequent failure, marked the end of his rivalry with Northcliffe. At that time he owned the *Daily Express*. He had also become owner of the *Standard* and the *St. James' Gazette,* the latter an evening newspaper. Under his management the *Standard,* which was one of the old London dailies, was modernized and advertised, but it failed to become a money maker, and ultimately went out of existence. In recent years Pearson, having lost his eyesight, disposed of his newspaper interests. During the war he has headed a movement for the aid of blind soldiers. As a recognition of his public services he was given the title of baronet.

The rivalry between Northcliffe and Pearson, it should be explained, was always of the friendliest character, their competition in business having aroused no ill feeling. This fact was mentioned by Lord Northcliffe in an interview two or three years ago, when he spoke of the loss British journalism had sustained through Sir Arthur Pearson's retirement. "He has been one of the great vitalizers of the profession to which he and I belong," added Lord Northcliffe. "His staffs have always been cheery and optimistic and devoted to him. We have been in good-

natured conflict most of the time since he and
I as boys first knew each other, but we have
always remained the best of friends."

Returning to the main subject, Northcliffe's ownership of *The Times,* it may be
asked why he should have regarded the acquisition of this paper as his supreme triumph. To the average American the term
" London *Times* " has a comparatively
uncertain meaning. Americans know, of
course, that *The Times* is a great newspaper,
but they do not realize that it is far more
than a newspaper, that it is, in fact, almost
as much a British institution as the British
constitution itself.

The very name, *" The Times,"* appears to
strike awe into the hearts of English people,
who have been taught to regard this paper
as the representative of public opinion. " I
shall write to *The Times* " was once the favorite threat of Britons traveling abroad,
when any incident occurred to disturb their
equanimity or which was contrary to their
insular experience. In America if a great
man has anything to say for publication he
has himself interviewed or, at least, contrives to convey his views to all the papers

at once. In England he "writes to *The Times*."

Why, it may be asked further, is this paper so great and powerful, and in what respect does it differ from any important American journal? The answer is that not only is it 130 years old, but from the start it has been unique in standing above its contemporaries and coming into close association with the British government, and while it has remained an independent newspaper, it has gained all the power and prestige of an official organ.

The story of *The Times* is a story of the evolution of the English people for a century or more. From the beginning of its career it has stood for great journalism and absolute independence in demanding efficiency on the part of the government, the very qualities that in later years, under changed social conditions, have given Northcliffe his success. During the course of a century this paper has become interwoven with the whole fabric of English life.

The Times, it has been said, is the most English thing in the world—English in its foibles as well as its strength, English in its independence of all excepting its customers, English in its strange capacity for accepting changes that are most vital and events of the highest moment as simple and natural consequences not deserving that much fuss should be made over them. The English alone revolutionize a suffrage or annex an unknown and vast state as part of the business of the year. *The Times* regards such things as the English think of them, with pleasure it may be or pain, but without a trace of emotion, much less of hysteria. *The Times* has been English in its fortitude under trouble, English in its occasional brutality, more than English in its persistency, while occasionally it has displayed unmistakable wrong-headedness. It has even been English in its method of expression.

The Times has linked the British Empire together. It forms a tie between Great Britain and Canada, Australia, South Africa, India, and other British dominions. In every quarter of the globe where the British flag is flying *The Times* is to be found. The daily and weekly editions are always on file at British clubs and libraries, to be read by those who wish to keep in close touch with the mother country. As a newspaper the word of *The Times* is taken as authoritative in all parts of the world. Whenever important events are occurring, it is almost impossible to look through an American newspaper without seeing a quotation from a *Times* editorial.

From this it can be easily understood that the man who owns the London *Times* not only gains an enviable amount of political and social prestige but has the means at his disposal of wielding a tremendous power. This serves to explain why Lord Northcliffe considered that he had reached the summit of his ambition when he secured possession of the world's greatest newspaper.

To the astonishment of the conservative element in England, Northcliffe did not alter the tone of *The Times* or introduce the slightest tinge of yellow into the columns of the venerable daily. On the contrary, while he gradually modernized its appearance and put new life into it, he maintained its dignity and integrity, its authority and power. That he intended to follow a conservative policy was made clear by a statement which he made soon after taking possession of the paper. "It is my highest ambition," he said, "to maintain the traditions that *The Times* has held for over a hundred years—traditions of great aim and breadth of view with regard to literary, scientific, and artistic matters and the higher progress of the nations outside of England." As the result of adhering to this policy *The Times,* under Northcliffe, has gained more prestige than ever.

No account of *The Times* would be complete without an outline of its remarkable history, however slight. As a story it is full of interest. The paper was started in an eventful period—toward the close of the eighteenth century, when George the Third was King of England, when Louis the Sixteenth and Marie Antoinette reigned in France, and four years before George Washington became President of the United States. At that time Belgium was part of the Netherlands, Greece part of Turkey, Italy a collection of independent states, German unity had hardly any more reality in men's minds than a nursery rhyme; less than one page of a textbook told all that was known of Africa. The Young Pretender was living in Rome, Warren Hastings was

awaiting trial, Lord Howe was the first lord
of the admiralty, and Sir William Herschel
was completing his great telescope. Every
year of that era was so full of events that
appear remote in modern eyes that it seems
an anachronism to bring an existing morning newspaper on the stage in their company.

It was in 1785 that John Walter, a London bookseller, issued a daily paper which
he called the *Universal Register,* changing
the name three years later to *The Times.*
The new daily consisted of a small double
sheet of coarse paper printed in small type,
and it sold for threepence (six cents). There
were no editorials in it, and none appeared
for some years afterwards; but in that respect *The Times* was not different from other
London newspapers of the period. Their
principal features were ponderous special
articles, correspondence, and literary contributions. They contained only a small
amount of news.

The Times, however, was different from
its rivals. In the first place it had a good
deal of news, considering its limited size,
and the news, moreover, was well selected.

It also contained a number of small paragraphs, written in lively style, relative to events in high life, some of which were almost libelous.

John Walter was an uncompromising man—a sturdy Briton, who would not be browbeaten by even an English king. He had strong convictions, and he did not fear to give them expression. He printed news in *The Times* of his day which would now be considered as the yellowest of the yellow. In fact, the original paper was a yellow journal of the purest type, and being outspoken and fearless, and even a little broad at times—in an era when newspapers were invariably suppressed—it became an immediate success.

Ever alert for news, Walter employed men to gather the gossip of the coffee-houses, then frequented by men of high standing, and these reporters brought in good stories. They made a hit with the public, and the circulation of the paper increased.

About five years after it was started *The Times* came to grief through its enterprise. In those days, to avoid the English libel laws the newspapers were accustomed to skeletonize the names of important people when they were mentioned. Apparently the editors of that time originated the " missing letter " puzzles which were used so profitably by English periodicals in after years. Following this custom, *The Times* printed a spicy item criticizing the Duke of York, one of the sons of George the Third, who filled most incompetently an important position in the British army. " A gentleman of quality " had been heard to remark, in the hearing of a *Times* reporter, that unless the D-k- of Y--k was removed from his high command the army would be in a bad plight.

To criticize a member of the royal family when George the Third was king was equivalent to *lèse-majesté* in Germany in these days, and there was a heavy penalty for the offense. The English public guessed *The Times'* missing letter puzzle at once, and so did King George and the duke. As a result the audacious publisher was arrested and convicted of libel. For this crime he was sentenced to pay a fine of £50 ($250), to stand in the pillory for an hour, and to be imprisoned for a year. He was excused from the pillory but was sent to Newgate, where he continued to give directions for the management of his paper.

Soon after Walter was sent to prison, two other libels appeared in *The Times*. On this occasion the Prince of Wales and the Duke of Clarence, two other sons of King George, were the victims. Although the prince and duke were referred to as the " P----e of W---s " and the " D-k- of Cl---n-e," everybody guessed the puzzle and Walter was again brought before the court. The judge fined him £200 ($1000) more and increased the term of imprisonment. He paid the fines, and through the influence of political friends he was released after serving four months.

When the first John Walter retired from business in 1803, at an advanced age, he transferred *The Times* to his son. Although the founder had regarded the paper, when it was first started, simply as an adjunct to his printing establishment, it had already become the most important part of his business and had taken second rank among the journals of the day. John Walter the second, who succeeded his father, concentrated all his energies on the paper.

Like his father, the second Walter was fearless and uncompromising, a stern, thoughtful, strenuous man of great intellectual capacity. At a time when the laws against newspapers were severe, he boldly exposed official inefficiency. He also published accounts of parliamentary proceedings, although reporters were not allowed to take notes. In the early years of the nineteenth century, when Napoleon Bonaparte ruled the destinies of France, *The Times* established a wonderful news service, considering the conditions in those days. In 1805 it published one of the best accounts of the Battle of Trafalgar and the death of Nelson.

When *The Times* criticized the government of the time for the manner in which the war with France was conducted, the government retaliated by stopping all mail addressed to the editor, while newspapers which supported the government were not interfered with. Foreign correspondence and other matter thus failed to reach the *Times* office. Walter was then informed that if he would promise to change the tone of his paper and support the government, he could have his mail promptly. He refused, and made arrangements to get his information through channels that the government could not reach. Among other plans, a swift cutter was kept running backwards and forwards across the English Channel, by means of which French newspapers, then contraband in England, were surreptitiously obtained. In this way *The Times* was enabled to supply interesting news to its readers and also received the first information of important happenings. In 1809, for instance, it announced the surrender of Flushing twenty-four hours before any other report reached London.

During the war at that time, as in later years, *The Times* was noted for its patriotic tone. It was also conspicuous for its bitter attacks on the Emperor Napoleon. Dr. Stoddart, who afterwards became Sir John Stoddart and Governor of Malta, was then editor, and he wrote in a most abusive style. " Corsican pirate, infamous despot, murderous ruffian," were among the mildest epithets that he used, even when France and Eng-

land were at peace. Napoleon winced so
much under these attacks that he consulted
some eminent English counsel to ascertain
whether he could sue the paper for libel in
an English court and get a verdict against
its publishers. He was advised not to bring
his action. *The Times,* however (possibly at
the government's request), moderated its
attacks.

In the early days *The Times* took the
position it has always since maintained, of
demanding that the British navy should be
twice the strength of its most powerful rival.
During the War of 1812 between Great
Britain and the United States, its editorials
severely criticized the government for allow-
ing British warships to be captured by
American frigates. It was the first London
paper to announce the result of the historic
fight between the *Shannon* and the *Chesa-
peake* in 1813, when the fortunes of war
were reversed. In 1815 it published the best
account of the Battle of Waterloo.

So great was the circulation of *The Times*
during the war between Great Britain and
France, in the time of Napoleon, that the
mechanical resources of the paper were found

to be inadequate to meet the demand, and although the presses were kept in operation throughout the day the sale of thousands of copies was lost. The printing was then done by means of hand presses, which turned out 450 copies an hour at most. The consequence was that before three or four thousand copies were printed the news would be comparatively old. Walter the second therefore turned his attention to improving the printing plant.

On the 29th of November, 1814, *The Times* for the first time was printed by steam. It was the first occasion in English newspaper history that a steam press had ever been used. This press, the invention of a German named Koenig, was capable of printing 1100 copies an hour. Later on an improved type of press was substituted which printed 2000 an hour. Thereafter improvements were steadily made that enabled the paper to be printed at much greater speed. In 1848 the output was 4400 an hour, and in 1857, 6000.

The appearance and make-up of the paper also improved in the course of years. In 1829 *The Times* appeared as an eight-page paper. In 1832 the circulation had reached 12,000 daily, and in 1837, when Queen Victoria ascended the British throne, it had increased to 30,000, an enormous figure in those days.

Walter the second kept pace with the progress of the age. Even in the early days he made *The Times* the most authoritative journal in the world. He not only introduced steam printing, but organized a complete system of foreign correspondence (afterwards vastly developed) and insisted on the accuracy of every item of news being proved before publication. All yellow-journal features having been eliminated, *The Times* became a highly respectable newspaper, solid and substantial, recognized as a power by the government.

Thomas Barnes, who had been employed on the staff as a reporter, succeeded to the editorship in 1817 when Dr. Stoddart retired. He was an able man, and did much to improve the news service and the tone of the paper. Under his management *The Times,* in 1834, established a system of expresses covering all parts of Great Britain, regardless of expense. There were few railways at that time, and some marvelous beats were made by using relays of horse-men when important speeches or famous trials were reported. On one occasion, when the British prime minister delivered an im-portant address in Glasgow, four hundred miles from London, *The Times* express cov-ered the distance at a speed of fifteen miles an hour, an achievement which created a great sensation.

During his editorship Barnes kept a sharp watch for unknown writers possessing the sort of fitness that would contribute to the popularity of the enterprising daily, and when possible employed them as salaried staff writers or occasional contributors. It was at this period that *The Times* not only aimed to be considered the leading journal of Europe but was universally admitted to have claim to that high distinction. Walter, as a rule, insisted on the paper supporting the government of the day, a policy which has been consistently followed ever since.

From the time that editorials appeared the views of *The Times* carried much weight, and, furthermore, its editorial writers were invariably well paid. In the 'twenties the position of chief editorial writer was filled by Captain Sterling, well known as an authority on politics. It was Sterling who originated the term "Thunderer," as applied to *The Times*. In one of his editorials he remarked: "We thundered forth the other day an article on the subject of—" Other London papers, referring to this expression, called *The Times* "The Thunderer." The term is now almost obsolete in England, but in this country, strangely enough, it has survived and is in common use.

It was in the 'thirties that *The Times* excited much comment by its high rates of remuneration for special articles. At that time the paper conducted a crusade against the election of Alderman Harmer as Lord Mayor of London, on the ground that he was owner of the *Weekly Dispatch,* which printed articles from a well-known radical writer of the time, who was not only an infidel but blasphemous. Ten special articles on this subject were sent to *The Times* by an outside contributor, and when the crusade proved successful he received a check for £200 ($1000), or £20 ($100) for each article of the average length of a column—

a wonderful rate for those days. It established a precedent, however, and since then the paper has been noted for its high rate of payment to the writers of special articles.

In 1837, when the Victorian age began in England, *The Times* had recently celebrated the first half century of its existence. During that time the world had undergone a complete change. The French Revolution had come and gone, the wars of Napoleon and the modernizing of Europe belonged to the past, democracy had arisen, tyrannical governments had been overturned, and the United States had become a great nation. In the 'thirties the Reform Bill was passed, which not only gave the British people a broad measure of liberty, but removed restrictions on the press, while every facility was given for the reporting of parliamentary debates. From the early days *The Times* had made a specialty of parliamentary reporting, and in the middle of the last century it had eighteen parliamentary reporters, including two summary writers.

The third John Walter, who succeeded to the ownership of the paper on the death of

his father in 1847, continued the family
record of able journalism. At that time
Barnes had retired as editor, having been
succeeded in 1841 by the greatest editor *The
Times* ever had, John Thaddeus Delane, who
ruled the destinies of the great daily until
1877. Under his direction it gained remarkable power, not only exercising an enormous
influence in England, but even attracting
the attention of foreign monarchs and their
prime ministers. During the editorship of
Barnes, Lord Durham called at *The Times*
office one day on behalf of King Leopold of
Belgium, whose complaints against the paper
had embarrassed the British ministry. In
1859, Napoleon the Third was the subject
of editorial attacks, which aroused so much
resentment in France that Lord Palmerston
requested the paper, for public reasons, to
moderate its tone. Similar cases have been
recorded in which the influence of *The Times*
was recognized by foreign governments.

Delane had been a close friend of the
third Walter at Oxford. He was a man of
good family, of high attainments, of extraordinary grip, and a born journalist. He was
at once courted by fashionable society and

politicians, and from his influence he obtained news that no other London paper could get. His social position was remarkable. He was the intimate friend of Lord Palmerston and other statesmen, and his sources of information were innumerable. Through his high position he induced men of eminence, such as Benjamin Disraeli, Sir William Harcourt, and George Grote, the historian of Greece, to write for *The Times*. He also had wonderful skill in selecting men for his staff and getting the best work from them.

For over thirty years Delane dined out every night in fashionable society, meeting the leading people of England, ever honored, ever feared; and at eleven o'clock every night he was at his desk in *The Times* office, dashing off brilliant editorials with an old-fashioned quill pen and laying down the law with an authority that no one dared question. In his day the " Thunderer " literally formed English public opinion.

The great editor was the best-informed man in England. Even Disraeli, when prime minister, openly sought his advice and support. By most politicians he was dreaded. When the Earl of Beaconsfield, in 1876, asked Lord Granville what he thought of Delane, the reply was: " I think I would prefer not to answer until Delane is dead."

The dramatic and tragic history of *The Times* was imbued with the romantic under Delane. When, for instance, the decision of the Peel ministry on the Corn Law was announced exclusively in the paper in 1842, it was instantly suspected that a ministerial secret of high importance had been betrayed by one of the most fascinating women of the period, and George Meredith has made this incident the dramatic climax of his thrilling story, "Diana of the Crossways." As a matter of fact, however, *The Times* was used by the ministry itself as the most effective medium for breaking the news to the public. Delane has figured in other novels, including Anthony Trollope's great story, " The Warden."

Like its famous editor, *The Times* has had a conspicuous place in English literature. Charles Dickens, Thackeray, and a number of other writers have made the great daily the subject of eulogy. In a speech in Par-

liament on one occasion, Bulwer Lytton said:
" If I desired to leave to remote posterity
some memorial of existing British civilization, I would prefer not our docks nor our
railways nor our public buildings, not even
the palace in which we hold our sittings—I
would prefer a file of *The Times.*"

While *The Times* has never posed as a
journal with a particular mission, political,
social, moral, or intellectual, it has never
failed to voice public opinion and expose
whatever needed to be exposed. During its
early career it confined itself to being solely
a purveyor of news, aiming to get ahead of
its competitors and contriving to outdistance
the government. Later on its opinion had
weight.

In the 'fifties *The Times* exposed the
Crimean War scandals, when William H.
Russell, one of its greatest correspondents,
sent thrilling descriptions of the privations
and hardships of the British troops, due to
criminal negligence in the commissariat.
During the American Civil War, Russell
again represented the paper, but owing to
his partiality for the South and his criticisms
of the North, especially after the Battle of

Bull Run, he was recalled. In all the wars since that time, *The Times'* news from the front has been distinguished for its accuracy as well as its speed in reaching the public.

From the start *The Times* was fortunate in having the most able editors of the day. Delane was succeeded in 1877 by his assistant Chenery, and he, in turn, was succeeded by his assistant Buckle, who filled the editorial post in recent years. *The Times* was equally fortunate in its selection of permanent correspondents, among whom one of the best known was de Blowitz, who represented the paper in Paris for many years. He had the entrée at most of the European courts, and his beats were innumerable, notably during the Franco-Prussian War and the years of reconstruction that followed.

After a century of achievement, *The Times,* in 1889, received the greatest blow it had ever sustained, when the Piggott forgeries ended in the utter failure of the paper to prove its case against Charles Stewart Parnell, and were followed by the tragedy of Piggott's suicide. Such a blow to prestige would have crushed any other paper, but the centenarian daily survived the storm. It was shortly after this episode that the third John Walter died, far advanced in years, and was succeeded by a fourth Walter, who, with other members of the family, controlled *The Times* until it was acquired by Lord Northcliffe.

Under its present owner this famous newspaper has not only gained more influence than it possessed in former years, but it is better managed. With increased energy and resources a remarkable improvement in the technique of production and presentation has been effected, and with this is combined a wide knowledge of political events at home and abroad, unwavering independence, and measured sanity. The foreign service of *The Times* is unrivaled, its special articles on political and social happenings in all countries are unsurpassed, while its impartiality in throwing open its correspondence columns to arguments on all sides of public questions makes the paper a national forum. As a national journal *The Times* still remains without a peer. It speaks for England as no other paper speaks.

In the period of one hundred and thirty

years that has elapsed since it was started, not only has the paper undergone a remarkable development in size and appearance, but its machinery of production has kept pace with this evolution. Instead of the printing plant turning out 2000 copies an hour,—the record figure in the early days,—the great Hoe presses are able to print over 100,000 copies an hour. The circulation of *The Times* has also shown a corresponding growth, and while it is not as large as that of some of the other London dailies, yet the fact that the paper circulates chiefly among people of the well-to-do classes, and also has a world-wide circulation, enables it to command higher advertising rates than any other English newspaper.

One of the early numbers of *The Times* contained thirty-seven small advertisements, for which extremely low rates were probably charged. Every decade since then, however, has witnessed a marked increase in advertising space and a corresponding increase in advertising rates. From the start patent medicine advertisements were refused, and this rule has always been maintained. At the present time the advertising profits are unusually large and would assuredly surprise the early Walters, who could never have dreamed what the future was destined to bring forth.

The progress of the editorial branch of the paper has been fully as impressive as the growth of the business departments. As already mentioned, the news service, domestic and foreign, is still unsurpassed. In the early days *The Times* secured the first news by means of sailing boats and horsemen. It has witnessed the evolution of railways, steamships, the telegraph, the cable, the telephone, wireless telegraphy, and aeroplanes, all of which figure in its news beats at the present time.

Under the direction of Lord Northcliffe, *The Times* maintains its precedence in the newspaper world, and although not an official organ its representatives are supposed to have the entrée in all departments of the government and to receive the first news of any important political event. It is, moreover, still recognized as the most suitable medium for official announcements. As an instance of this, it may be mentioned that a few years after Lord Northcliffe took possession of the paper, Mr. Asquith, then prime minister, broke all precedents by sending it an interview, which was the first time that a British premier had ever done such a thing. Although the interview appeared exclusively in the highly respectable *Times,* the ultra-conservatives in England made a great out-cry, declaring that such a method of publicity was unbecoming to the head of the government.

To-day, as in the beginning, *The Times* is sold for threepence. A few years ago Lord Northcliffe caused a sensation by re-ducing the price to a penny, the first time such a reduction had been made in the his-tory of the paper. Since the beginning of the war, however, the rising value of white paper and the increased cost of production have necessitated a return to the former price.

The evolution of *The Times* is strikingly portrayed by the building in which the paper is produced. It is a somber, red-brick struc-ture, made up of additions, which start from an unpretentious section erected in the mid-dle of the last century, spread round what is called Printing House Square, and which,

The "Times" Office   The Home of the Famous "Thunderer"

in comparatively modern style, have a front-
age on Queen Victoria Street, where the
principal entrance is situated. In the older
parts of the building there is a maze of corridors and staircases in which a visitor can
easily get lost. It was the old part of the
Times Building, in Printing House Square,
that the youthful Alfred Harmsworth described as " a great British institution, typical of John Bull's conservatism," when he
predicted that he might some day own the
famous newspaper.

Impressive and somber outside, a great air
of mystery pervades the *Times* office itself.
Callers seldom are permitted to see the editor. Inquiries are answered by uniformed
messengers, usually men of middle age, the
personification of dignity, silence, and mystery. In one of the corridors of the central
wing there is a mahogany door inscribed
" Lord Northcliffe," which gives entrance to
the office of the owner. It is an impressive
sanctum, quiet and restful, with antique fit-
tings, and a heavy Georgian mantelpiece at
one end. From the windows can be seen the
huge grey and white dome of St. Paul's.
Here Northcliffe, conserving his energies by

his separation from noise and irritation,
meets his editors and receives important
visitors.

Adjoining this office is a large, square,
high-pitched chamber known as the " council
room," and here the owner confers with his
editorial staff. Since the beginning of the
war this apartment has become almost a
part of the British government. The " conference," essentially an American newspaper
institution which Northcliffe introduced into
England, is held in this room every afternoon
at a quarter to five. An American writer
who was present at one of these gatherings
has thus described the scene: " Around an
octagonal table sit the men who make *The
Times* and who also make history. At the
head sits Geoffrey Robinson, the editor, with
Northcliffe in the third seat from him. It
is really a cabinet meeting, for often *The
Times* gets later news than does the government itself. At these meetings, especially
those held in crucial hours, you see Northcliffe in action. It is a study in contrasts to
watch him. He crouches in his chair, an
intent listener, or else leans forward as the
sharp, pithy, and pointed interrogator. With

a single question at an expert he gets at the heart of the whole business."

Such is life at the office of *The Times,* which, as already explained, is not only a newspaper but a British institution. In fact, employment on the great daily is regarded by many English people in the higher walks of life as equivalent to employment under government. Many fathers have endeavored to find careers for their sons by securing places for them in Printing House Square in preference to the diplomatic service. There is always a waiting list of applicants for positions, sometimes five or six years elapsing before an important place is filled. It is said that the editor of a London newspaper once received a letter from *The Times* stating that he had been appointed to a modest position at a small salary, his application having been filed eighteen years before.

While *The Times* to-day leads, in influence and importance, as the representative of British public opinion, it has maintained its popularity as the journal of the educated classes, all of which is in striking contrast with its humble beginning. In reviewing the developments of a century or more, perhaps the most astonishing of all is the fact that a family which, originally, was hardly ranked as belonging to the middle class, should have seized and kept for over a hundred years the function of expressing public opinion in England, should have made of a compound of reports and comments a powerful factor in the government of an empire that, during that time, has never ceased to grow, and should have transformed a paper which they neither directed nor edited, although they governed it, into the leading newspaper of the world. The continuous existence of any kind of newspaper is a species of miracle, but in the case of *The Times* it is unparalleled.

After a century or more, and the meeting of boundless competition, *The Times* still remains so completely the first English journal that no Englishman of position ever thinks of quoting any other paper. Wherever he may be, it is to this paper that he sends the announcement of his marriage or of his child's death. The journal of the best elements of English society, *The Times* has always been conducted on a high plane,

ever independent and courageous, and consistently representing the dignity, secrecy,
and omniscience of the British press. These
have been its characteristics for over a century, and they have placed it in the position
it holds to-day, in which it is supposed to
wield a power second only to that of the
English throne.

Such is the newspaper which Lord Northcliffe acquired as the greatest prize of his
career, and through which he has become an
increasing power in the political and social
life of Great Britain.

VIII

NORTHCLIFFE AT WORK

HAVING followed the career of Lord Northcliffe from his unpretentious beginning as an ambitious youth, Alfred Harmsworth, to his highest point of achievement as owner of *The Times,* the reader is likely to wonder how the man himself has developed in the course of thirty years. The question may be asked, What sort of a man is this newspaper magnate at the present time?

As a succinct answer, it may be stated that while the years have naturally changed the appearance of Lord Northcliffe, yet he has lost none of the enthusiasm and love of hard work that were his characteristics in earlier days. He is still the chief inspiration and motive force of his periodicals and newspapers, with their millions of readers.

Physically, Lord Northcliffe fulfills the picture of a big man. He is powerfully built, rather thick set, and somewhat under six feet in height. His rather florid face is clean shaven. His well-shaped, massive head and strong jaw combine the qualities of thoughtfulness and combativeness, and when in repose the head is thrust slightly forward. His steel-grey eyes are ever alert.

He gives one the instant impression of possessing an enormous amount of vitality and reserve force, courage, capacity, imagination, and the ability to concentrate. Although he is fifty-two years old, it is difficult to guess his age from his appearance, for he is one of those unusual men who seem to be ageless, and whose actual age, in point of years, is of secondary importance. He is the embodiment of health. His muscles are as hard as iron, and he takes care of himself like an athlete in training.

In his youthful days Northcliffe was said to have some resemblance to Napoleon, and even now his resemblance to the Emperor is striking. The profile of Northcliffe is much the same as that of Napoleon in the prime of life. There are the same characteristics, the finely shaped nose, the determined chin, and the same lock of hair straying negli-

gently over the high forehead, which have
been made familiar the world over by De la
Roche's celebrated snuffbox portrait of Napoleon. Other resemblances between the
two men have been noted,—their vivacity,
their eager, questioning manner, their curiosity about all new inventions, their versatility, determination, and rapidity of
thought, the accuracy of their observations,
and their fondness for travel and comparison. The energy and quickness to see and
act, the resolute determination to push an
enterprise to success, which made Napoleon
famous—those are the qualities that have
landed Northcliffe, in an astonishingly brief
period, on the pinnacle of success.

Northcliffe has a multiple personality. In
certain moods he is as tender as a woman,
with an almost feminine sense of kindliness
and sympathy, but in directing his big
moves or shaping some public policy he is
unyielding and ruthless. Like Roosevelt,
he has a magnetism that dominates any
gathering in which he may be found.

In a conversation with him on serious
topics one perceives at once that the bent of
his mind is toward great affairs, and his

way of handling them has in it more of the statesman than of the journalist. His manner is simple, direct, and sincere, his thought original, individual, and far reaching. His concentration as a thinker is shown in his manner of speaking. He uses short sentences and goes straight to the point without unnecessary circumlocution. His voice is low, pleasant, and cultivated. He uses good English and occasionally employs some apt American term.

Northcliffe made his way in the world through ignoring the conventional and striking out on new lines. This disregard of the commonplace is shown in his dress. In summer and winter he invariably wears an unstarched shirt with a soft collar, and a subdued red tie, although such an attire is not considered the best form in England. He prefers comfort to good form, however, and is therefore sensible enough to defy convention.

In his working methods Northcliffe is a lover of schedule and promptness. His way of doing business is by means of a system of appointments in which a certain number of minutes are devoted to certain propositions, and the discussions are sped up so briskly that the day's work involves no slack. Like most successful men, he always finds time for everything. He is the personification of punctuality. When he says that he will see you he means that you are to be there when the clock is striking the hour. This orderliness marks all his habits. It represents a high degree of concentration in business, and it also provides time for home life, quiet study of big questions, exercise, and travel.

Northcliffe has a large staff of secretaries and experts in various branches of editing and publishing, and these are called into frequent consultation. Sometimes he has quite a gathering of them at one of his country houses in the summer time, when all sorts of business matters are discussed. He has three offices in London,—one in the Times Building, one in Carmelite House, and another in Fleetway House. He is generally to be found at one of these during working hours. As in former years, he directs everything, leaving the execution to subordinates, and does not waste time on petty details. When he works he brings all his energy into play. He has been called a stern taskmaster by some of his English critics, but even if that be true, it is also a fact that he demands more of himself than of any of his subordinates. Possessing colossal energy, he regards it as a treasure, and while he will spend it with reckless prodigality to accomplish definite aims, he will not dissipate it for mere pleasure.

A man who is closely enough associated with Northcliffe to know his impulses says that one of the causes of his decision to agitate for the overthrow of a recent British prime minister was the statesman's waste of vitality at formal dinners, which rendered him incapable of acting masterfully on important problems of the day. In marked contrast to this, Northcliffe reserves his energy for useful purposes. Sir Thomas Lipton, it may be added, has a motto hanging over his desk in his London office, which reads: " Work is my fun." That might be Northcliffe's maxim, too, for he is undoubtedly the most energetic worker in England.

Before the average Englishman is out of his morning tub, Northcliffe has done some hours' work. He rises at five o'clock in the morning in the summer time and at six in the winter. During most of the year his working day is arranged as follows: Rising at five, he has a cup of coffee at quarter-past five and begins work at half-past. At that time all the London morning news-papers, including his own, are brought to him for inspection. He glances through every column in order to learn what is go-ing on in the world, and also to see what rival papers are doing. Incidentally he compares them with his own papers. While reading, he jots down notes and criticisms on everything, from typesetting to sugges-tions which may be useful to his editors. These notes are embodied in letters to his staff, which are written later in the day.

His vast store of energy enables him to handle an immense amount of material con-nected with the various subjects in which he is particularly interested. Yet so great is his power of concentration that he imme-diately reduces a myriad of petty details to definite impressions tersely expressed. Oftentimes he makes a criticism of one of his papers in a single word written on the front page of a copy that is sent to the editor.

Even during breakfast he gives orders to one of his secretaries, dictates important letters, and occasionally telephones. His midday meal is usually devoted to conferences upon important matters with people who have been asked to luncheon for that purpose. The business of the day is supposed to end at half-past seven in the evening, but during war time conversation invariably drifts to topics connected with work. Retiring at ten o'clock, Northcliffe is read to for fifteen minutes, and is asleep by half-past ten. Six and a half hours of sleep suffice. Then at five o'clock he is at work again. The war has not interfered with this routine, which goes on week days and Sundays and is only interrupted by an afternoon's golf, an occasional visit to the front, or a trip to New York.

All those who have come in contact with Northcliffe receive the impression of tremendous reserve force and dynamic aggressiveness lying alertly latent, and subsequent meetings emphasize this impression. To one visitor he seemed to be like a caged lion, not because he roared, for roar he never does, but because it seemed as if his pent-up energy were trying to break through invisible bars that intervened between him and the immediate attainment of a multitude of purposes. Walking back and forth in a restricted alcove, he paused suddenly from time to time to speak sharply and briefly. Thus he settled three or four vital matters every minute. As soon as there was an instant's delay, one saw again the caged-lion phase.

Yet all observers agree that Northcliffe never gets flustered or beyond himself. It is noticeable that whenever an atmosphere of flurry surrounds him, it is caused entirely by office boys, clerks, and other one-cylinder subordinates, puffing and tearing to keep up with his smooth-running two-hundred-horsepower engine. It is impossible to enter a room where he is working and not be drawn irresistibly into activity. One of his guests at a country house, after greetings were exchanged, withdrew to a corner of the work room, but within a minute he had been dragged out and set to correcting the proof of an article which Northcliffe had written about the war. When that was finished he was given a cablegram to an American newspaper to revise.

In his letter writing Northcliffe's characteristics shine brilliantly forth. Despite the fact that the letters are dictated, and are typewritten by competent secretaries, he reads every one slowly and carefully before signing it. In a batch of letters that he disposed of while a visitor was present, he altered only a single word, which he crossed out and replaced with a synonym. In almost every third letter, however, he underscored a clause or sentence. Each letter was typewritten upon a single, medium-size sheet of blue paper with " The Times " engraved at the top, and consisted of only a few lines. The lines were single spaced, and in most cases were in one paragraph. This applied even to a letter to the prime minister which touched upon three important and separate topics. There was no waste of words, no use of such bromides as " I have received your letter," and never the address of the recipient. The letters began with " Dear So-and-So " and were signed in the lower right-hand corner, usu-

ally in pencil, with the one word " Northcliffe " written at an oblique angle mounting
toward the right.

Even for a genius in journalism Northcliffe is an amazingly prolific writer of good
stuff, throwing off signed interviews, articles, and essays with the speed of a rotary
plow. In the early days of his newspaper
ownership he occasionally wrote editorials
and other copy, and even in these days he
finds time to write many special articles.
He writes in the style in which he would
talk out of a buoyant and busy mind, dic-
tating clearly and rapidly, his copy need-
ing very little correction.

As in his earlier years, Northcliffe is still
a believer in the vigor and optimism of
youth. Consequently, in visiting his business establishments one is impressed by the
youthfulness of the men who hold important
positions. The editor of *The Times* is
barely forty, and none of the directors of
the Amalgamated Press are over middle
age. That is part of the Northcliffe system. Having managed a great business
himself before he was thirty, he knows the
value of the strength and resourcefulness

which accompany fruitful years. The first two questions that he hurls at any applicant for employment are: "How old are you?" and "What can you do?"

With all his mercilessness toward inefficients and incompetents, it is agreed by nearly all who have been employed by Northcliffe that he is a delightful man to work with. In spite of his vast and widespread interests he will come into the reporters' room of the *Daily Mail,* sit on the edge of a table, smoke cigarettes, and talk to the men as if he were one of themselves. He likes them and they like him.

Frank Dilnot, a former *Daily Mail* correspondent, relates in his book on Lloyd George an incident of a young writer who was sent to investigate a series of happenings in a Midland town, but was rather badly hoaxed and was responsible for a good deal of ridicule directed against the paper. This, of course, is a deadly sin for a newspaperman, and the chiefs of the office were naturally severe about the matter. The writer in question, feeling that his career on the paper was over, went out of the office to lunch, and as bad luck would have it en-

countered Northcliffe's automobile drawing
up at the entrance. He knew that " Alfred," as Northcliffe is familiarly called,
would be fuming and was the last man on
earth whom it was desirable to meet in such
a mood. The young fellow braced himself
for the attack as Northcliffe beckoned him
forward. " What is this I hear? " exclaimed
the newspaper owner. " You have had your
leg pulled, haven't you? Don't take it too
much to heart. We all get deceived sometimes. I have had my leg pulled before
now. It's annoying, but don't worry about
it."

Northcliffe frequently goes through his
editorial departments, making the acquaintance of new men and exchanging a few
sentences of conversation with the established members of the staff. Once he
stopped before the desk of a junior sub-
editor whom he had never seen before and
inquired: " How long have you been with
me? "

" About three months," was the reply.

" How are you getting on? Do you like
the work? Do you find it easy to get into
our ways? "

" I like it very much."

" How much money are you getting? "

" Five pounds a week."

" Are you quite satisfied? "

" Perfectly satisfied, thank you."

" Well, you must remember this, that I want no one on my staff who is a perfectly satisfied man with a salary of five pounds a week."

Members of any of the staffs who break down are, when necessary, sent to recuperative climates, their full salary and expenses being paid until they recover. One of the assistant editors who became afflicted with a lingering malady was ill for three years before he died, but during that time he received his salary, while his medical expenses also were paid. Subsequently Northcliffe invested a considerable sum of money for the maintenance of his widow. This, however, is but one instance of Northcliffe's charities, which are practically unending. His private pension list, which is very large, not only benefits the widows of deceased members of his staff, but includes the names of old and deserving workers who were with him in the days of his early struggles. To what extent these charities reach no one knows, for he never lets his right hand know what his left hand does.

To the older of his men Northcliffe to-day is still affectionately known as "Al-fred." He has a sense of humor, often ironical, and likes to send little jabs that will keep his employees up to the mark. Just before the war began, for example, he sent to some of his chiefs an illustration of a beehive surrounded with bees, which con-veyed the hint, " Be busy." One of the spe-cial writers of the *Daily Mail,* the oldest in point of service, received one day from Northcliffe a magnificent gold-mounted fountain pen. As the journalist in question was rather inclined to take his ease when-ever opportunity offered, he saw the point at once. In showing his gift to a friend, later on, he remarked: " Here's a nice gift from Alfred. Evidently he wants me to do some writing." " Well, have you done any? " asked the friend. " Indeed, I have," was the reply, " I've just made out two nice big expense accounts with my gold-mounted pen."

In his office in the queer red-brick building which houses *The Times,* close by the Thames with its grey fogs and orange-colored mists, Northcliffe has a comfortable resting place, a sort of exaggerated Morris chair, and in this he reclines rather than sits. Yet he manages to arrange matters with his visitors on a basis of intimacy sufficient to enable him to recline without any one feeling ill at ease. It is part of his system of conserving energy.

His dynamic force, as already observed, impresses every visitor who has the privilege of seeing him in action. Will Irwin, the American correspondent, who visited the *Times* office, observed that while Northcliffe greeted him with an approved English accent, its staccato style was almost American in its nervous force.

" I noticed Northcliffe's slight stoop, which is characteristic," says Irwin. " It does not suggest midnight hours over a desk, but a kind of general peering curiosity about life. His smooth-shaven face was in repose when I caught sight of it first. It looked able and massive. It was crowned with a thatch of brownish hair,

and there was about it a kind of proportion and comeliness. As he advanced
toward me his prominent, broad, and restless eye glanced sharply as he took me by
the hand. I can't recall the color of that
eye, for I was too much absorbed in its
expression of keen, live interest in everything. He settled in an easy chair, rang
for tea, and started to talk. When I first
glimpsed his face I thought it massive. In
conversation it became boyish. His sharp,
straight nose, his crisp mouth, were as points
of light."

Irwin continues: "When I entered the
room Northcliffe had just settled an important point of policy for the *Daily Mail*.
Then his secretary announced the editor of
a comic weekly, one of the papers that he
controls. Before the editor could reach the
desk Northcliffe had the latest copy of the
comic spread out before him and started
the conversation.

"'Smith, sit down,' he began. 'Why
don't you put paunches on those policemen?
The public expects comic policemen to be
fat. And the persecuted husband must always be thin. That fellow doesn't look hen-

pecked; he looks as if she had fed him well. Be careful or we shall get too refined.'

"With that joke he dismissed the editor of the comic weekly, laughing. The next visitor was one of the editors of the *Daily Mail*. Again Northcliffe was deep in conversation before the visitor had taken a seat.

"'Excellent article on page three,' he said; 'I like the way it runs on from one thing to another. But it should have been on the editorial page. There is too little news to it. People look for news on page three.' On another page of the current *Daily Mail* Northcliffe or his secretary had marked an item from a continental correspondent.

"'That is good,' he said. 'That man can write. Watch him.'

"There entered presently the head of one of the mechanical departments. Something had gone wrong with a rotary press. Northcliffe took this occasion to inquire into the state of the presses in general. Number three was below her guaranteed run the last time he had heard from her. Had they found out yet what was the matter? How was the flying paster working?

"Out of this talk grew the impression that Northcliffe knew every machine in the shop, with its powers and its latest improvements. And he seemed to take as much delight in his knowledge of his machinery as in his understanding of European politics.

"In fact, when the session was done and he looked across at me with that peering, searching glance of his, I felt the Celt in him coming to the surface. 'Oh, man, am I no a bonny fighter?' quoth Alan Beck in his moment of triumph to David Balfour. 'My boy, do I not know this business?' Northcliffe seemed to say."

As explained in previous chapters, Northcliffe is a strong believer in the maxim that an efficient laborer is worthy of his hire. "Make your employees contented," is his rule. Adequate compensation, he is convinced, is the secret of contentment, and he has found that it is a good investment. Like most successful employers he is deeply interested in those who work for him. On busy mornings, when it is impossible for him to glance through all his personal mail, he has been heard to remark: "Run through it quickly and see if there are any letters from my work people." They always receive his attention.

Personality, it has been remarked, is a very mysterious thing. A man cannot always be estimated by what he does. In Lord Northcliffe's case a very good idea of him can be formed from what he says. When interviewed he invariably speaks to the point and says something that is worth recording. He is, in fact, one of those fortunate people who talk well. In one of his recent chats he discussed success in life and the best means to attain it. His own success he largely attributes to concentration, the instincts with which he was born, and good health.

" A good physical condition," he observed, " is fundamental. Then comes regular living. In my own case I manage my life, as far as possible, with machine-like regularity. I have regular hours set apart for exercise and fresh air. Most business men spend too much time at their desks, thus losing their sense of proportion, their correct perspective, and become buried in details. I have to leave England to see my business in its true perspective. I do not follow the de-

tails of my affairs, but I know them. Then
I put them into the hands of men I can
trust. My faculty for selecting the right
men is, of course, one of my most valuable
assets. I made some serious mistakes in
this respect when I was younger, but none
in late years. I select men entirely on my
own judgment, without reference to their
past records. Other things being equal, I
believe that university men are the best."
The last remark is interesting because Lord
Northcliffe is not a university man.

On another occasion, the great publisher
again emphasized the importance of concentration as the secret of success. "Men
fail," he said, "because they dissipate their
energies in pleasure or in meddling with a
dozen different concerns. I have centered
myself on one thing, journalism. That is
my business, my recreation, my all. To
concentration, of course, must be added
other essential traits, but that alone will accomplish a great deal. As to the other
qualities which bring success, I should place
first: industry, self-culture, cheerfulness,
self-reliance, determination, confidence, initiative, ambition, and optimism. Then

come foresight, leadership, ability to select and inspire, great mental and physical stamina, superior judgment, willingness to incur big risks, personal magnetism, dynamic force, imagination, and common sense. Above all things, avoid worry, for that has killed more people than hard work ever killed."

In discussing his method of selecting efficient subordinates Lord Northcliffe said: "In our own case we place great value on early training. We are even particular about hiring our office boys, who may eventually become department managers. In Napoleon's army every private, figuratively speaking, had a marshal's baton in his knapsack, and all our young men, on the same principle, are encouraged to be ambitious. Their work speaks for itself, and that enables us to make judicious selections when important places have to be filled."

When anxious fathers come to the famous journalist and ask him how their sons should make a start as newspapermen, he invariably says: "The first essential is the best possible education, including a knowledge of French and Spanish, then a period of initiation in a newspaper office in a small town." Such advice is eminently practical, for the beginner who finds employment in the office of a small-town daily undoubtedly gets a better insight into newspaper making than the young man who starts out as a cub reporter on a newspaper in a large city.

As the result of his own experience, Lord Northcliffe has expressed the following opinion in regard to some other requisites for success in journalism and the publishing business: " I believe in hard work," he says, " but hard work is not enough. Many people work with their eyes on the ground. I believe in travel. Our young men don't go abroad enough. I attribute our family success in no small measure to the fact that all my brothers and I have traveled extensively.

" Originality is important. I believe that half the journalistic notions of what the public wants to read are wrong. They are largely based on old-fashioned tradition or upon the journalist's personal tastes. I believe the public is a far better critic than is usually imagined. And I do not believe that any amount of advertising will keep up a bad thing. The public does not care one

iota about size; if anything, a small journal is preferred to a big one. It is a broad
principle of our business never to compete
in size with anybody. More money has been
lost in journalism on the theory that the
public wants bulk than on any other theory.
What the public wants is quality, character,
individuality."

Having climbed from obscurity to fame
unaided, Lord Northcliffe is well qualified
to give advice to young men who wish to
rise in the world. When he was asked recently to give some suggestions for the
guidance of other climbers, he said: " My
advice to every young man would be this:
Concentrate your energies and work hard.
Specialize, be original, launch out on new
experiments, and be sure to have the courage
of your convictions. I think that special-
ization is the keynote of success, and this
principle will be even more essential in the
future. The world's effective workers are
constantly increasing in number. Competition is steadily growing keener. The man
who wins recognition in this twentieth century will have to do some one thing extremely well. If I were giving just one

word of advice to a young man I should
say—concentrate. When you have fixed
the lines on which you want to travel and
know that you are right, keep to them and
do not listen to what other people say.
Every young man has a chance to rise, but
it needs good judgment to know when to
seize opportunities, and persistence to keep
hold of them when they are caught."

World famous as he is to-day, Lord
Northcliffe's advice is full of encouragement
to those earnest workers who have not yet
reached places of eminence. As he wisely
points out, if only the right kind of seed be
planted the fruit will ripen by and by. Nor
are results always attained in a hurry. Indeed, one of the great lessons derived from
the life of this successful man is that
patience, perseverance, determination, and
unflagging courage are qualities which, given
a suitable environment, will surely win their
reward.

IX

SOCIAL GLIMPSES

THERE are two Northcliffes, one who is known in public life, the other who is known at home, and they differ in many ways. The stern fighter of inefficiency, the incessant worker and busy man of affairs, becomes transformed when he crosses the threshold of his home. In this busy man's life there is, in fact, one definite rule which might be copied with advantage by overworked American millionaires. His resting hours are devoted to complete relaxation, although in war time he has had to keep a sharp watch on the news and the direction of his newspapers, especially *The Times*.

An English wit once remarked: "It is vulgar to talk about one's business in social life. Only people like stockbrokers do that, and then merely at dinner parties." Lord

Northcliffe apparently takes a similar view. Except in a time of a great national crisis his work for the day ends when the time for dinner begins, and from that moment no guest at any of his houses ever discusses business. Unlike so many men of decided talent, Northcliffe reveals at home one of the best sides of his nature. His bubbling wit, brilliant conversation, and good cheer are for his own fireside; all that is cutting, critical, and denunciatory is for public enemies or inefficients who wear a rhinoceros hide. At home one sees the real Northcliffe, filled with all the youthful impulses and vitalized energy of a Peter Pan who is never likely to grow old.

Neither his tremendous business responsibilities nor his activities as newspaper owner, editorial director, and public man consume his whole energies. In spite of his busy life he has found time to become an expert at any game which he has taken up, and has carried his spirit of thoroughness even into his recreations. He plays a swift game of tennis, and he is an enthusiastic golfer. Having been one of the first Englishmen to take up motoring, he knows all that is worth knowing about an automobile. He has more than a dozen cars, of all varieties, and before the war it was his custom, in the winter season, to travel from London to the south of France in one of his motor vehicles whenever he went to his villa at Beaulieu on the Riviera coast.

Northcliffe has taken a great deal of interest in automobile racing, and has offered prizes in connection with the sport. He has also taken a foremost part in promoting motor-boat racing, the race for the Harmsworth Cup having been one of the great events in these contests. It is quite possible that some day he may become an aviator, for he has been interested in aircraft from the time they first appeared. For years he has been well known as an angler —not with hook and worm, but as a manipulator of a slender rod and artificial flies in fishing for trout. He has written many articles describing his fishing experiences, which include tarpon fishing in the Gulf of Mexico and exciting tussles with giant tuna on the Pacific Coast.

Although as a man of wealth and position Northcliffe has moved in every grade of

fashionable society, his inclinations are not
so much for the life of fashion as for that
of achievement. On this account the guests
at his houses are usually people who have
done something useful in the world, either in
the domain of government, in the industrial
realm, or in literature, science, or art. Any
one who visits him is practically certain to
find society that is interesting.

The famous newspaper owner attributes
no small measure of his success to his married life, which has been singularly un-
clouded and happy. To-day Lord and
Lady Northcliffe are as charming, unaffected, and delightful a couple as when their
joint efforts yielded barely fifty dollars a
week.

Not only is the wife of the great journalist one of the most interesting and attractive
women in English society, but she is also
one of the most popular. Her manner is
English in its graciousness, her voice is
English in its softness and beauty of modu-
lation. From the start she was a great
help to her husband, both through her keen
powers of observation and through her unusually good judgment in literary matters.

Lady Northcliffe

From a recent portrait

At a later period her help was equally important in the social realm.

On the leading questions of the day Lady Northcliffe has pronounced views, and especially concerning the question of suffrage. A lover of the home, she is opposed to the suffrage movement, and while a firm believer in vocational life for women, she does not consider it necessary for women to have votes in order to effect reforms.

On one of her visits to New York, Lady Northcliffe was interviewed by a woman writer, and in the course of this chat she gave some thoroughly practical views on the subject of marriage. Among other things she said: " Everyone ought to marry, because marriage is a woman's sphere and a man's success. I don't believe that single men ever develop the best there is in them. It is but natural that they should not, because their natures are incomplete without the softening, tempering influence of woman. It may be said that a bad marriage wrecks many a man's life, but that simply goes to prove how greatly marriage counts.

" The way to be happily married is to marry one who has the proper attributes to

complement one's nature. There is nothing
in the world that will not yield to such a
combination—social success, professional success, financial success, and the greatest success of all, real happiness in the home. All
these are possible to the men and women who
marry well. To find a suitable affinity it is
necessary to follow that oft-repeated maxim,
' Know thyself.' That is quite possible, for
we are not such enigmas as we sometimes
like to think. And if we are perfectly hon-
est, which it is to our interest to be, we
must recognize our shortcomings as well
as our good qualities; then all that remains is to find some one to fill up the
gaps."

Such words of plain common sense need
no comment, but they serve to prove that
Lord Northcliffe was as fortunate in matri-
mony as in the great enterprises which
brought him wealth and fame.

The charities of this interesting couple are
unbounded, especially since the war began.
Having no children of his own, Lord Northcliffe has not only taken a deep interest in
the families of his brothers, but has been
practically father by adoption to a host of

children among the members of his staff and other associates.

Mrs. Harmsworth, the mother of the distinguished journalist, who is now in the seventies, is a splendid old lady, with a most kindly manner, and just the suspicion of a high-class Irish accent. An intellectual woman, familiar with the best in literature and art, her influence on her sons has largely shaped their destinies. She has the peculiar distinction of being the only woman who has four sons in the British parliament—Lord Northcliffe and Lord Rothermere in the House of Lords, and Cecil and Leicester Harmsworth in the House of Commons.

Besides having a London house near Hyde Park Corner, Mrs. Harmsworth has an old-fashioned country place, Poynters Hall in Hertfordsire. Wherever she is, her eldest son, Lord Northcliffe, when at home, seldom allows a day to pass without calling upon her, and his invariable custom is to set aside one day each week to be spent with her. She is often consulted on matters of importance, and her advice is greatly prized. On her side she wields a firm maternal despotism in guarding the health of her sons, who are obedient to her slightest wishes.

In addition to the members of the family already mentioned, there are three Harmsworth brothers and three sisters, all but one of whom are married. Of the brothers, Hildebrand, who was connected with the periodical business for a short time, had some attraction to journalism and bought the *Globe,* an old, conservative London evening paper. St. John, who had much of the enterprise and originality that characterize his brother, Lord Northcliffe, was preparing to enter the newspaper business twelve years ago when he met with an automobile accident which crippled him for life. In spite of this he has taken an active part in the management of a successful company which he formed to promote the sale of a table water, which has found a large market throughout the world. Vyvyan, the youngest brother, had no inclination for journalism, and having bought a country estate, he became what is called in England " a gentleman farmer."

As already mentioned, Lord Northcliffe, when plain Alfred Harmsworth, received a baronetcy in 1904 and became Sir Alfred

Harmsworth. In 1906 he was created a peer with the title of Baron Northcliffe of the Isle of Thanet, and in 1917 he received the title of viscount. On his accession to the peerage he adopted the unique armorial crest shown on the title page. Two rolls of paper, crossed on a shield, are surrounded with bees (presumably busy), while above the shield a hand grasps a third roll of paper. The shield is supported by two gladiators armed for the fray, typical of the eminent journalist's combats in the realms of newspapers and politics. Beneath this design is the appropriate motto, " He who acts diligently acts well."

Lord Northcliffe's brother, Harold, who was raised to the peerage in 1914 as Baron Rothermere of Rothermere, Hemsted, Kent, had also been a baronet for several years. He has an attractive personality and is extremely popular among his business associates and employees. Recently he has held the important post of Air Minister, having charge of the department which superintends the construction and maintenance of Britain's aerial squadrons.

The terrible sacrifices entailed by the war

have been experienced by Lord Rothermere
to the fullest degree. In February, 1918,
his eldest son and heir to the title, Lieutenant
Harold Vyvyan St. George Harmsworth,
died in England from wounds received at
the Battle of Cambrai. Lieutenant Vere
Sidney Tudor Harmsworth, his second son,
was killed in action in 1916.

In these days Lord Northcliffe is seldom
at one place for more than three or four
days. Being a man of action, he finds relaxation in movement. He has a London
house, a country house, and at least four
nooks in remote places in which he finds rest
and recreation. One of them is a cottage on
the banks of a celebrated trout stream, and
another is what he calls a "sleeping box,"
perched high on a lovely hill in Surrey,
its whereabouts being known to only a
few people. He calls it "No Hall, Nowhere."

Lord Northcliffe has entertained so many
of his American friends at Sutton Place,
formerly his largest country house, that it
may be of interest to mention that he has
disposed of the property to the Duke of
Sutherland, who intends to make his home

there when living south of the Tweed.
There are few English manor houses to compare with Sutton Place, either in charm of
design or in setting. This venerable mansion
was built between 1520 and 1530 by Sir
Richard Weston, one of the " Councillors "
of Henry VIII. He was also ambassador
to the court of France. While in France Sir
Richard was greatly influenced by the Ren-
aissance architecture, and the manner in
which he blended it with the Tudor style in
building his home at Sutton resulted in a
mansion unique of its kind. It was there
that Sir Richard entertained Henry VIII,
and other distinguished men of the
time.

Sutton Place is about thirty miles from
London and not far from the quaint old
town of Guildford. Constructed of red
brick and terra-cotta, now mellowed by age,
it is in a wonderful state of preservation.
Surrounding it is a beautiful park in which
there are many trees centuries old, while
the flower gardens are noted for their beauty,
gardening and the culture of roses being
one of Lady Northcliffe's hobbies. A few
years ago some American robins and grey

squirrels were imported and turned loose on the estate. These are familiar objects to-day, having increased rapidly.

The old mansion is superbly maintained, the fine oak paneling having been preserved, while the antique furniture and objects of art in the principal rooms have been gathered with rare taste. Many charming portraits hang in the ancient hall, the walls of which are ornamented with armor and implements of the chase. In recent years Lord and Lady Northcliffe managed to recover many of the belongings of the place which had been sold or otherwise alienated. Equipped with all the comforts and conveniences of twentieth-century life, there is no discordant note in the atmosphere of this picturesque Tudor manor.

Sutton Place has a romantic and tragic history. Francis Weston, son of Sir Richard Weston, who built the house, was one of the reputed lovers of Anne Boleyn, queen of Henry the Eighth. Having been convicted of treason, with several other young men, he was beheaded on Tower Hill. His ghost is traditionally supposed to haunt Sutton Place, and on the anniversary of his death is

Sutton Place

Lord Northcliffe's recent country house, a famous Tudor mansion

Courtesy of Macmillan Co.

said to pass through the corridors bearing the severed head and clanking a chain.

The tragic fate of Francis Weston made no difference in the friendship between Henry the Eighth and Sir Richard, the entire Weston family—father, mother, and the son's young widow—having continued to accept and enjoy the king's favors. The last male Weston died in 1730, leaving a daughter from whom the present owners of the property are descended. As the estate is entailed, it was leased to Lord Northcliffe.

A number of distinguished Americans have been the guests of Lord and Lady Northcliffe at Sutton Place, including Colonel Roosevelt, William Jennings Bryan, and William Dean Howells.

Northcliffe still retains his first country house, Elmwood, on the coast of Kent, which he bought with the early profits of *Answers*. A sentimental interest thus attaches to this attractive little mansion, which is a quaint structure, the interior very homelike and comfortable, with charming rooms, much old furniture, and many books.

Elmwood is situated in a part of Kent known as the Isle of Thanet and adjoins the village of St. Peter's. About half a mile from the house are the white chalk cliffs that overlook the English Channel. On one promontory, the North Foreland, stands an important lighthouse, and adjoining this, on part of the Elmwood estate, is a point described in old documents as "Ye North Cliffe." It was from this place that the title Northcliffe was derived.

When the German destroyers attacked the coast of Kent in the summer of 1917, it was easy for them to aim at Elmwood, which is almost on a line with the lighthouse. On that occasion a shell passed through the house and partly destroyed the library. Northcliffe, who escaped injury, at once telephoned to the staff of *The Times* that " they would hear with mixed feelings that he was not hurt."

Until recently the eminent journalist had a house in the ultra-fashionable quarter of London adjacent to St. James' Palace, Marlborough House, and Buckingham Palace, the abodes of royalty. Lord Northcliffe's former residence, 22 St. James' Place, a charming old mansion, was occupied in the early part of the last century by

Thomas Rogers, the banker poet, contemporary and friend of Lord Byron, Tom Moore, and other literary celebrities. Many men and women who figured conspicuously in the history of that period visited the mansion of the poet, who violated all precedents by being a man of wealth.

The war has changed Lord Northcliffe's domestic arrangements, and like many other people of distinction he has been caught in the wave of economy that has swept over England. An American writer who called on him at the *Times* office recently, and afterwards went home with him, was surprised to find that he was occupying quarters in a less select district. "Northcliffe's car passed Buckingham Palace," says this writer, "and after making several turns it entered Buckingham Street, a narrow thoroughfare, almost like an alley. It stopped in front of a row of small houses, and Lord Northcliffe got out, remarking: 'This is my home, number eight. The house next door is Lord Lytton's.' I was much interested, and went inside to see more of this change of state as compared with the palatial residence in St. James' Place.

"On the ground floor there was a room about eighteen feet square which was the dining room, furnished neatly and plainly; in the rear the 'den,' and then a large hall with a stairway. The house fronts about twenty-five feet and has three stories. I should say that $100 a month would be a pretty stiff rent for it.

"'What did you do with the fine house in St. James' Place?' I asked.

"'We let it to a man who had spent five million dollars in building a fine house,' replied Lord Northcliffe. 'It was too expensive to maintain in war times, so the owner closed it up and came down to what he regarded as contraction and economy in St. James' Place. We, in turn, moved to this little house, displacing people who find a flat good enough, and their predecessors in the flat doubtless now content themselves in lodgings. We keep three servants here when we can get them. With the money saved by living in Buckingham Street instead of St. James' Place, Lady Northcliffe is able to keep and support a hospital of her own. So far from finding it a deprivation, my wife and I like it. It is less trouble and there are fewer complications.'"

The war hospital which Lady Northcliffe conducts has been reserved for officers. It contains three general wards and a private one, which has had the honor of accommodating a general. From the windows can be seen the grounds of Mortimer House, one of the famous London mansions. In describing the establishment, a correspondent of the *Pall Mall Gazette* recently said: "The wards have been decorated with unerring good taste under Lady Northcliffe's personal direction, the furniture having been obtained from one of Lord Northcliffe's country houses. A large bowl of flowers beside each bed completes an unmistakably comfortable, homelike scheme. Lady Northcliffe herself, in the most becoming of white nursing outfits, moves about like the presiding angel of the house, with a smile on her lips and a cheerful word for all. She is as much at home in the little white marble operating theater (the most complete of its kind) as in the cosey, firelit apartment where the nurses take their rest, while the officers' day room, furnished and decorated under her direction, lacks nothing the most ideal home could provide. The house, which ranks as a primary hospital, accommodates twenty-one cases, and for months there has not been a vacancy."

Since he became a prominent figure in England, Lord Northcliffe's activities in the social world have been usually turned in a useful direction, a tendency which was noticeable even in his youthful days. As long ago as 1894, for instance, when as Alfred Harmsworth he had achieved success and made a fortune at the early age of twenty-nine, he created a stir by promoting an Arctic expedition. The Jackson-Harmsworth Expedition, as it was called, was headed by Frederick Jackson, F.R.G.S. In September, 1894, the party sailed for the Arctic Ocean in a staunch whaling vessel, the *Windward,* the plan being to establish a camp in Franz Josef Land and to make a dash from there to the pole. This project, however, ended in failure, although the expedition proved successful in other ways. Not only were some important observations made, but one day Nansen, who had left his ship the *Fram* drifting in the polar sea, came

walking over the ice in an attempt to reach
a settlement on land, and was unexpect-
edly rescued by a hunting party from the
Windward. Nansen returned with Jackson
to England. In 1898 the *Windward* was
presented to Lieutenant Peary for use in the
Arctic region.

Another early social event which excited
much interest occurred in 1897, when Northcliffe, then Alfred Harmsworth, entertained
at his house in Berkeley Square the premiers
of the British colonies who visited London to
attend Queen Victoria's jubilee.

Lord and Lady Northcliffe have traveled
extensively, and to this fact is largely due
the busy journalist's thorough knowledge of
the world. He has seen practically every
country in Europe, and in addition to frequent visits to the United States and Canada
his travels have taken him to Egypt and
India.

During his visit to India in 1897, he made
a careful study of native questions, and since
then has done much to dispel misconception
and pave the way for warmer relations between the Indian Empire and Great Britain.
His efforts in fostering good will between

the two countries cannot be easily gauged as to results, but it is certain that they have done much toward drawing the bonds still closer together.

In the course of his travels Northcliffe has seen most of the world's famous sights. Those that made the greatest impression upon him were the Roman Forum, the Taj-Mahal in India, the Grand Cañon of Arizona, and Niagara Falls, which, he says, "one does not begin to understand until it has been studied for at least three days." Naturally, he has met many celebrities, and there are probably few heads of European governments, crowned or uncrowned, with whom he has failed to become acquainted. A monarch for whom he has a great regard is King Alfonso of Spain. One of his first meetings with that able ruler was at Pau, in the south of France, about nine years ago, when a number of distinguished people gathered there to witness the first trial flights of the Wright aeroplane. At that time King Alfonso and Northcliffe discussed the future of aviation and agreed that the Wright brothers had created a new era. The king, it may be added, is numbered

among the readers of the London *Times;*
and the same is true of other monarchs, including even the Kaiser, who, in spite of the
war, is said to insist on getting his *Times*
regularly.

True democrat that he is, however, Northcliffe prefers the company of newspaper folk
to that of fashionable society, and would
probably rather meet a newspaper ruler than
a crowned head. If the nobility are on one
side of the road and the members of the
journalistic profession on the other, give
Lord Northcliffe a chance and he will always herd with those who have been his life-
long associates, with whom he retains sympathy and affinity, and whose ability he rates
higher than ability in any other line of human endeavor. He is quick tempered, but
also good hearted to the core, and no fellow
craftsman ever applies to him in vain for
legitimate assistance in his work. He is
never ashamed but always proud of his profession, and is willing in any company to
stand up and be counted with a reporter.

The versatile journalist has been described
as a man who has the hardest shell and the
softest heart in England. As an instance

of his good will toward newspaper workers
a story is told of a kindly act that he performed when the Supreme War Council met
at Versailles. Just before the first session
opened, the British Prime Minister,—Lloyd
George,—Mr. Balfour, Lord Milner, and
Earl Reading held a preliminary meeting at
the Hotel de Crillon. At that moment a
little woman reporter stopped Northcliffe at
the door of the hotel and asked for his help.
She wanted to get an interview with Lloyd
George, which seemed to be utterly impossible at such a time. Northcliffe, however,
had known her and regarded her highly, and
was at once keen to render assistance in obtaining what she wanted. He went into the
meeting to see what could be done, and when
he came out, he said: "I interrupted them,
but apologized and explained matters." On
the way from the room to the carriage the
woman reporter, through Northcliffe's good
offices, was enabled to have a chat with the
Prime Minister and get a story that went
all over the world with credit to herself.

In private life Lord Northcliffe, as already observed, makes it a rule to find rest
and recreation, but the war, which has

created abnormal conditions, has compelled him to modify this excellent rule. In these days of unexpected happenings, it is necessary for him to keep an eye on the news as he rests, and occasionally he must find that the softer pleasures of repose and the further reaches of reflection are beyond him. By no stretch of imagination could any one picture Lord Northcliffe watching the clouds and indifferent to the hour at which the postman should bring the morning papers.

A glimpse of Northcliffe's strenuous life at the present day was recently given by Major Eric Fisher Wood in an article that appeared in the *Century*. On his arrival at Elmwood, where he was a guest, Major Wood had a chat with his host in the library, a high-ceilinged apartment, lined with shelves containing every conceivable kind of reference volume. Several tables were piled up with letters, telegrams, and papers which the secretaries were required to find instantly whenever needed. On one table were placed several telephones, which were in almost constant use.

" After dinner," says this writer, " we adjourned to a little sitting room and there sat

around an open fire, while Lord Northcliffe lay down at full length on a couch by
the fireside. His secretaries were com-
manded to bring the gramophone and to
play furiously. They played ragtime and
one steps from 8.45 until 10 o'clock, taking
turns at shifting the records and changing
needles. Meanwhile conversation continued
uninterruptedly except when the telephone
bell in the adjacent hallway rang because of
business so important that his editors felt
obliged to call Northcliffe even in the midst
of his sacred period of ' rest.' A secretary
wrote down the message and then came to
report.

"During the period between dinner and
10 o'clock Lord Northcliffe positively refused to get up from his couch and pretended to be resting constantly. It was easy
to see that even when his body rested his
subconscious mind was as alert as ever. On
one occasion a secretary, having answered
the telephone, reported the message, and
having been told what answer to transmit
went out again to telephone, shutting the
door behind him, while Northcliffe resumed
his conversation. The secretary in the hall

outside, in repeating in the telephone North-cliffe's reply, got one word wrong, saying 'Thursday' instead of 'Monday.' Despite the discussion which was going on, North-cliffe heard it instantly, and through the door, as quick as a shot, sent another secretary rushing out to correct the mistake.

"At 9.30 he ordered a secretary to telephone to the *Times* office and obtain the details of the next day's news. This is done every evening, that Northcliffe may run over the day's items before he retires. The secretary was gone about ten minutes and brought back six or eight pages of shorthand, beginning with a report of a destroyer's fight in the North Sea and ending with a résumé of a violent attack upon Northcliffe by some hostile newspaper.

"It is always a most illuminating light upon any man's character to observe the attitude with which he sustains the abuse of his opponents, and it was therefore with the keenest interest that I watched the little scene. Before beginning to read the attack the secretary grinned cheerfully and expectantly, while Lord Northcliffe lay at full length upon the couch with his head turned

in attentive interest, smiling a smile of
happy contentment as would have shamed
the famous Cheshire Cat. It was not difficult
to see that he is a man who would be wretch-
edly unhappy without a plentiful supply of
enemies, and that he values their attacks
more highly than the plaudits of his friends."

Like Harriman, the railroad magnate,
who had a telephone in every room, Northcliffe usually contrives to keep in touch with
his newspapers, no matter how far from
London he may be. Sometimes he picks up
a piece of important news and loses no time
in telephoning it to one of his papers. With
him the instinct of the newspaper man is
always in evidence. How well it is put to
use the author had an opportunity of ob-
serving on one occasion when motoring with
the keen-eyed journalist from London to
Elmwood, a distance of nearly seventy miles.
On the way a halt for luncheon was made
at an old-fashioned inn close to a small village.

Afterwards, while standing at the doorway and waiting for the car to come from
the garage, Northcliffe started conversation
with an old man who was seated on a bench

The Hall, Sutton Place

In use since the days of Henry VIII, this ancient room is
the embodiment of quaint picturesqueness

near by. A quaint old figure, wearing a smockfrock, the venerable countryman might have stepped from a painting by Moreland. He was almost ninety years old, he said, and although the village was only forty miles from London he had never been to the city. He seemed to have been quite indifferent about the wonders of the great metropolis and had been content to pass his days in working as a farm laborer in the neighborhood, seldom venturing more than a few miles away.

"An excellent idea for a fourth-page article in the *Daily Mail*," remarked Northcliffe, as he made a note in his memorandum book. "There must be many villages of this kind, with old-fashioned people and queer customs, even in these days of automobiles and aeroplanes."

Having obtained an idea, Northcliffe was anxious to pay for it. "Now, grandfather," said he to the old inhabitant, "if you could have anything that you liked in this world and could have it this minute, what would you choose?"

Dazed by this unexpected visit of a modern Santa Claus, the old man stammered that he would like nothing better than two pounds of the best tobacco, some new clay pipes with long stems, and a sovereign ($5). His grandchildren, he explained, took good care of him, but there were times when he felt that he would like to have a little change of his own to do what he pleased with, and occasionally his supply of "baccy" ran short.

"You shall have them at once," said Northcliffe. Turning to the landlord of the inn, he asked him to have the tobacco and pipes brought out immediately. When they were produced and handed to the near centenarian, Northcliffe gave him the sovereign, with a shake of the hand, and told him that he hoped he would live to be over a hundred.

It was clearly a red-letter day in the life of this ancient toiler, whose delight was evident as he tried to find words to express his thanks. That, however, is not the end of the story.

A few moments later a woman came along the road, tired and bedraggled from a long tramp. Stopping at the inn doorway, she asked Northcliffe for a few pennies to get food and drink. He handed her some money and asked her how far she had come and how she made her living. She had walked over ten miles that morning, she answered, and she followed the races for a living. "I am a gipsy, sir," she added; "I sell papers and other things at the tracks, and sometimes when the police ain't looking I tell fortunes."

"You won't tell mine," remarked Northcliffe, with a smile, "because I'm opposed to every form of superstition, and I have never had my fortune told."

"You don't need to have it told, sir," replied the woman as she studied him closely. "You have gained everything you ever set out to get."

"A good character reader, at any rate," said Northcliffe. "Now," he went on, "you say you follow the races. I suppose you bet whenever you have any money."

"Yes, sir," answered the woman, "sometimes I do put a few shillings on one of the horses."

"Now, what paper do you get the best tips from?" asked Northcliffe.

To quote the reply would be a breach of confidence, but the gist of it was that one of Northcliffe's papers had formerly beaten all others with its sporting news, but recently it had fallen behind and a rival paper was giving better information on racing topics.

"I have suspected that for some time," commented Northcliffe, as he made another note, "and I know the reason of this falling behind. It will be remedied very promptly."

The result was that a few days later there was a shake-up in the editorial department of the offending paper, which had such a good effect that the sporting news was soon in the lead again and this paper once more eclipsed all its competitors.

While he has an eye for news, Northcliffe seldom loses sight of the humorous side of things, and keenly enjoys a queer situation. Perhaps it is his ability to extract humor from daily life that has enabled him to cope with the heavy responsibilities and hard work that he has had to face. One of the most amusing incidents that he ever noted occurred in Scotland. On one occasion he visited the Hebrides Islands, where Gaelic is the prevailing language. Many of the people there are so poverty-stricken that they live in rude stone huts, thatched with heather. During a storm, the observant traveler sought refuge from the rain in a rather pretentious hut which served as a village store. He soon noticed that bare-footed children came in at intervals, handed the storekeeper two or three eggs, said something in Gaelic, and received little packets in exchange.

"What is the meaning of this?" asked Northcliffe.

The storekeeper, who spoke English, explained that as money was scarce among the people, they used eggs as currency, and children were sent to buy an egg's worth of tea, coffee, sugar, or other things. When he had a sufficiently large supply of eggs he shipped them to the mainland for sale.

While the conversation was proceeding, a little girl peeped through the doorway somewhat bashfully and at last summoned up courage to enter the store. She whispered something, whereupon the storekeeper, smiling, handed her a packet without receiving anything in payment.

As she disappeared, Northcliffe said, "I'm sure there's a good story in this."

"You're right," said the storekeeper, "it was funny. She said: 'Mother says will you trust her for an egg's worth of tea, as the hen hasn't laid yet.'"

Like the Caliph Haroun-al-Raschid of old, Northcliffe is able to wander about the country without being recognized by those whom he interviews. For, strangely enough, while he is declared by his admirers to be the biggest man in England and has even been termed the biggest man in the world, he is less known by sight to the people of his own country than many a minor celebrity. His power in Great Britain surpasses that of any man who does not hold office, his name is on everybody's lips, his portrait frequently appears in the newspapers, and articles, interviews, and editorials concerning him are constantly published in the British and American press; yet he can walk about London without recognition except by a few people. During the months that he spent in New York in 1917, as head of the British War Mission, he was seen almost daily by many people as he left his offices in Fifth Avenue, but only a few newspapermen were able to identify him.

King George cannot leave Buckingham Palace without attracting a large crowd. Lloyd George is as well known by sight as his views are known by his speeches and political actions. Alfred James Balfour's attenuated form is immediately recognized; while Kitchener, from the days of his South African triumph to the time that he went to his death off the Orkneys, was greeted whenever he appeared in public. Even Colonel Roosevelt found that his identity was familiar to the people of London when he visited England on his return from Africa. Northcliffe, however, retains and enjoys the fullest degree of anonymity.

Most celebrities would resent this lack of popular recognition, but to Northcliffe it is a manifest advantage; for while he is the world's foremost newspaper owner, he is able to experience all the variety and excitement of the journalist's life, and this is worth more to him than any amount of public acclaim. His social life is full of variety and originality, and that is probably the reason why those who have glimpsed it find that it abounds in what newspapers term deep human interest and material for live stories.

X

'AMERICAN EXPERIENCES

EVERY American who meets Lord Northcliffe is impressed by what might be termed
his adopted Americanism, a characteristic
which was noticeable even in his youthful
days. At the present time no other living
Englishman knows or understands us as
well as he. Having traveled extensively in
this country, he is one of the few Englishmen who have really caught the American
spirit, and who can enter into the American
point of view.

Northcliffe's journeys have taken him
from Maine to California, from the Great
Lakes to New Orleans; and he has seen
Canada from east to west. He is a close
observer, and life in the great American
cities has always interested him. By his
thorough knowledge of local conditions, he
can discuss the enterprise of New York, the
culture of Boston, the growth of Chicago,

and the attractions of Washington. He
knows all about our great industrial centers.
The wonderful possibilities of San Francisco
have not escaped his attention, and he has
made the rounds of Cincinnati and St.
Louis.

During his frequent visits, in recent years,
he has become acquainted with large numbers of representative Americans. He is
known to a legion of newspapermen, from
reporters to newspaper owners; he has
talked finance with our great financiers and
manufacturing with our captains of industry, and has also found time to discuss
public affairs with some of our foremost
politicians. He has been greeted by two of
our Presidents. In New York, at Newport,
and elsewhere he has penetrated the inner
circles of fashionable society and has many
friends among the leaders of wealth and
culture.

As the result of his study and observations Lord Northcliffe's knowledge of American history and social conditions surprises
every American who talks with him.
When he wants to illustrate society, for
instance, he links the Bowery with White-

chapel or Wall Street with Lombard Street.

Once when he was traveling from Washington to New York with some newspapermen, one of them happened to mention that the inventor of the first submarine was Robert Fulton, and added that a monument ought to be erected in Fulton's birthplace. Northcliffe took obvious satisfaction in interjecting: "Yes, I know—Robert Fulton was born about ten miles from where the train now is, in Lancaster County, Pennsylvania."

While a band in New York was playing some ragtime selections, somebody in Northcliffe's party started to tell the story of Irving Berlin. Northcliffe stopped the would-be story teller by remarking: "I have met Berlin. Isn't it extraordinary that he should write all that music without knowing a note?"

Even in his great liking for America's national game, baseball, Northcliffe's Americanism is distinctively shown. Whenever he is in the United States during the baseball season and has time to spare, he is sure to attend at least one of the principal games

An Exciting Moment

Lord Northcliffe as a "fan," watching a baseball game
in New York. ©*Western Newspaper Union*

of the World's Series.   In 1917 he was
among the spectators in the press gallery
when the Giants and White Sox contested
for the championship in New York.   A
photograph of the distinguished " fan," taken
on that occasion, has been reproduced as an
illustration for the present chapter.

When the White Sox and Giants visited
London a few years ago, in the course of
their tour round the world, Lord Northcliffe did everything in his power to make
their public appearances a success.   His
newspapers devoted a large amount of space
to explanations of baseball and aroused so
much interest in the sport that the king,
accompanied by his suite, attended one of
the games, which was witnessed by 25,000
spectators.

In his familiarity with such matters as
baseball Northcliffe reveals his amazing store
of knowledge and equally amazing memory.
He has met almost everybody worth knowing, and he never forgets.   When a man
becomes preoccupied with his own greatness,
he likes to do most of the talking.   Northcliffe, on the contrary, still listens more than
he talks, as a good journalist should.   He

gives much information, but he receives much in return. In fact, he is the sort of man who always interviews the interviewer.

Northcliffe's knowledge of American local history surprised a New York friend who took him on an automobile trip through an interesting part of New England. Not only was the British visitor thoroughly well informed in regard to colonial history, but he was equally familiar with the details of the Revolutionary War and their connection with towns which were passed on the journey.

This recalls the fact that while Northcliffe has always been an admirer of the United States and his newspapers have been consistently pro-American, he is intelligent enough not to be a strong believer in much of the " Hands across the Sea " talk that is heard at times. What he believes is that the chief community of ideals between the Briton and American lies in their mutual love of fair play and their adherence to the principles of freedom achieved in the English Revolution of 1640 and the American Revolution of 1776.

In discussing this subject not long ago,

he remarked: " There ought to be a strong feeling of sympathy between the people of Great Britain and of the United States because of the fact that they are largely of the same race. There is a great friendship for Americans on our side of the Atlantic, and we take pride in the achievements of the United States during the past hundred years under the leadership of men who, in every stage of the country's development, have usually borne English names."

Most international misunderstandings, Northcliffe believes, might be prevented if the nations were better acquainted with each other. He is therefore a strong advocate of travel as an educator. Britons and Americans, he is convinced, would be much better friends if they traveled more in each other's countries, although conditions in this respect, he admits, are improving. In giving his views on British-American relations, he said recently: " The vast masses of people in Great Britain and the United States are really inlanders; they seldom travel out of their own country. I suppose that the number of Americans who know anything of the British Empire by personal travel is less than a half per cent. The Englishman who has lived for three or four months in the midst of American family life, or an American who has resided in any part of the British Empire, begins to realize that Britons and Americans are singularly alike. The fact that they speak the same language, with minor variations, renders it speedily possible for those who have not advanced in years of prejudice to understand and therefore to like each other."

Northcliffe paid his first visit to this country in the early part of 1894, when, as Alfred Harmsworth, he had started his weekly papers, laid the foundation of his fortune, and reached the first stage of his journey toward fame. Although he had become well known in England, at that time, as the publisher of *Answers,* his visit to New York was unnoticed by any of the local newspapers.

During a stay of two months on this side of the Atlantic, the young publisher visited Boston, Montreal, and Quebec, and also made a trip to the Gulf Coast of Florida for some tarpon fishing. Before leaving New York he investigated publishing conditions thoroughly, and among other things made a study of the distribution methods of the American News Company, into which he was given an insight by the late Patrick Farrelly, at that time president of the great organization.

Some New York publishers who were told of Harmsworth's success were highly skeptical, and were unable to believe that a mere youth had started some cheap papers and had made a large fortune in less than five years. When told the story they shook their heads and frankly confessed that they could not credit it.

Nearly seven years later—at the end of December, 1900—Alfred Harmsworth visited New York again, but on this occasion the news of his coming had preceded him. On his arrival he was interviewed by reporters and snapped by camera men, the newspapers having reserved a large amount of space for accounts of the enterprising founder of the Harmsworth publications and the *Daily Mail*. Later on illustrated articles appeared in the Sunday supplements, some of which filled an entire page, while "Harmsworth stories" were sent to all parts of the country by the news agencies,

The famous journalist obtained still further publicity a few days later when it was announced that, at the request of Joseph Pulitzer, he had arranged to take charge of the New York *World* on the night of December 31, and superintend the issuance of a Twentieth Century Edition, based on his own ideas of what the newspaper of the future was likely to be. This experiment was watched with great interest by newspaper proprietors throughout the United States.

On December 31 the *World* published the following address from Alfred Harmsworth to readers of the paper: "I have come to the United States to exchange ideas on journalism, to learn, and to suggest. The editor of the New York *World* has given me complete control of his magnificent organization for twenty-four hours, and though the time is brief and I only reached this country on Thursday last, I shall appeal, to-morrow, to the fair, able, and intellectual discrimination for which Americans are noted the world over. I feel confident that my system of portable, pocketable, logically arranged journalism will meet with careful consideration, and that from the invitation I shall make to the American people to offer suggestions as to what is wanted in the newspapers of the twentieth century I shall receive invaluable advice."

On assuming charge of the *World* on the evening of December 31, Harmsworth delivered a short and breezy address to members of the staff, in which he asked for their coöperation in making the new paper a success. As a joke the *World* men all appeared in evening dress, with the idea of impressing the editor pro tem. Harmsworth, however, was in his usual businesslike attire. As he glanced round the room his eye lighted on one of the editors who was also in working garb. "That man has the right sense of humor," he remarked briskly. "He shows some originality, too." A few years later this *World* man was invited to join the staff of the *Daily Mail* at an unusually large salary, and to-day he has become one of the principal stockholders.

On January 1, 1901, the Twentieth Century Edition of the New York *World* made its appearance. Harmsworth had issued the paper in what he called "tabloid form," or about the size of *Collier's Weekly,* with thirty-two pages and four columns to the page, the news being condensed to the smallest limits. No story exceeded 250 words in length, and illustrations were dispensed with. In an article which appeared on the editorial page, the originator of this new idea in journalism declared that the paper of small size had the following good points: " It is an advantage to advertisers. It is convenient for reading in the street car or for carrying in the pocket."

Among new ideas which he suggested was this: " It is impossible for the busy man to keep track of new books. I would therefore employ a staff of competent editors to examine all new books that are coming into the world each year, by good authors of all countries. I would provide a careful condensation of every new book or publication worth reading."

As to the suggestion last mentioned, that has already been followed by the American press in recent years, most of the important newspapers having issued weekly literary supplements.

That Harmsworth was right in his idea of news condensation has been proved by the

experience of most newspaper readers, the
majority of whom simply glance at the headlines and seldom take the trouble to read
entire stories of a column or more. On the
staff of the *Daily Mail,* it may be added,
reporters are not paid by the amount of
space they fill, as in this country, but according to their ability to produce an interesting
story in the smallest compass.

What the proprietor of the New York
World thought of the "tabloid" idea was
shown by the fact that on January 2 the
paper was issued in its usual form. Many
publishers, it is true, commended the Harmsworth idea, and Thomas A. Edison, among
other celebrities, hailed tabloid journalism as
a great improvement; but the general verdict in American newspaper circles was decidedly against it. Newspaper experts who
criticized the tabloid form contended that it
was unsuited to American conditions, that
American readers preferred long stories, and
that advertisers required large space. Frank
A. Munsey, who expressed this opinion,
said: "The large sheet is not only easier to
read but is more impressive, while it also
gives advertisers greater room. What is

still more important is the fact that the small paper is not a money bringer."

In spite of these unfavorable views, the far-sighted British journalist has never changed his mind in regard to the tabloid principle, and still believes that compactness of form and brevity will distinguish the newspaper of the future. In an interview a few years ago he said: "American newspapers are afflicted with what I call the size disease. A great deal of space is wasted on trivialities, such as unnecessary illustrations. For instance, in a New York paper that I was reading to-day I noticed a story of a woman who had been run over by an automobile. This story was accompanied by a picture of the car. Now what is the use of such a picture? It is just a common automobile, seen by hundreds. Who is wiser for seeing the picture? The story could have been told in four lines, but half a column was devoted to it.

"Condensation will be the feature of the coming newspaper. In fact, we have educated the British public to appreciate condensed news, and you will come to it, in this country, in time. American business men

A Snapshot (1901)

At the St. Augustine, Florida, Golf Club

have told me that they cannot read half the stories in the newspapers, because the articles are much too long. They simply read the headlines. That is why I say that American newspapers are suffering from the size disease in their news reports, in the size of their pages, the number of their pages, and their general make-up. They are too unwieldy."

As to the size of American newspapers, strangely enough the managers of the New York subways have apparently been converted to the tabloid idea. Illustrated posters were recently placed in all the trains requesting passengers to fold their newspapers while reading them, because large sheets, held at arm's length, frequently cause annoyance to fellow travelers. The paper famines in recent years, with the consequent increasing cost of white paper, have also served to call attention to the advantages of smaller newspapers, and some adaptation of the tabloid idea may eventually become general.

It is interesting to add that as long ago as 1875 Charles A. Dana, of the New York *Sun,* made a strong plea for condensation.

"The American newspaper reader," he said, "demands of an editor that news and discussions shall not be presented in solid chunks, but so condensed and clarified that he shall be relieved of the necessity of wading through a treatise to get a fact or spending time on a dilated essay to get a bite at the argument." No one had a better idea of newspaper making than the *Sun's* famous editor, so that his opinion is of special value.

Since 1908 Alfred Harmsworth, like his famous "tabloid," has disappeared from view, and Lord Northcliffe, as he is now known, has supplied plenty of copy for the newspapers on his frequent visits to this country.

In 1908 it was announced in Washington that Lord and Lady Northcliffe and Mrs. Harmsworth, Lord Northcliffe's mother, had been entertained at the White House by President Roosevelt. At that time the British and the American advocates of the strenuous life formed a friendship that has since continued. Northcliffe on that occasion not only had an opportunity to observe Colonel Roosevelt's energetic methods of dis-

patching public business, but also enjoyed
the privilege of hearing him address a visiting delegation with all his characteristic
vigor of speech and manner.

Subsequently, in commenting on the ac-
cessibility of public men at the capital and
their lack of reserve in giving interviews to
reporters, Northcliffe remarked: " There
are no secrets in America. Big men in this
country don't shut themselves up, but can
be seen and criticized. It is doubtless for
this reason that they come in for such a
large share of discussion, advice, and con-
demnation from the press."

The visitor found much to attract him in
Washington. " The capital," he said, " has
impressed me as a city of rapidly increasing
beauty and one well worthy of the world's
greatest republic. It is of a size and dignity
which might be expected for the headquarters of the United States government." At
the same time he declaimed against the idea
that Philadelphia is a slow town. " The
Baldwin Locomotive Works there," he remarked, " are the largest in the world. As
for newspapers, one of the Philadelphia
evening newspapers is not surpassed in any

part of the world for appearance, make-up, and quickness of production."

In speaking of New York, at that time, Lord Northcliffe said that he had been much impressed by the improvement of the city architecturally, the business districts having been almost rebuilt since his first visit in 1894. There had also been a notable advancement, socially, artistically, and otherwise. "The most remarkable thing about New York," he added, "is the splendid spirit of optimism by which it is animated." An admirer of New York, Northcliffe, in 1908, presented a memorial window to Plymouth Church in Brooklyn. It is included in a series of twelve windows which illustrate the influence of Puritanism on democracy and liberty in America.

In a recent interview American progress was discussed by the British journalist, his opinion being that the advancement of the next hundred years would far surpass the achievements of the last century. The following extracts from this interview are of peculiar interest as conveying the result of a thoughtful observer's ideas and impressions:

" Mechanically the United States is so far ahead of the rest of the world that I doubt whether Europe will ever be able to catch up. Even in the matter of surface transportation you lead all other nations. The inventive genius of this country is the admiration of the entire world. Without American inventors we might never have had the telegraph, telephone, sewing machine, modern printing press, typewriter, phonograph, and innumerable other devices that now play such an important part in everyday life.

" In newspapers, in which, of course, I am chiefly interested, we surely lead you in style and accuracy. On the other hand, you beat us with your quick production and general mechanical proficiency. Rotary presses, typesetting machines, and the stereotyping processes—things quite essential to newspapers the world over—are entirely, or almost entirely, American inventions.

" The American public school system serves as a model for the world. As an educative force it has been wonderful. No other nation could possibly have assimilated, in a single generation, the sort of people that have been dumped on your shores from Europe. The public school has done much in transforming their children into useful American citizens."

A staunch friend of the Wright brothers, the pioneers in aviation, Northcliffe believes that the United States may, some day, outstrip all other countries in the manufacture of aircraft. " I am glad," he said, " that Dayton, Ohio, the home of the Wrights, has become an important aircraft center. It is possible that Dayton may eventually become the aircraft capital of the world, which it is fitting that the home of the Wright brothers should be."

While Northcliffe has been unstinted in his praise of everything in this country that is worthy of commendation, he has not overlooked some of our national weaknesses. A few years ago, for example, he declared in an interview published in the New York *Times,* that the people of the United States had a genius for being commonplace. Here is what he said in part:

" The early settlers in America were people of marked individualities, who thought

for themselves. They read and wrote original things, and were not afraid of the opinion of the majority. Many of them had
left Europe, in fact, as a protest against
the power of the majority. They were original thinkers and they produced an original
mind in the American.

"In recent years the vast influx of immi-
grants of a lower type, all aping American
ways, has produced a sameness throughout
the country. It is impossible for a stranger
traveling through the United States to tell
from the appearance of the people or the
country whether he is in Toledo, Ohio, or
Portland, Oregon. Ninety million Americans cut their hair in the same way, eat
each morning exactly the same breakfast,
tie up the small girl's curls with precisely
the same kind of ribbon fashioned into bows
exactly alike; and in every way all try to
look and act as much like all the others as
they can—just as the Chinese do. In other
words, Americans, in many ways, are white
Chinese.

"The whole tendency, in these days, is to
destroy individuality. Anything like individuality in dress, thought, or action on the

part of any of your people is decried as un-American.

"I believe in individuality. I do not believe in standardizing human beings. I believe that one of the reasons why so small a country as Great Britain maintains so vast a place in the world is that we produce individualities. Scotland has never had a population of more than five millions, and yet the highly individualized Scotchmen are found at the top in all parts of the world. In developing resources and building cities wonderful attainments have been made in the United States, but most of these things have been done by the old American stock which made America what it is to-day."

The general impression among American newspapers was that Northcliffe did not intend to be taken seriously. Most editors, in fact, hailed the interview with delight and fairly chuckled over it. As an editorial writer has since remarked: "No one resented the interview. American readers, after digesting it, exclaimed: 'He's done it very well. Three cheers for him!' That, of course, is the American attitude. Abuse us, if you like, but don't do it stupidly. Recently the Germans have been doing it stupidly."

While, to a certain extent, this may be true, yet it is scarcely a correct interpretation of Northcliffe's views. What he undoubtedly meant was that in this country there is a tendency toward standardization among people. For example, somebody declares that young men in order to succeed must be " clean cut and aggressive." Forthwith this phrase is circulated far and wide until it becomes fairly bromidic. Then the newspaper and magazine artists get to work and portray their ideals of " clean cut and aggressive young men," who are represented with hair brushed back, looking keen eyed and resolute, ready for any emergency. The same young men are even depicted in the ready-made clothing advertisements. Tens of thousands of young men, all over the country, make desperate efforts to model themselves after this pattern, thinking much the same thoughts, inspired by the same ambitions, following the same beaten paths. That is why Northcliffe tells us to standardize our engines, but warns us not to standardize our men. The world does not want standardized human beings. It wants originality.

On one of her visits to New York, Lady Northcliffe discussed with an interviewer that always interesting subject, the American woman. She had been much impressed by the types of femininity that she had seen in this country. "American women," she said, "are assuredly the most beautiful that I have ever seen. They have a grace and distinction all their own, and as for the attractive young girls, I have never seen anything like them. In no other country does one see so many well-dressed women as in the United States, and this applies not to any particular class, but to all classes. An observant visitor, moreover, cannot fail to be impressed by the intellectuality and sound common sense as well as the brightness, vivacity, independence, self-reliance, initiative, and other good qualities which distinguish American women of the best type." As already mentioned, Lady Northcliffe is an "anti," and does not believe that the extension of the franchise to women is necessary for the world's progress.

Lord Northcliffe, who indorses all that

Lady Northcliffe has said of American womanhood, and who shares much the same opinion in regard to votes for women, nevertheless admires the way in which American women have set to work to get what they want in the matter of political rights. He considers it a great pity that in England the suffrage movement has been characterized by violence rather than by grace and attractiveness. As to suffrage in England, he believes it is a dead issue as far as militancy is concerned. "The militants who made the most noise," he says, "were the leaders of an immense number of superfluous women who could not get husbands and had to do something."

In an interview expressing his belief in the supremacy of man, Northcliffe remarked: "There are 1,700,000 more women of voting age than men in England, Scotland, and Ireland. If they were given the same franchise rights as the men, they would dominate the British Empire. No self-respecting man is going to be dominated by women. The men of England will not tolerate rule by women. Personally I am not against giving women the vote on a property basis, but the suffragists will not be satisfied with that."

As already noted, Lord Northcliffe has seen a great deal of this country and has visited many of our winter and summer resorts. In the autumn of 1917, while heading the British War Commission, he gathered some impressions of Atlantic City when he attended the Chambers of Commerce Convention which was held there.

In a chat with a reporter after the meeting, Northcliffe said that he had been very favorably impressed by this popular resort, which he compared to Brighton, one of England's liveliest seaside places. As he strolled along the Board Walk, a number of objects attracted his attention. He gloated over the big electric advertising signs on the piers, and asked if a certain advertising scheme on the beach front had not derived its effectiveness from its clever unobtrusiveness. He commented on the similarity between Atlantic City and that famous corner table in the Café de Paris in the French capital, where, if you sit long enough, sooner or later you will see the whole world pass by. "Everybody," he

observed, "seems to go to Atlantic City."
Then he wanted to know why there was not
an adequate convention hall in Atlantic
City, with proper acoustics. Speakers at
the Chambers of Commerce Convention, he
remarked, had not been heard to good
effect.

As he walked on, making these observations, Northcliffe met an editor from Philadelphia with whom he was acquainted. The
editor was accompanied by two of his reporters. "This is surprising," exclaimed
Northcliffe. "Is the whole staff down
here?" Then he added: "I suppose they
have sent you to Atlantic City to escape
from the gunmen."

The dramatic quality of Philadelphia's
Fifth Ward political reign of terror had
apparently interested this observant journalist. "A wonderful story!" he declared
in admiration. "Blackjacking and murder
going on just around the corner from Independence Hall. Good copy for the newspapers, eh?"

Northcliffe's judgment regarding American news values was lightninglike. Apparently he would be well qualified to edit an

American newspaper, but when somebody told him so and suggested that he might enter the newspaper field in this country, he replied that such an idea was absurd. "I have been asked frequently," he added, "whether I intend to embark in the newspaper business on this side of the Atlantic. My answer has been invariably that no man living can manage a paper by cable. For a foreigner to compete from a distance with your live and vigorous press would be an act of brief and expensive foolishness."

In the course of this conversation Northcliffe showed that he had been a close observer of American methods of newspaper distribution. He asked why a certain New York daily paper was not delivered promptly in Washington, which he characterized as now being, in every sense, the capital of the nation. That he still adheres to his tabloid idea of journalism was shown when he asked why the newspapers could not be made a quarter of their present size in order to cut down the amount of white paper they needed. He scoffed at the idea of charging three cents for a newspaper instead of cutting down its size.

It was at Atlantic City that the alert journalist inspected a mammoth typewriter placed on exhibition for advertising purposes. The machine was ten feet high, with a keyboard like a cellar door and keys the size of saucers. He examined it closely, peering into its inwards from every angle. Then he said: "I see, I see! It works like a printing press." Then he departed, smiling with delight at this Yankee trick of advertising.

The spirit of fraternity toward American newspapermen which Lord Northcliffe displayed at Atlantic City was typical of his attitude at all times. In May, 1917, his friendship for the American press was shown in a thoroughly practical manner when he came to the rescue of newspaper publishers who were suffering from the paper famine.

Owing to the scarcity of news-print paper some minor newspapers were almost on the point of suspension. As a means of relief, Lord Northcliffe offered the entire output of his Newfoundland paper mills to the American Publishers' Association. At that time the Newfoundland mills were producing two hundred tons of paper a day, and there were thousands of tons of ground wood and sulphite for sale to American paper mills at prices considerably lower than the American quotations.

Lord Northcliffe's offer having been accepted, the American Publishers' Association formed a company to receive and distribute the paper which he arranged to supply. In spite of the difficulty of freight transportation, this new corporation—the Publishers' Paper Company—proved that Newfoundland paper could be sold at lower prices than paper produced in the United States, although manufacturing costs are higher in Newfoundland. Many American publishers were thus enabled to get a supply of cheap paper, a fact which had some influence in causing a general reduction of paper prices.

An admirer of efficiency, Northcliffe has inspected some of our largest manufacturing establishments, such as the Edison Works at West Orange, New Jersey, the Baldwin Locomotive Works in Philadelphia, the Remington Arms factory in Bridgeport, Connecticut, the Bethlehem Steel Works,

and the automobile plant of Henry Ford in
Detroit. He was so much impressed by
what he saw at the Ford factory that he
wrote a special article on this subject for
the London *Times*. Among the things that
particularly interested him was the factory
school in which English is taught to those
unfamiliar with the language, fully a hundred dialects being spoken by the workmen.

On leaving the factory, he remarked that
he had been greatly impressed by the good
physique and healthy appearance of most
of the workers. " I hope," replied Mr.
Ford, " that you also noticed that there is
no hustling. I don't allow it." On this
point Northcliffe was in perfect accord with
the automobile manufacturer, as one of his
favorite maxims is that work done in haste
is seldom done well.

In discussing the Ford plant and the
system of high wages that prevails there,
Northcliffe said: " The high-wage idea is
very good in its way, but I recently met a
business man named Filene, who has a
large store in Boston, and he has adopted
a better system. He pays his employees
a certain percentage of his profits, and

every worker, being a sharer in the business, is thus inspired to do his best. That plan will eventually be adopted in all large businesses."

The profit-sharing plan, it will be recalled, was introduced into the Harmsworth periodical business in the early days, and has done much toward building up the great organization now headed by Lord Northcliffe.

Having visited this country during a period of twenty-four years, the keen-eyed British newspaper owner has constantly found much to interest him, and he has undoubtedly derived much benefit from a cosmopolitan exchange of views. Always on the lookout for new ideas, he has been able to adopt some that he has noted, for the benefit of his great enterprises. In this respect he has not only shown good judgment but has also displayed traits that are usually supposed to be distinctively American. In other words, Lord Northcliffe possesses, to a marked degree, that restless, tireless, ambitious nature which makes up what is universally regarded as the American spirit.

Fishing for Tarpon

Lord Northcliffe cruising off the Gulf Coast of Florida

XI

AT THE FRONT

As a virile writer and well-trained observer, Lord Northcliffe has found scope for his talents on the battlefields of Europe. In the course of several visits to the front he has had opportunities to see the vast armies of Great Britain and France in active service, and he has also studied the wonderful organization which has made their operations effective. He has noted what sort of men compose these armies, and incidentally he has interviewed the generals in command.

Having gained a clear idea of the principal features of the world's greatest war, Lord Northcliffe embodied his impressions in a highly interesting book, entitled "At the War," * which appeared about a year ago. Every page of this work fairly bristles with facts, incidents, and picturesque details,

* See note page 355.

while at the same time the author has disclosed phases of his own complex nature by remarks that attract and impress the reader. Lord Northcliffe, in short, has presented, comprehensively and concisely, just the sort of information that people wish to get in regard to modern warfare.

By some of his opponents Lord Northcliffe has been called ruthless, and in the hard, crushing blows that he has directed at certain things which displeased him he has justified that description. On the other hand, his praise of bravery and efficiency is just as frankly enthusiastic. He has also shown a spirit of deep sentiment in his touches of the pathetic, such as his account of the landing of young British soldiers in France and their departure for the front. What he witnessed took place at a port where transports constantly arrived and departed.

At three o'clock one morning, so he relates, he was awakened by an English bugle call. Opening his window and looking out, he saw in the glare of the tall arc-lights a regiment of English soldiers which had just debarked. He heard the roll call. A few minutes later the transport on which they had arrived steamed away, and the young Britons, all new recruits, boarded trains to be conveyed to the front. When the arc-lights were extinguished and the soldiers had gone, the whole thing seemed like a dream, queer and mysterious.

The next occasion on which he observed some fresh arrivals was in the daytime, when another contingent landed. The departure from England of those bright, fresh English lads—their faces looking so red beside their darker French allies—had been so recent that many of them still wore the flowers their sweethearts had given them on part-ing. They looked about earnestly and curi-ously, their officers obviously a little nervous as they marshaled them for the roll call. There was apparent an air of anxiety as to what the busy townspeople, hurrying to their mid-day meal, would think of them.

But the French peasants, long accus-tomed to these scenes, took very little no-tice of the newcomers. A few women venders went among the soldiers, however, selling them oranges and cigarettes, and encouraging them with good-natured chaff. Then these men were stowed away on trains and taken off to points all over northern France, so that eventually he found them in the most unexpected places, building great bridges, running trains and steamboats, digging trenches, making roads near railways, and erecting huts. Wherever they were they always looked neat and spruce.

Northcliffe confesses that he took great pride in the fact that the faces of the British soldiers differed from those of the Germans. They were full of individuality. He was also proud of an outstanding characteristic of the "Tommy," his insistence upon smartness, and in wearing his clothes in a manner that clearly distinguished him in a war that caused English, French, and Belgians to work together.

It was at Verdun that the observant author gained one of his first glimpses of the war. He went there from Paris, making the journey of 150 miles in an automobile, as the railways were blocked with cannon, ammunition, food supplies, and troops. Long before he reached the French lines he found signs of war. Even thirty miles away the villages were filled with soldiers, resting or waiting to be called into

action. There were great fields full of artillery—" parks," as they are called—and
vast plains covered with wagons.

The first impression of the war, at close
range, says Northcliffe, is the immensity
and complication of it. The war zone is a
world apart. Immersed in it, one becomes
so absorbed in its activities that the outer
world is forgotten. These activities continue night and day.

The idea of generals galloping into battle
at the head of their armies, of Napoleon
and Wellington glaring at each other
through telescopes, as they are said to have
done at Waterloo, is destroyed in modern
warfare. As Northcliffe points out, army
operations are not directed from the battlefield as of old. Far away from the firing
line—from five to twenty-five miles—are
the headquarters of the various armies. The
German and French generals at the battles
of Verdun were at least twenty miles
apart.

The headquarters of a modern general
might, with a slight stretch of imagination,
be compared to the offices of a great railroad
contractor, with its clerks, typists, and in-

numerable telephones. Everything is conducted in a matter-of-fact, business way. Indeed, the author heard much less talk of a particular battle at the front than he would have heard at home.

Modern warfare is a horrible, grim, mechanical business, says Northcliffe. Very seldom is there a touch of the color or romance which surrounds it in the popular imagination. He rarely heard a band playing in the war zone, and the only sign of picturesque warfare that he saw at Verdun was a squadron of lancers that he passed one day, with their pennants gaily streaming, preceded by a corps of buglers.

Northcliffe was much impressed by the splendid organization of the French army, and the physique, efficiency, and fighting spirit of the French soldier. The superb calm of the French people and the equipment of their cheery soldiery convinced him that the men in the German machine could never have conquered, even if France had not been helped by Russia, the five British nations, and Belgium, Serbia, Italy, and Japan.

When Northcliffe gathered the material

for his book, General Joffre was in command of the French army. The author visited the French headquarters, where he found that the pride and panoply of war had gone, if indeed they had ever existed. Excepting for the presence of two orderlies at the gate, the official residence of the commander-in-chief had the appearance of an ordinary hotel. Père Joffre received the distinguished British visitor at the appointed hour, in a small room, where he was seated at a long, narrow table with a white-felt top. His manner and conversation were unaffected and direct.

The famous general's routine, at that time, was simple in the extreme. He conferred with the leaders of his staff at 6.30 A. M., when all reports and dispatches of the night were discussed and orders given for the day. Lunch was served at eleven. At noon there was another conference, and at one Joffre went out driving or walking until four. At 8.30 P. M. there was a third conference, and at nine o'clock punctually— no matter what happened—Joffre went to bed. At the Battle of the Marne, which began September 5, the orders, written by

Joffre, had been drawn up on August 27. Most of the French officers are young men, and even General Petain is still in his fifties.

Northcliffe's description of the campaign at Verdun abounds in vivid incidents. The town, he says, lies in a great basin, with the river Meuse winding through the valley. Some groups of fir trees on the hills give the country a certain resemblance to Scotland.

As one approaches the firing line the volume of sound becomes louder and more terrific. When he visited the front, two young officers who accompanied him explained what was taking place. This they did by means of signs, for the noise was sometimes too great to permit conversation except in yells. He had several narrow escapes. Everybody at the front has had similar experiences. He did not like it, and does not believe that any one else does. Nevertheless, it is not true that every bullet has its billet and that every shell does material damage. In April, 1916, the Germans fired 15,000,000 shells during the battles of Verdun. Probably not one in a hundred had any bearing upon the military result.

The effect of these terrific bombardments is peculiar. In some villages both sides of a street were laid in ruins, while here and there a cottage remained undamaged. Deep holes were made in the earth, as if some convulsion of nature had taken place. Occasionally a whole area had been bombarded out of recognition—buildings, trees, and trenches so smashed and destroyed as to resemble the effects of an earthquake.

The district of Verdun is in one of the coldest parts of France, and one subject to frequent and sudden changes of temperature. On one occasion the opposing French and German trenches were so close to each other as to be within talking range. The trench parapets, which had been frozen hard, suddenly melted and subsided, leaving two lines of men standing face to face without any obstacle between them. It was a case of wholesale murder on one side or the other, or a temporary unofficial peace until fresh parapet protections could be made. The French and German officers, grasping the situation, turned their backs, as if un-

willing officially to countenance such an un-
warlike proceeding, while the men on each
side rebuilt their parapets without firing
a shot.

After seeing Verdun Northcliffe visited
Reims, where he found the inhabitants wearing gas-masks as part of their ordinary ap-
parel. Excepting that the stores were
closed, as on Sunday, and the streets de-
serted, the city showed at first sight no signs
of bombardment. Later on, however, in
passing through the Boulevard de la Paix,—
strangely named,—he noticed whole mansions
in ruins, and the cathedral square was devas-
tated. Fragments of the famous colored
glass, the author remarks, have been gathered and set in rings. It is difficult to distinguish the blue glass from sapphire.

In portraying the havoc wrought by German shells, Northcliffe adds a dramatic
touch. It was late in the afternoon when
he entered the cathedral, and a sunbeam,
undiluted by the broken windows, disclosed
a horrible discoloration on the stone pave-
ment. "That," said the guide, with much
feeling, "is the blood of the wounded German prisoners who sought refuge in the

cathedral and were done to death by their own incendiary shells. That sign we shall keep forever as a warning to the world of Hun ferocity."

The strangest scene in Reims was in the great champagne cellars, where the majority of the native population, chiefly feminine, was at work. Deep underground, thousands of women were busily filling and turning the acres of bottles that were arranged in wonderful subterranean highways, the Pommery cellars alone forming whole streets of wine.

On his various trips to the front, Lord Northcliffe had ample opportunities to see the British army in action. He pays a high tribute to the unswerving efficiency of the "Tommies" of England, the Highlanders of Scotland, and the fighting Irish. He has also words of unstinted praise for the contingents from other parts of the British Empire, notably the Canadians, Australians, and New Zealanders.

As to the colonials, he was quick to answer the much discussed question of discipline, and to point out that when it comes to fighting their discipline is as rigid as the most exacting commander could desire. In

time of battle the men obey their officers
implicitly. The spirit of the colonials is excellent. When General Birdwood, commander of the Australians, praised his men
for their bravery, and asked: "Are you
ready for more when the time comes?" the
answer came back in a great shout, "Yes!"

A strong believer in the unity of the British Empire, Northcliffe rejoices at the
meeting of Englishmen, Scotchmen, and
Irishmen on French soil. Their interchange
of views will, he prophesies, materially alter
British politics when the boys get home.
The advent of Canadians, Australians, and
New Zealanders, with their attachment to
the mother country, foreshadows, he believes,
an indissoluble bond of empire which will
have a vast influence on the world's future.

Lord Northcliffe seems to take great
pleasure in destroying most illusions about
war. For instance, in describing the British
headquarters, he says they were not established in a palatial château but in a modest
dwelling, while outwardly the life of the
commander-in-chief, General Sir Douglas
Haig, might have been that of a Scottish
laird at home on his estate.

He quickly sketches the habits and appearance of the famous leader, who is known to the British public only by name. Lithe, alert, of distinguished bearing, and good looking, is the author's description. "He does not waste words," says Northcliffe, "not because he is silent or unsympathetic—it is because he uses them as he uses soldiers, sparingly but always with method." When General Haig is interested in his subject, as in expressing his admiration for the new armies and their officers, or in testifying to the stubborn bravery of the German machine gunners, it is not difficult to discern from his accent that he is what is known north of the Tweed as a Fifer, and possessed of the Fifer patience and oblivion to all external surroundings that makes him so difficult to beat in golf, in business affairs, or in war.

Neither good news nor news not so good seems to affect this blue-eyed commander or to interfere with his day's work. There are all sorts of minor criticisms of the commander-in-chief at home, mainly because the majority of people know nothing about him. Sir Douglas Haig is fifty-four years

of age. Many of his staff are much
younger. A grave, serious body of men,
they have inspired confidence from one end
of the line to the other. With them, in
every case, " Can it be done? " takes precedence of " It can't be done." One of General Haig's favorite maxims is that war is
a young man's game.

Northcliffe praises the brave little Belgian army, which gave the Allies invaluable
breathing time when the war began, and has
been fighting longer than any of them.
Since the early days of 1914 the army has
been much renewed, and considering its size
it is a perfect force, excellently organized
and efficiently directed. That the Belgians
are well equipped with big howitzers, 75's,
and machine guns, and that every gun has
a plentiful supply of shells, is known to
Hans and Fritz everywhere along the Belgian front.

Roughly speaking, the British have raised
an army of about four millions. Part of
these troops hold the western front, some
are in reserve along the line, others are in
Macedonia, Egypt, Saloniki, or Africa,
while a certain proportion are training at

home. The men in this vast army must have three meals a day. Their clothes, boots, underwear, and equipment must be kept in good order and renewed at regular intervals. Their horses, mules, and motor vehicles must have the wherewithal to live or be used. In short, the British army must be maintained as a going, effective concern. Consequently, a wonderful system of organization, managed by experts in every branch, has been built up until there is neither muddling nor inefficiency.

An admirer of efficiency and economy, Northcliffe was much impressed by the improvement in army organization which had taken place since the war began. His admiration was particularly aroused by the telephone system, which would have done credit to an English city far away from the war zone. At points where men were burying the blackened corpses of Germans, and where the sound of big guns made it necessary to shout in order to be heard, he found that telephone wires had been installed. War without the telephone would have seemed impossible. Every head of a department in the British lines had a tele-

phone close at hand, and the wires were
even connected with the trunk system of
the French government. Interpreters were
stationed in the exchanges.

With almost an American fondness for
speed, the author was delighted to learn
that a staff officer at the front was able to
call up London, Paris, and seaport bases
in France within an hour. He describes
additional means of communication, such as
line and wireless telegraphy, and bestows a
compliment on the Signal Corps, on whose
achievements so much depends.

Of particular interest to American readers
is Northcliffe's description of the army behind the army, of which the public has but
little knowledge. Thousands of men in the
rear are engaged in every conceivable kind
of occupation, from railway construction to
preparing food or salvaging waste products.
Over two hundred trains a day and 35,000
loaded cars every week are required to supply the British army with food, ammunition,
engineers' stores, broken stone and other
material for road making, and trench sup-
ports of wood and iron.

One of the largest field bakeries turns

out 222,000 loaves a day, or 440,000 rations. At one base on the northern line there were 40,000 tons of oats and 32,000 tons of hay for the horses. Thousands of trucks, cars, and motor cycles—fifty million pounds of equipment on rubber tires—make up the mechanical transportation equipment of the British army in France alone. Four million gallons of gasoline are used every month. A complicated system of repair shops is in operation.

With his customary news sense, Northcliffe realized at once that what every mother, father, sister, and sweetheart wanted to know was, how the boys were treated at the front. He has graphically shown that the British army is well fed, and as a vivid illustration of this he describes huge pyramids of jams, pickles, bacon, beef, butter, and cheese that he has seen.

Having been one of the first advocates of auto-mobilization, Northcliffe admits that the motor dispatch riders—"the noisy nuisances of peace-time roads," as he terms them—have become a prime factor in the prompt waging of war.

The cry which has become familiar to

American ears, "Speed up!" was raised by Lord Northcliffe in the early days of the war, and some of his advice to his own people seems applicable on this side of the Atlantic. Those at home, he declares, can help to speed up the machine if they will only put their strength into the task. He was prompt in seeing the necessity for standardization, especially in motor trucks and other branches of mechanical transport.

He found that two score different types of motor vehicles were in use at the British front. Each required its own spare parts in order that repairs might be speedily made. He lays stress on the fact that delay in war time is fatal. The Germans, he explains, have comparatively few types of motor vehicles, and for that reason are not obliged to keep such a large variety of spare parts. The British equipment, on the other hand, requires 50,000 different kinds.

Northcliffe devotes much space to descriptions of aeroplanes, and particularly to the fighting planes which are fitted with searchlights and carry one or two machine guns. What the development of the aeroplane means to England is a subject of supreme importance to Britons, especially in view of the fact that England is now less than twenty minutes by air from the continent of Europe. He adds: " Let it be realized that aeroplanes are very cheap to make and will become cheaper. The vast change that this invention has produced in the position of England does not even now seem to be understood by one person in a hundred."

In emphasizing the fact that the world's great war is a war of machinery as well as bravery, the author says that the first impression of it is chaos, confusion, and immensity. Then follows the more mature impression that everything is conducted with the clockwork regularity of a great business. He describes the supplies at a base which furnished 100,000 men with horses, bicycles, rifles, guns large and small, munitions, observation balloons, aeroplanes, medical stores, portable hospitals, ambulances, foods of every description, cartridges, forage, and harness. By multiplying 100,000 ten or twenty times, some idea of the immensity of the war business is gained. Its colossal expense is shown by the fact that every

British soldier costs the nation between
twenty-five and thirty dollars a week to
maintain.

The salvage system impressed Northcliffe as one of the wonders of the war.
To-day, before the fume and reek of a
battle have disappeared or the dead are
buried, the Salvage Corps begins work on
the shell-churned field, collecting unused
cartridges, machine-gun belts, unexploded
bombs, old shell cases, damaged rifles, haver-
sacks, steel helmets, and even old rags.
The latter are sold for $250 a ton.

According to official reports, it may be
added, the Department of Salvage has
saved the British government $12,000,000
a year on uniforms alone. Four thousand
women are engaged in the work of renova-
tion and repairing. Army blankets, boots,
capes, and coats of rubber and leather are
also gathered for reclamation. One million
pairs of boots were salvaged in 1916. The
salvage system extends everywhere, and
nothing is immune. Every gasoline can,
for instance, is used and reused. Even
hospital dressings are sterilized and sold as
cotton waste. Wooden boxes and nails are

put to use. Grease is collected at the camps and employed in the manufacture of glycerine and soap. Even potato peelings are sold to French farmers as hog feed.

Briefly, yet clearly, Northcliffe describes every phase of the training that new British troops undergo behind the lines, such as trench practice in actual facsimile, trench gas attacks in which the deadly gas is used, bombing with real bombs, crater fighting, and machine-gun practice. In fact, all the elements that enter into real warfare are assiduously demonstrated at the rear until the men are perfectly drilled.

At the end of 1917 Lord Northcliffe had an opportunity of seeing the American forces in the field, and although his account of what he saw forms no part of his book, it can appropriately be added to his other impressions.

The alert British journalist traveled to American headquarters with Generals Pershing and Bliss, Admiral Benson, Colonel House, Ambassador Sharp, and other officials. The party left Paris at eight o'clock in the morning in a special train, and returned at ten at night. This, Lord

Northcliffe says, will give some idea of the distance.

At a small railway station, some miles from headquarters, a guard of honor was waiting to receive the American army chiefs, and the party, on leaving the train, passed through half a mile of grim, hardy young Americans in trench helmets, standing at attention. They appeared to be in fine health and spirits.

"Eastern France," says Northcliffe, "was under a frost—not the dazzling, keen atmosphere of New York, but a sunny, damp atmosphere to which Americans are unaccustomed but are bearing well. The air was full of the thudding of great guns in an artillery battle which a young West Point officer told me had been proceeding without cessation for three days and three nights some miles away to the east."

In American automobiles the visitors were taken straight across the country, ignoring the roads, until the crest of a low ravine was reached, where thousands of the first contingent of the American expeditionary force were being trained. Here an exhibition drill was witnessed. American aeroplanes were circling overhead, and violent clangs of bursting hand grenades indicated that the bombing schools were practicing. The first exhibition was rifle practice with landscape targets. It was good shooting, the high average of 75 per cent of hits being recorded.

Then followed practice with a trench mortar, well known to the British army. The men had thoroughly mastered the principles of this. Later on some bomb throwing took place, in which the participants demonstrated that the throw is not the baseball pitch, but a complete over-arm semicircle, somewhat resembling over-arm cricket bowling. Then came an exhibition of trench fighting, bayonet practice, and a fine quarter of an hour's work with French 75 guns at a range of a mile and a half. The target was a little wood, and after the first four shots the gunners got the range almost every time. The spotting was done by an aeroplane which hovered overhead and indicated hits by wireless.

Colonel House, who is a Texan, took up a rifle and did some good shooting himself. Excellent wooden models of enemy snipers

were concealed among the rocks and foliage
at a distance of some hundreds of yards.
It was the object of the pupils in this part
of the war game to draw a sudden bead on
an enemy dummy and get it. Many had
become adepts in sniping.

The party returned to the railway, and
after a short journey reached General
Pershing's headquarters, a large French
barracks that had lately been occupied by
a distinguished French regiment. The buildings had been refitted, steam heated, and
electric wired, and were in telephonic communication with Paris and the various parts
of the American army. Interesting information was given at headquarters by members of General Pershing's staff, which
showed that American adaptability had very
quickly assimilated the best points of the
British and French training arrived at after
three and a half years of actual warfare, to
which had been added certain ideas and alterations necessary for an army whose home
base was three thousand miles away.

Lord Northcliffe was much impressed by
the strong personality of General Pershing,
who has been described by an American

writer as "erect, square jawed, with keen eyes, and a mouth firmly indicated beneath a close-clipped mustache, having all the concentration of a master chess player." The British observer also gained a highly favorable impression of the spirit of the American officers and men, and the state of their preparation. Every branch of the organization was admirably managed, with young men, full of energy, at the head of each department.

In addition to describing the armies in the field, Lord Northcliffe has devoted much space to the auxiliary organizations that are at work, such as the Red Cross societies. All the profits resulting from the sale of his war book, it may be added, have been presented to the British Red Cross Society and the Order of St. John.

In an account of the Red Cross hospitals, he describes how the world's greatest surgeons, including King George's doctor, attend the wounded of the rank and file. There is, in fact, no finer tribute in the book than that which the author pays to the war doctors. "We are so accustomed," he says, "to considering doctors as part of our daily life, or as workers in speckless, palatial hospitals, that we have hardly visualized the man who shares the hell of the front trench with the fighters, armed with only two panniers of urgent drugs, instruments, and field dressings, his acetylene lamp and electric torch. If there be degrees of chivalry, the highest award should be accorded to the medical profession, which at once forsook its lucrative practice in a great rally of self-sacrifice."

Some idea of the dangers which army doctors have to face is shown in the figures for the three months of June, July, and August, 1916, when 53 officers of the Royal Medical Corps were killed and 208 wounded, while of non-coms and privates 260 were killed and 1212 wounded.

The elaborate and efficient system of caring for the wounded is carefully explained by Lord Northcliffe, who traces the progress of the wounded from the regimental head base, where the doctor with his stretcher bearers waits alongside of the men. As the stretcher bearers pass in with their loads, there is a rapid diagnosis, an antiseptic application, a hastily written label tied upon the victim's breast, and the wounded man is borne away in the open to the next stage, the advance dressing station, which is sometimes pushed right up to the firing line. The stretcher bearers thereupon begin again another dangerous journey rearwards.

The comforting assurance is given that by far the greater proportion of the wounded are slightly hit and are walking cases—so lightly hurt in large numbers of instances that where the stretcher bearers themselves have fallen, slightly wounded soldiers have borne them out of danger.

Northcliffe's picture of an advance dressing station at West Péronne is vividly interesting. "We reached it," he says, "on a heavy, sultry afternoon, by hiding ourselves behind anything possible. Dust and smoke gave the atmosphere of a coming thunder storm; the thudding of the guns on both sides was incessant. Now and then was heard the brisk note of a machine gun, which sounds exactly like a boy rasping a stick along palings.

"There was no sign of anything in the nature of a hospital or anything above ground. I was getting tired of being told to lie down flat every few seconds to avoid

bursting shells, when I saw a couple of
stretcher bearers coming through the haze
as from nowhere, and then disappear underground. 'It is underneath there,' I was
told by my guide, whose daily duty it was
to inspect medical outposts."

Getting down into a trench, Northcliffe
was guided through an underground maze,
part of a former German trench system,
which had been turned into a hospital. He
never saw a more touching sight, he says,
than this underground station, where seventy
wounded men were being attended to by
doctors and assistants, and waiting to be
removed as soon as the place could be va-
cated. One of these collecting stations which
he had visited two days previously had been
shelled by the enemy. By a strange chance
the only victims were a number of German
prisoners.

To prevent mistakes, each wounded man's
label is checked at every point that he
reaches, with as much care as a registered
letter receives on its way through the post.
The casualty clearing station, with its nurses
and sunny gardens into which the beds are
carried so that the wounded men can enjoy

the birds, flowers, and trees, seemed like an oasis after the grim desolation of the Somme heights. Although he is a " bear " for work himself, Northcliffe was astounded at the tireless activity of doctors and nurses. He frankly admits that he had never thought it was possible for human beings to work so many hours, although the war, it is true, seems to double the energy of every one engaged in it.

One of the most important hospitals of the British Red Cross is at Rouen, where the Grand Séminaire, a modern building, has been reserved for wounded officers. Here there are accommodations for 250 patients, who receive the attention of a large medical staff. In addition to an X-ray department, there is a pathological laboratory in which important work is carried on by an expert bacteriologist. A room equipped for massage and general electrical treatment has also been provided.

An interesting branch of war work is the Record Department, which keeps complete data of every British soldier from the moment of his arrival in France until his departure or death. A branch office enables relatives to ascertain the time and place of burial of every officer or private who is killed, whether he comes from Great Britain or the colonies. This information is important in cases where wills are probated.

With delicacy, Lord Northcliffe describes how the effects of dead soldiers are collected when the bodies of the slain are reverently searched. All property is carefully listed, and the list accompanies the familiar belongings to one of the great bases on the lines of communication. Here the bag containing the mementos is opened by two clerks, who check the list once more. The bag is then sealed and sent home. He watched the opening of one of these pathetic parcels at the time of its final checking. It contained a few trinkets, some pennies, a pipe and tobacco pouch, a photograph of wife and baby, a trench ring made of an enemy fuse, and a small diary.

Northcliffe has much praise for the Y.M.C.A., which has provided huts and clubs in which war-worn soldiers can find rest and recreation. The Church Army, the Salvation Army, and other organizations have also

done excellent work in supplying comforts
for the men.

He pays an eloquent tribute to the women
of the war, whose self-sacrifice as nurses and
volunteer workers leaves him at a loss for
appropriate words of praise. " Women," he
says, " have taken to every kind of war
work with a rapidity and adaptability that
have certainly not been shown by all members of the ruling sex. It has been openly
admitted that in many ammunition factories
women in their eagerness to defeat the
enemy are expending more energy than men
working in the same shops."

As the result of his interviews with British officers and men, Northcliffe confirmed
the impression gained by other investigators,
that the German is a good soldier when ad-
vancing with numbers under strict discipline, and is undoubtedly brave, but when
left to himself he lacks the initiative which
distinguishes the British and American soldier. He has harsh words for the Germans,
especially the Prussians and Bavarians, who,
he says, are extremely cruel. The German
non-coms when taken prisoners treat their
men with a bullying savagery that is aston-

ishing, while German officer prisoners pay absolutely no attention to their men, even those who are wounded.

He was told that the Germans treat their slightly wounded with great care because they wish to get them back into the firing line quickly. The badly wounded are neglected. Indeed, he observes, the wounded man is not the hero in war that he is supposed to be. The object of both sides is to win, and while every care is taken of the wounded, priority is given to the forwarding of fighting men.

Like many other observers, Northcliffe was impressed by the wretched appearance of the German prisoners, many of whom were undersized, ill fed, and untrained. He refers to the difference between the treatment accorded to German prisoners in France and in England. The authorities in England seem disposed to hide the prisoners, while in France they work in public and are contented with their lot. Excepting for the letters " P. G." (*Prisonnier de Guerre*) on the tags on their coats, he found it difficult to realize that middle-aged Hans with his pipe and young Fritz with his cigarette were prisoners at all. This caused him to declare emphatically that the sooner the German prisoners in England were put to work to assist in shortening the war, the better it would be.

On one of his trips to the Continent, Northcliffe visited the Italian front. That was in the early days, when the Italian army had pushed forward into Austrian territory. He has described the gallantry of that advance over the Dolomite Alps in the face of almost insurmountable difficulties.

The brutalities of the Austrians, he discovered, were similar to those practiced by the Germans. The Italian slain were constantly found mutilated. He was shown some terrible spiked maces habitually used by the Austrians to break the skulls of the wounded. Equally barbarous were thongs with leaden balls attached to them, which the Austrian non-coms used in driving laggards into the fighting line.

General Cadorna, who was then the Italian commander-in-chief, has been described by Northcliffe as a quick-moving man of sixty-six, and the most humorous of the generals in the war. He had a glitter in his grey eyes that reminded one of Pierpont Morgan. The resemblance also applied to the character of the two men, for Morgan, like Cadorna, was kindly disposed, although merciless and adamant when necessary.

Northcliffe was surprised to find that in the talks between Italian soldiers and Austrian prisoners English was the only language in which they could converse. Investigation disclosed that thousands of Italians and Austrians had worked in the United States. The English they used was not the English of England, he observes, but in many cases it was a New York dialect.

As a newspaperman, Lord Northcliffe was gratified to notice that the lessening of the censorship had permitted real war news to come from the front. The fact that able correspondents are allowed to tell freely and frankly what is going on enables readers with imagination to grasp the magnitude of the war, and to realize that the equivalent of the South African campaign or the Crimean War is being fought in France practically every month.

What is needed by the Allies as well as neutrals is a continuous demonstration by

skilled writers, artists, lecturers, cinemato-
graph operators, and photographers of what
is happening, in order to impress the facts
of the war on the people who are so lavishly
pouring out their blood and treasure to overthrow German tyranny and to make freedom
possible throughout the world.

All the profits accruing from the sale of Lord Northcliffe's
Book "At the War" (George H. Doran Company, New York;
Hodder & Stoughton, London) are devoted to the work of the
Red Cross. Nearly $40,000 has been so raised and disbursed.

XII

THE BRITISH WAR MISSION

When it was announced, in May, 1917, that the British government had decided to send Lord Northcliffe to the United States as head of a special mission, for the purpose of reorganizing the vast system of purchasing and forwarding supplies, which had been in operation since the war began, it was agreed that no better choice for the position could have been made. His tact, his energy, his wide experience of American affairs, and his genius in handling great business matters were all factors in favor of his success in directing this important work.

By the American press Lord Northcliffe's coming was hailed as a great event. Most Americans had heard of his wonderful career. They had not forgotten his great fight against British military inefficiency in 1915, when his victory in the famous " Battle of Shells " saved England from disaster. They also remembered that for years he had been at the forefront of every progressive movement in Great Britain.

On the fourth of June the British commissioners embarked secretly on a fast ship, and made the voyage from England to New York. Every precaution had been taken against German spies before leaving, and during the trip a sharp watch was kept for submarines, but fortunately no periscope was sighted.

When the commissioners arrived at New York, they were greeted formally by representatives of the United States government and other officials. Lord Northcliffe was also greeted informally by a large gathering of newspapermen. He was interviewed and photographed. Stories of his arrival, coupled with biographical sketches, appeared in every important newspaper.

As in England, Lord Northcliffe was not oblivious to the humors of the censorship. The day after his arrival one of the New York newspapers, in attempting to follow censorship rules, naïvely announced that " Lord Northcliffe arrived at an American

port yesterday and went at once to the
Hotel Gotham." When a reporter asked
him what he thought of the censorship, he
remarked drily: " I cannot discuss the subject, but that sentence, I think, speaks for
itself."

Lord Northcliffe's headquarters at the
Hotel Gotham in Fifth Avenue at once became a center of attraction. From day to
day they were crowded with visitors of
every description, from financiers and heads
of important industries, military men, and
politicians down to " men with schemes,"
men with something to sell, and the usual
throngs of reporters. One afternoon the
callers included the president of the largest
banking institution outside of Wall Street,
the president of an important Chicago bank,
and the head of a great manufacturing company. A staff of secretaries was kept busy
receiving and sorting these visitors, a large
proportion of whom were seen by Lord
Northcliffe himself.

In spite of the hot weather which prevailed at the time, Lord Northcliffe dispatched his business with an amount of
geniality that impressed all who saw him.

He met newspaper representatives as often as possible, outlined to them the work of the mission, and incidentally counteracted many false reports concerning British inactivity in the war which had been circulated by German propagandists. The American press, keen and eager, new to the war, drew upon his experiences at the front with avidity. He was able to dispel many erroneous impressions regarding the actual state of affairs.

Shortly after his arrival, Lord Northcliffe opened offices for the mission in a new building in upper Fifth Avenue, and a large staff was speedily organized in order to deal with executive matters. At the same time another department was established in a skyscraper situated in the center of the financial district. Here another staff was installed. Numerous branch offices already existed in various parts of the country, and these were included in the general plan of reorganization.

As soon as the preliminary work was completed, Lord Northcliffe went to Washington to carry on his work there. After meeting the President and the principal leaders in the government and receiving the coöperation of the British Embassy, he opened offices in one of the largest buildings and gathered another capable staff.

With President Wilson he was at once on cordial terms. Their respect and liking for each other gained with each meeting. To Lord Northcliffe the President appeared to be " a mixture of Scottish caution combined with tenacity and American unexpectedness —a man of great determination, clarity of vision, and fair-mindedness."

During his stay in Washington, Lord Northcliffe's sunny disposition had its usual effect upon all whom he met. His witty comments upon men and affairs entertained them. He was all that Americans supposed an Englishman not to be. Whether he was among university professors, politicians, members of the learned professions, or business men, the impression made was the same—that of a swift observer, of a man quick to grasp essentials, of a nature slow to impute evil, but impatient of dullness or incapacity, of a personality which compelled the epithet " great."

While he was at the capital he made a

number of new friends in official circles, with whom he discussed politics and played golf. He won the hearts of the local newspapermen by his readiness in giving interviews that were full of interest, and with the freemasonry of journalism he did everything possible to help even the humblest reporter.

Thenceforward he made New York his headquarters, occasionally visiting Washington and also making trips of inspection to various industrial centers. Later on he visited Detroit, Chicago, St. Louis, and other cities of the Middle West. During his entire stay in the United States he observed his usual custom of rising at five in the morning, and working almost incessantly until half-past seven in the evening. In this interval he met important business men and others, arranged big deals, worked on his system of reorganization, and gradually brought order out of chaos. He retired promptly at ten o'clock, and was up again at five the next morning, ready for another day's work. His marvelous endurance astonished his American friends.

During most of his stay in New York,

Lord Northcliffe made his home at Bolton Priory, one of the largest houses in Pelham Bay Park, a well-known suburb, adjacent to Long Island Sound. Here he entertained visitors and found rest and quiet, the essential antidotes for his life of strenuous action.

To give some idea of the colossal task which Lord Northcliffe had undertaken it is necessary to explain how the British system of army supplies had been developed from the early days of the war. It is a story that reveals the magnitude of modern war operations, in which millions of men must be equipped, clothed, and fed.

In 1914, when the great conflict began, the visible supplies of provisions and war materials in each of the Allied countries were insufficient for the purposes of a long war. The Allies were therefore compelled to enter neutral markets as buyers on an extensive scale. The United States, by reason of its immense resources, became the greatest market of all.

Early in the war the British government enlarged existing departments and organized still greater special departments of na-

In Paris, 1917

Lord Northcliffe starting out to attend a preliminary
meeting of the Allied War Council

tional service to control the purchase and
distribution of supplies. Some of the latter
eventually surpassed even the greatest private businesses in the enormous extent of
their dealings and expenditures. At that
time the purchase of supplies in the United
States was placed in charge of J. P. Morgan & Co., the New York banking firm,
this important business being ably directed
by Edward R. Stettinius, a member of
the firm and a well-known financial
expert.

In the case of certain other Allied powers,
notably Russia, the buying and awarding of
contracts was at first managed somewhat
loosely by special representatives who were
sent to New York. Realizing this, a number of enterprising Americans were struck
with the idea of getting options on war materials of all kinds and making profitable
deals with these officials. In some cases men
without any capital obtained important options on chemicals, munitions, rifles, lumber,
foods, metals, and other commodities, and
by acting as middlemen cleared large fortunes. In the vernacular of Wall Street
any enterprise that is launched with little or

no capital is said to have been " started on a shoestring." These fortunate option dealers were consequently termed the " shoestring millionaires." It was probably because of these loosely arranged options that much confusion arose in regard to supplies in the first years of the war. In some cases deliveries could not be made, and in several instances large quantities of defective equipment were rejected.

At the beginning of 1915, when the New York Stock Exchange reopened after having been closed for some months because of the outbreak of war, the newspapers were publishing sensational reports of huge contracts awarded to American companies by the Allied governments, amounting to untold millions of dollars. Orders were pouring in for munitions, rifles, guns, motor boats, electrical equipment, locomotives, metals, foods, cotton, leather, and other commodities. Some of the enormous orders for copper seriously taxed the production of American mines.

The stocks of companies which had received orders immediately began to advance, speculation became rampant, and thus the

great war boom commenced in Wall Street.
Advances of a hundred points or more were
common. Bethlehem Steel (common), for
example, rose from $50 to over $600 a share.
Electric Boat, which had been quoted below
ten dollars, went above $400 a share in
a few weeks. Railroad-equipment shares,
automobile shares, and many others scored
sensational advances. Fortunes were made
and lost daily by frenzied speculators in
these stocks, which were popularly termed
" the war brides."

When the United States entered the war
in April, 1917, the competition for war supplies was greatly increased, and it became
more important than ever for the Allies to
prevent any serious reduction in the quantities they were receiving. At that time
the buying for the Allies—Great Britain
excepted—had been coördinated and had become better managed. Some confusion had
arisen, however, in regard to the British
buying, which had been transferred from
Morgan & Co. to less efficient hands. The
numerous branch offices engaged in purchasing supplies were loosely connected.
What the British mission was empowered

to do was to reorganize the entire system and make it businesslike.

An idea of the vast dealings of the American branch of the British supply system can be gathered from a brief mention of some of the things that are required for the British army of four million men. Since the beginning of the war the value of the purchases made by the Contracts Department in London has aggregated $3,750,-000,000. The gross outlay in 1917 was about $1,750,000,000, and this did not take in guns, munitions, aeroplanes, or mechanical transport.

Since the war began the purchases have included 105,000,000 yards of cloth; 115,-000,000 yards of flannel; 400,000,000 pounds of bacon; 500,000,000 rations of preserved meat; 26,000,000 cans of jam; 167,000,000 pounds of cheese; 35,000,000 knives, forks, and spoons; 35,000,000 pairs of boots; 40,000,000 horseshoes; and 25,-000,000 gas helmets. The British armies in France alone require every month 95,000 tons of oats; 4,000,000 gallons of gasoline; 20,000 tons of flour; 10,000,000 pounds of ham and jam; and 75,000 tons of hay. In the economies effected by the Contracts Department and the mobilization of materials that has been achieved, the highest degree of business efficiency has been attained. It has done away with excessive war profits, the supplying of inferior materials, and other evils that formerly resulted from war contracts.

At the Contracts Department in London over 70,000 manufacturers or dealers are listed. These firms are in every neutral or Allied country, but mainly in Great Britain, Canada, Australia, and the United States. They can produce anything that the British armies require. When the armies cannot get what they want from some outside firm, the government makes it on its own account. On the index, for instance, under the head of " Biscuits " or " Crackers " are the names of every available biscuit-producing establishment in Great Britain and the United States. There is also a record of every contract that each firm has had with the British government, with the date and the price.

Thousands of contracts of all kinds are made in the course of the year. Some sections of the Contracts Department control such a vast amount of business that they have become separate and self-sufficient groups. The Royal Army Clothing Department, for example, spent about $250,-000,000 in 1917. After food, the next important item is clothes. The contracts are awarded to regular manufacturers, and each manufacturer produces one definite article, such as a jacket, trousers, puttees, socks, shoes, or a cap. Inspection plays an important part in this department. Every garment must conform to specifications or it is returned.

Some idea of the scope and effectiveness of the inspection can be gained from the fact that in July, 1917, out of 3,000,000 pieces of clothing inspected 117,000 were rejected. Out of 2,000,000 pairs of shoes sent in 68,000 were turned down. In one lot of 184,000 sheepskin coats—worn by motor-truck drivers—27,000 were below standard.

As a recent writer has remarked: " The business of war as represented by the system of supplies and transportation of the British army is nothing more or less than a colossal piece of merchandizing that has become a triumph of standardization. It expresses the genius of organization of a hundred United States Steel Corporations, Standard Oil Companies, and International Harvester Companies rolled into one."

The American branch of this great system which Lord Northcliffe reorganized, had control of expenditures that were roughly estimated to range from fifty to eighty million dollars a week. One newspaper calculation placed the amount at $3,996,816,000 a year, or at the rate of $10,958,400 a day, $456,600 an hour, $7610 a minute. In commenting on this enormous outlay Lord Northcliffe said: " I was sent to the United States not only because I have been here twenty times before, but because I am accustomed to directing large organizations, and it was felt by the British government that some one should supervise these huge disbursements which are passing into American pockets every week. Until my coming all the great purchasing departments in the United States were without a head. Now the business is working smoothly and efficiently."

Certain pro-German newspapers had mis=

stated the facts about these expenditures, and had asserted that Great Britain had borrowed billions from the United States to spend in England. Lord Northcliffe dispelled this illusion by a prompt explanation: " The credit of $185,000,000 monthly arranged by the United States government was intended to be used by Great Britain for the purchase of war supplies in the United States. This amount has been supplemented by our own expenditures. These expenditures mean a substantial sum every day for every man, woman, and child in the United States. I do not mention this in order to glorify war but merely to show that it indicates an appreciation of American products, which are invariably excellent."

Operating under Lord Northcliffe's direction were three principal British departments, besides many representatives dispatched to this country by the British Ministry of Munitions, the War Department, and the Admiralty. The three departments —Production, Inspection, and Railway and Shipping—had their headquarters in New York. Of these the Production Department is probably the most important. It records all progress that is being made in the United States in the manufacture of big guns and high explosives, and in fact everything connected with munitions. It also arranges railway rulings for munitions. Its third important function is to check quantities and weights of various parts from contractors or factories right down to the ships. The work of the Inspection Department differs from that of the Production Department, being confined to inspecting the quality of the munitions supplied. The Railway and Shipping Department controls the movements of British shipping to and from this country and the forwarding of supplies from interior points in the United States to the coast.

Few people in the United States have any idea of the extent of the British organization. To an interviewer with whom he discussed this subject, Lord Northcliffe said: "Most people think of the British supply system in this country as consisting of a thousand men or so. Of course there is a small group at the head of it, but as a matter of fact we have ten thousand men in the United States and Canada who are engaged directly or indirectly in purchasing, inspecting, checking, or arranging the transportation of food, munitions, and all the rest of our supplies. At the present time I am responsible for all of them."

The astonished interviewer added: "The picture was complete. Here was indeed the greatest spender in the world's history, responsible for the disbursement of nearly four billion dollars yearly, so gigantic a task that there were needed ten thousand agents under him whose daily task it was to spend, spend, spend!"

Lord Northcliffe was asked whether bids had to be made in open market, and if so, whether it tended to drive prices up. He replied: "We formerly had to bid in the open market and had to pay eight and a half cents a pound for steel, for example. But that was before the Exports Administrative Board was established under Judge Lovett, to pass on priority of demands. Now the United States and England buy side by side. We used to be represented in this country by Morgan & Co., but now all our buying of metals is done through the Lovett board, as it should be. But we have

our own offices, of course—two or three big
suites in New York, and others at a hundred
other points."

Lord Northcliffe did not fail to grasp
the humorous side of the war-contract business, and the devices employed by "men
with schemes," who secured options with a
view to becoming "shoestring millionaires."
In talking of this he said: "Before the
American Exports Board was established we
had salesmen of every conceivable sort over-
running our offices all day long. Hordes
of them crowded into our anterooms. It
seemed to me that most of them had nothing
in stock but nerve. Why, they hadn't a
factory to their names—just depended on
getting an order from us, and then going
out and finding a factory on the strength
of that order."

When Lord Northcliffe was asked in what
direction most of England's money went in
the United States, he dispelled the notion
that fifty per cent of it was devoted to
purchases of grain, meat, and other food-
stuffs. He said that food was a big item,
but not so large as fifty per cent or anywhere near that proportion. Commenting

on this statement, one editorial writer remarked that investigation disclosed that of
six billion dollars' worth of exports from
the United States during twelve months
ending in June, 1917, meat and dairy products, breadstuffs, refined sugar, and glucose
all put together did not make up much
more than a tenth part of the whole. Still
the amount of breadstuffs exported in that
period, valued at $113,000,000, was double
the amount exported in the year before the
war began.

It has been estimated that in 1917 Great
Britain purchased $250,000,000 worth of
copper in the United States and half a billion dollars' worth of explosives. On this
point Lord Northcliffe observed: " It is impossible to say what commodities make up
the bulk of our American purchases, because
they vary from day to day. One week we
are buying grain, the next something else—
copper, for instance, tremendous amounts
of copper. Iron, steel, brass, cotton and
woolen goods, oil and meats, autos and
trucks, and a myriad of other things are
purchased. I am the responsible buyer, it is
true, but one cannot go wrong with the

hundreds of inspectors that we have over here, extremely keen young fellows all of them. This, however, is a young man's war."

Throughout his life Lord Northcliffe has owed much of the success of his ventures to his shrewd selection of those whom he always speaks of as his " associates " or " colleagues." When he became head of the British War Mission he secured the most competent men he could find to help him. His staffs were made up of experts in their various lines. He concentrated most of his efforts on perfecting the directing organization in New York. When he returned to England he was able to feel that the great business of purchasing and forwarding would run smoothly under the capable direction of Sir Frederick Black and Sir Andrew Caird, who were left in charge. Valuable aid was also given by Sir Charles Gadon, vice-president of the Bank of Montreal, one of Canada's ablest business men, who was stationed in Washington, by the Honorable Robert Brand, partner of the famous Paris house of Lazard Brothers, and by Edward R. Stettinius, who had man-

aged the buying for the British government
so efficient-y in the first years of the war.

The nature of the transactions which have
been conducted in the United States by the
British War Mission cannot be specifically
described, although they can be easily
guessed at from the brief account that has
been given. Few people, however, could
form an accurate idea of the extent of the
business done in New York alone or the
number of people engaged in doing it. The
Railway and Shipping Department, for instance, employs many hundreds of people,
both in New York and at other points. In
an article on the work of the mission a writer
in the New York *Evening World* gave the
following description of this department:

"On the second floor of a vast office building in lower Broadway there is a whole
range of big rooms, taking up 10,000 feet
of floor space, at a rental of $22,500
(£4500) a year. These rooms are filled
with busy workers. They are fitted with the
latest office appliances. You would say
they were the offices of some great industrial corporation.

"So they are. The British Empire is at

present the greatest industrial corporation in the world, though the United States will soon rival and very likely pass it when the war industries of the country are in full swing. All those people in the second floor of that vast Broadway office building are working out the transportation of enormous shipments of all kinds of freight from American ports to Great Britain.

" The other branches of the mission— and there are a great many of them—are buying all that this shipping department can send across the ocean. Buying munitions of war, which means shells, guns, rifles, cartridges, explosives; buying grain, buying cotton, buying oil, buying mules and horses, buying hogs.

" Britain has sent the best men she could find to the United States on this purchasing errand, because it is clear that at the present moment there is no more important work than this to be done. Upon the shipments from the United States depends in a large measure the issue of the war. Thus a short time ago there came a hurry call for oil that was needed urgently in the United Kingdom for war purposes. At once the mission headquarters got busy. The most prominent oil men in the country were asked for their assistance, which they gave generously, and with the most valuable effect. 'We swam in oil,' Lord Northcliffe said humorously, 'we breathed oil. The whole place seemed to reek of it.' The result was a steady shipment of oil across the Atlantic."

Such was the gigantic work of reorganization that Lord Northcliffe undertook in June, 1917, and successfully completed by December, when he returned to England. So pronounced was his success that before his return he received a message of congratulation from the British War Council, expressing the warmest appreciation of his services. That the mission succeeded so well was entirely due to his clear-headed business ability. In less than six months he had dispelled confusion, established an efficient system, introduced economies, and speeded up the purchasing and forwarding of supplies. When he left New York the whole machinery of organization was running with the ease of a perfect machine.

After his return to London, Lord Northcliffe had an audience with King George at Buckingham Palace, when he received His Majesty's thanks, and was also requested to thank the associate members of the British mission for their good work, in which they had been so effectively assisted by their American colleagues. In conversation with Lord Northcliffe at that time the king spoke in high terms of the American mission to the Allies and of Colonel House, whom he had known for some years. The mission, he said, displayed the energy and alertness indicative of American character and purpose. Lord Northcliffe was surprised at the king's intimate knowledge of the possibilities of aircraft production in the United States, his interest in the Liberty Motor, his knowledge of the men who had evolved it, and the manner in which it was produced.

As a further recognition of his services Lord Northcliffe was shortly afterwards honored with the higher title of viscount. His energies were not allowed to rest, for in less than a month he organized a London headquarters for the British War Mission, establishing them at Crewe House, one of the great London mansions, where a large staff was soon busily managing the British end of the great system of purchasing and forwarding carried on in the United States. Crewe House was at once prepared for the entertainment of representatives of the United States, France, and other Allied nations visiting England on business. The banquet hall and ballroom were renovated, and paintings to adorn the walls were brought from the National Gallery.

Apart from his arduous work in connection with the British War Mission, Lord Northcliffe found time in the United States to help the Allied cause by presenting the truth about the war in articles that he contributed to American newspapers and magazines. Although pressure of business prevented him from accepting many invitations to address business, political, and social organizations which poured in during his stay in America, he managed to speak on several important occasions in New York, Chicago, and elsewhere.

It is doubtful if any other British public man could have upheld the cause of the Allies so successfully as Lord Northcliffe. It is certain that none could have done it with more vigor, could have made a better impression upon the government and people of the United States, and implanted more forcibly the conviction of Britain's resolute will to conquer, of her faith in her resources and her Allies, of her steady confidence that victory can in time be won.

It was a difficult task for Lord Northcliffe, because he followed in the wake of the Right Honorable Arthur James Balfour, M.P., who had visited the United States in April, at the head of a special mission to emphasize the aims and ideals of the British people in conducting the war. Mr. Balfour's engaging manners won him immediate popularity. His deftly phrased speeches were read with admiration. But Mr. Balfour to the American people was an exotic. They were curious about him as one of the older statesmen of England. He was in appearance and speech what one of the newspapers, without offensive or even humorous intention, called " an interesting survival."

Lord Northcliffe, however, was fortunate in representing a completely different type of Briton. It was desirable from the British point of view to impress upon the American people that they had not come to the rescue of an effete civilization. It was necessary to show them that their allies, the British, as a race are no less virile and resourceful than they are themselves. Among Americans an idea had widely prevailed that England had become " played out " and that the British people were timid and unenterprising haters of innovation. That idea has diminished since the war began. Nothing could have done more to dispel it entirely than the vigorous work of Lord Northcliffe in the United States.

After his return to England Lord North-cliffe used all the influence of his newspapers in supporting the plan for an Allied War Council to meet at Versailles, and to bring about the concentration of effort which was needed to win the war. Each country had been fighting on its own initiative, and it was difficult to get satisfactory results, whereas the Central Powers had been united.

When this plan was recommended by President Wilson, an interview was given out by Lord Northcliffe, in which he said:

" Not one Englishman in a hundred understands the position and power of the President of the United States. By most Englishmen he is regarded as an American prime minister. Our prime minister, of course, is removable by a single adverse majority vote in the House of Commons. It is not understood over here that the President cannot be removed from office except in extremely rare circumstances, that he has more power than a constitutional monarch, and has supreme authority over the army and navy. This explains why President Wilson's message to Colonel House in regard to the Allied War Council was published so inconspicuously by most English newspapers."

After the council had been established Lord Northcliffe said: " It is no secret that at the suggestion of Secretary McAdoo, M. André Tardieu and I worked on this plan for months in the United States. It ought to have been put in hand long ago. If action had been taken at the time desired by Mr. McAdoo, the Italian disaster in December, 1917, might have been averted. Before the coöperative principle went into effect, the war was conducted in a manner that would have ruined even the United States Steel Corporation in less than two weeks."

In February, 1918, Lord Northcliffe accepted the position of Director of Propaganda in Enemy Countries, while continuing his work on the British War Mission. He had agreed to use his intimate knowledge of enemy countries to enable reports of important speeches and statements of war aims to reach the peoples of the Central Powers and their allies, and thus disseminate the truth in communities where it had been persistently suppressed.

XIII

A MESSAGE TO AMERICA

SINCE the war began, it has been remarked, the people of the United States
and Great Britain have discovered that they
are in closer community of essential thought
and purpose than they had previously suspected. There has been a striking similarity in the methods which both nations
have adopted in dealing with the intricate
problems of war time. Furthermore, allow-
ing for their greater distance from the firing line, Americans have thought about
the great issues of the war almost exactly
as the British have thought about them.

The American people have followed the
phases of the war in Great Britain, the
blunderings, the tenacity, the onset of conscription in an essentially non-military community, with the complete understanding of
a nation similarly circumstanced, differing
only by scale and distance. They have now

been through something of the sort themselves. It had not before occurred to many
Americans how parallel the two countries
are. They begin now to have an inkling of
how much closer the resemblance may presently become.

More than any other British public man,
Lord Northcliffe has a profound understanding of this similarity in national aims
and methods. Through his wide knowledge
of American affairs he has been enabled to
view the important questions of the war
from what may be termed an Anglo-
American standpoint, and this has been evident in much that he has written in the last
three years.

During his visit to the United States as
head of the British War Mission, Lord
Northcliffe, as already mentioned, contributed some highly interesting articles to
newspapers and magazines, in which he discussed a variety of topics incident to the
war. He also addressed a number of important gatherings. One of his most notable
speeches was delivered at the British re-
cruiting celebration held at Madison Square
Garden, New York, where an audience of

14,000 greeted him with enthusiastic applause. Another interesting occasion on
which he spoke was in Kansas City, where
he addressed a convention of 2000 newspaper editors of the Middle West.

The introductions at the meetings at which
Lord Northcliffe appeared led his hearers
to expect a great deal from his speeches.
They were not disappointed, for he made
an instant impression of forcefulness and
sincerity. As he had none of the wiles
of the professional orator, there was nothing
flamboyant in his phrases. He did not attempt to work up effective points with the
aim of inviting applause. But there was
meat in every one of his sentences. He invariably paid his audiences the compliment
of assuming that they did not want mere
rhetoric. Therefore he did not speak as
one who talked for the sake of talking.

In most of his speeches what he had to
say was not very palatable. He could have
won cheap and easy applause by telling
people what they would have liked to hear
—that the war was almost won, that the
submarine menace had failed, and that the
task of the United States would not be diffi-

cult. Instead of that, he told his audiences what he believed to be the truth about the war, sending them away thoughtful, but braced to the necessity for effort and sacrifice. His criticism was constructive,— "Build ships, save food, pull yourselves together for a long war." He treated the war as a grave calamity affecting everybody, a calamity which everybody could do something to combat if they were only told what that something might be.

Lord Northcliffe discussed the war as it had never been discussed by politicians in England. At all points his wisdom of talking plainly and frankly was entirely justified by the manner in which his speeches were received. One of the newspaper editors after the Kansas City gathering began his description of it by saying that the talk they had heard had taught them a great deal which they did not know before. He also said that Lord Northcliffe had not only made every one feel sure that he knew what he was talking about, but that he meant every word that he said. It was his obvious sincerity, his evident desire not to make a showy effect, but to thresh the wheat of reality from the chaff of illusion, which won his audiences over as soon as he began to speak and which held their attention.

The plain-spoken utterances of Lord Northcliffe, typical of his character as an observer and thinker, did much toward counteracting the mischievous work of German propagandists. He lost no opportunity to state the case of the Allies, and to explain why they had united against the common foe of democracy. His views on the war in its relation to the United States showed plainly that he had a thorough understanding of our national ideals and purposes. In many ways his public utterances constituted a stirring message to America, and one that is particularly interesting at the present time. For that reason the following résumé of some of the things that he said in his articles and speeches forms an appropriate addition to his biography.

In discussing the striking resemblance between the United States and Great Britain before and since the war began, Lord Northcliffe, in one of his addresses, pointed out that both countries had been over wealthy

and equally unprepared for defense against
the attack of a powerful enemy. "If England," he said, "had possessed only a mild
form of military insurance there would have
been no war. Like yourselves, however,
we were eternally talking about money,
business, or territorial expansion. The
United States has been like an over-rich
corporation and has invited trouble from
hungry competitors. We were in precisely
the same position. It is a curious fact,
moreover, that the richer people become the
more they preach peace. It pleases them
and their pockets. We were all purse and
no fist.

"The Germans knew of our weak points,
and they suddenly fell upon us. Fortunately for ourselves, a certain number among
us had insisted upon having a modern navy,
although some of our richest people, as well
as those most politically strong, advocated
a reduction of the fleet. Great Britain,
however, had only a small army and was
unprepared for aerial warfare. In the early
days of the war if the Germans, instead of
fooling with Zeppelin gas-bags, had been
enterprising enough to land fifty thousand

troops from aeroplanes in England, and
these invaders had intrenched themselves,
we should have had considerable difficulty
in ejecting them. If we had only spent
as much in the right kind of preparedness
each year as we are now spending in two
weeks of the war (our daily expenditure is
over $30,000,000) this war could not have
happened."

As to Germany's reasons for beginning
the war, Lord Northcliffe expressed the
opinion that they were not commercial but
dynastic. "No doubt there were commercial interests in Germany that were foolish
enough to believe they would be benefited.
But the aim of Prussian Junkerdom was to
establish a world domination. Commerce
was to lend its aid, but commerce was to be
a means towards the attainment of the
war party's object and not an end in itself.
So much is certain. Equally certain it is
that commercial ambitions had nothing to do
with Austria-Hungary's reasons for fighting,
nor for those of Turkey or Bulgaria. They
joined with Germany because Germany alternately threatened and cajoled their rulers.

"The German people have been pur-

posely deluded into the belief that they are
defending themselves against foes who are
set upon crushing them out of existence, a
design which nobody but a lunatic would
conceive or imagine possible of execution.
Austria fancies that she went to war to de-
fend herself against Russia, the truth being
that she was used as a cat's-paw by the
Hohenzollern gang." *

The Kaiser's grandiose scheme for an
empire of Middle Europe that would
stretch from Antwerp to Bagdad, dominate
the world, smash the Monroe Doctrine, ab-
sorb South America, and levy tribute upon
the United States has been revealed since
the war began. In referring to this menace,
Lord Northcliffe remarked: " So you know
what Germany was after. She envied the
people with the goods and had a great desire to control countries that possess coal,
iron, and other valuable resources. There
is no sentiment about German warfare. We
are very wealthy in Britain and so are you
in the United States. Germany did not
want a little country like Belgium. She was
after something bigger."

* *Current Opinion.*

In reviewing the position of the Allies, Lord Northcliffe said: " Here, in the United States, I am told, and I have discovered proof for myself, there are people who have been deluded by German and pro-German propagandists into supposing that this is a ' commercial war,' although it is not easy to make out exactly what they mean by that expression. As far as I can learn, they suppose that the combatants are each seeking to obtain control of the world's markets. They even suggest that it was a motive of this kind that brought the United States in. The argument runs thus: The big American interests were so heavily committed by their dealings with the Allies that they forced the government of the United States to intervene in order that they might not lose their money. It will be useful to examine this delusion and to knock away the props on which it stands.

" No one in England was ever insane enough to propose that Britain should try to meet German competition by fighting Germany. The proposal had been made that Britain should abandon her system of free trade under which Germans were able to do business as freely as Britons in any British dominion or dependency. But that proposal was not adopted. What would have been the good of Britain going to war with Germany in order to secure markets? As soon as she had secured them they would have been open to German as freely as to British trade. The German Vice-Chancellor, Dr. Helfferich, has asserted that Great Britain's object was ' the economic oppression of Germany.' How could Britain oppress any nation economically as long as she allowed the traders of all nations to compete with her own traders upon equal terms?

"Further, if Britain had planned a commercial war, is it likely that she would have been caught unprepared? How unprepared she was all the world knows. Britain had no motive for taking up arms beyond the saving of Belgium and the assertion of the right of all peoples to develop freely and securely as they desire, except the motive which led her to fight Philip of Spain and the Spanish Armada in the sixteenth century, and that which made her the leader of the nations in the struggle against the at-

tempt of Napoleon to become the master
of Europe in the early eighteen hundreds.
She saw that she must fight for her life, for
the security of her communications, which
are the arteries carrying her life blood.
'The war,' Sir Robert Borden said in New
York last year, 'has taught us two things.
First, that the liberty, the security, and the
free existence of the British Empire are dependent upon the safety of the ocean path-
ways, whether in peace or war; next, that
sea power is the most powerful instrument
by which world domination can be effectually
crushed.'

"The peoples of the British Empire did
not want war. They had nothing to gain
from war. They were threatened. They
were attacked. Whether Prussia had invaded Belgium or not, Britain would have
been obliged to fight in self-defense. It was
not Brussels that the Germans wanted when
'for strategic reasons' they marched their
troops across the Belgian frontier which they
had signed a solemn treaty to respect. They
wanted Antwerp, which Napoleon called,
with clear-sighted understanding, 'a pistol
pointed at the head of England.' They

wanted an outlet for their ocean-going submarines. They wanted Calais."

In spite of governmental watchfulness, the evil effects of German propaganda have been experienced in England and France. This possibly explains why certain misconceptions regarding the causes of the war still exist in both countries. "A number of English people still fancy," said Lord Northcliffe, "that Britain could have kept out of the conflict if Belgium had not been invaded. These people cannot understand that Prussia's object in forcing war upon France and Russia was to clear them out of the way and be able to attack England and, in course of time, the United States, with a good prospect of success, later on. I have even heard French people speak as if France took up arms to regain Alsace and Lorraine, whereas we know that France would never have brought upon the world the frightful calamity of war for selfish aims."

As to the motive which impelled Russia to enter the war, that country, as Lord Northcliffe explained, could not be accused of having had commercial ambitions. Al-

most all the commerce that Russia possessed
had been in German hands for many years.
" Russia," said Lord Northcliffe, " was
goaded into mobilizing her armies by the
attempt of Prussia and Austria to establish
German influence in the Balkans: to insult
and injure Russia by showing that she could
not save her Slav brethren, the Serbs, from
being crushed out of existence as a free
nation. It would be just as stupid to suggest that France made war for commercial
aggrandizement. France stood by her ally,
Russia, as she had bound herself to do by
a ' scrap of paper.' France is an honorable country. Her people keep their en-
gagements. If France now asks for the
return of Alsace and Lorraine, it is because
she desires a guarantee against further
Prussian aggression and because the populations are in favor of French instead of German rule."

In summing up the reasons which compelled the United States to enter the war,
Lord Northcliffe referred to the fact that
German scientists had, for many years, persistently spread the idea that Germans were
supermen, a chosen race, and that it was

necessary for the progress of humanity that
they should impose their will upon the rest
of the world. "German intelligence," he
remarked, "was devoted to this object, and
no scruple about honor or pity was to be
allowed to stand in the way. Every means
to victory was to be used, without caring how
brutal and devilish it might be. 'We are,'
it was declared, 'the most advanced, most
efficient nation; therefore we are meant to
crush out the less advanced. That is our
idea of progress.'

"Such an idea, however, the United
States could not accept or tolerate. This
country refused to accept Kaiser Wilhelm's
insulting boast to Ambassador Gerard in
Berlin: 'There is no international law now.'
He meant that Germany had done away
with it. She claimed to have put her will
in place of law.

"If a ruffian stood in the street and declared: 'There is no law now. I have abolished it. I will kill any one who comes this
way without groveling to me for permission,' would American citizens say: 'Oh,
very well, we must do as you think fit'?
No, American citizens would very quickly

have that ruffian out of the way, either
locked up or buried with holes through him.
That, I think, would be the attitude of
Americans as individuals, and the attitude
of the nation is the same towards the ruf-
fianly attempt of the Hohenzollern party to
substitute their will for the law of nations
and to ' bulldoze ' the United States.

" Prussia, in the course of her savage and
criminal rage, injured the United States,
and added insult to injury by telling American citizens that if they did not want to be
injured further they must keep out of the
way, and only move about, by kind permission of the Kaiser, where Germany was
pleased to let them go. It was because of
this that the United States declared war
upon the Central Empires. If this country
had meant to take up arms in defense of
British or French interests, or in the interests of Belgium, or in order to spread
democracy, it would not have waited until
April, 1917. If its aims had been commercial, it would have been in the war long ago.
The motive which brought the United States
in was not sympathy with any other nation,
was not desire for gain, was not an abstract

fondness for democratic as opposed to auto-
cratic government; it was self-interest, self-
preservation, self-respect. The American
people are not fighting to make the world
safe for democracy, but to make the world
safe for themselves.

"For this cause American armies are being sent to France. That is where the
enemy of the world's peace must be brought
to book. Mayor Thompson of Chicago is
reported as having said, ' I do not believe in
sending our youths to the trenches of Europe instead of providing an adequate army
to prevent home invasion.' The war can be
ended, the world can be made safe for us
all to live in, only by fighting the Germans
where they are. History shows that all nations which have waited to be attacked have
suffered in consequence. Ask any French-
man whether he thinks it an advantage to
France that the war is raging on French
soil. There could be only one answer to
such a foolish question. The American
army must fight the Germans in Europe
in order to prevent them from bringing the
war to the United States.

"The task which the United States has

taken up in consequence of the Prussian attack upon its sovereign rights is the task of throwing into the scale the last weight which will turn it against Germany. That task may be summed up in the three F's—Feed, Finance, Finish. When there are two million American troops, which put Right before Might, facing the common foe of all nations, the Finish of the war will be at hand. The world looks to American initiative, enterprise, and innate love of freedom to put an end, let us hope for all time, to an attempt to tyrannize, unprecedented in history."

In Lord Northcliffe's opinion it has been difficult to arouse the American public to the gravity of the war because the fighting line is so far away. Certain hardships, resulting from war conditions, have been experienced in the United States, but no actual suffering. In discussing this subject Lord Northcliffe said: " People in America read about the wonderful victories of the Allies and the sinking of hundreds of German submarines; they are told that Germany is on the point of starvation. Most of these stories are untrue, but they believe all of them. It is impossible for the American people to realize what war actually is, because they are so far away from it. They have not seen wounded soldiers coming back, and they have not had their homes destroyed by aeroplanes. They cannot understand such things until they are brought home to them."

The same is undoubtedly true of the reports of German atrocities, which lose much of their effect in traveling three thousand miles. Being far removed from the war zone, and having no visible evidence of the horrors of war as waged by the Germans,— the massacres of women and children, the maiming and murdering of male civilians, the enslavement of whole populations of non-combatants, the systematic starvation of prisoners, the ravaging of towns and countries,—it is difficult for the great mass of the American people to grasp the full significance of these terrible happenings. As an observer Lord Northcliffe was much impressed by this fact.

The people of the United States, as a well-known American war correspondent has remarked, do not seem to understand the difference between the treacherous, brutal-ized German soldier of reality and the inoffensive German of popular imagination. " The French and English," says this writer, " are not fighting the Hohenzollerns. They are fighting the Germans. They have been at it a long time, and they ought to know them. When will Americans begin to believe what those who have been fighting the Germans over three years tell them? How long will they continue to believe that the German is not what he is, but what they think he ought to be? That is to say, what he used to be."

Having a thorough knowledge of the insidious methods of German propaganda, Lord Northcliffe warned Americans to be on guard against this treacherous and dangerous force which has been so persistently employed. As is well known, since the present atrocious conflict was forced upon the world by the Prussianized Germans they have won more by deceit than by arms. The treachery, bribing, propaganda, and wholesale corruption which led to the collapse of Russia have been practiced, on a less gigantic scale, in other countries. Prior to April, 1917, the pro-German movements, with their

misrepresentations and distortion of facts,
which were carried on in the United States
constituted a national menace.

This method of warfare is not of recent
origin, however. As a matter of fact, many
years before the war almost every country
had been gathered into the meshes of the
German secret service. In some countries
newspapers were subsidized to create pro-
German feeling, revolutionary societies
were supported, strikes were fomented, and
criminals of the lowest type were enlisted to
commit murder and arson whenever it became necessary for the Kaiser's government
to strike a blow. The work of spies and
propagandists in the United States proved
conclusively that Germany had for years
been preparing for the possibility of war
with this country. As investigations disclosed, the German ambassador at Washington had been supplied with large funds
for the payment of secret agents commis-
sioned to blow up ships and munition plants.
In addition, support was given to opposers
of conscription and to emissaries of the I.
W. W., engaged in precipitating strikes in
mines and factories. President Wilson is on

record to the effect that scores of American citizens, while the United States was at peace with Germany, were killed by murderers in the employ of the German government.

In one of his speeches Lord Northcliffe asserted that before the outbreak of the war German intrigue had been at work in England. "Many Germans," he said, " were then holding high positions in the United Kingdom, such as mayors of towns, and we were amazed to discover that they had been working against us for years. They had provided Berlin with valuable information. Like yourselves, however, we were an unsuspicious people, and it took us some time to realize what these treacherous enemies were doing. Nor could we conceive that the German ambassador, whom we supposed to be a high-minded, honorable gentleman, would busy himself with schemes of revolution, arrange for the burning of our munition factories, and concoct other plots, when he should have been trying to straighten out affairs between our country and his own."

That it is difficult to cope with the in-

tricate German spy system Lord Northcliffe
frankly admits. He believes that a large
amount of information has been sent to
Germany in apparently innocent cable messages addressed to business houses in neutral countries. Such messages can give news
of departing transports and other ships in
order that they may be attacked by submarines. "Outgoing cables," he says,
"should be closely watched. It was only
by checking back cables to neutral countries that we succeeded in catching some of
our spies.

"I don't know whether the United States
government has an alert censorship on letters and cable messages to Spain, but I
venture to think that if this is not the case
and a censorship is installed, a large amount
of secret information might be detected. I
would also point out that newspaper illustrations may easily convey dangerous information. The Germans have a system of
enlarging newspaper pictures to see if they
can get any useful ideas from them. For
that reason no picture of any new tank,
aeroplane, or other war machine should be
published."

Lord Northcliffe has been surprised by the quickness with which the Germans ascertain what is going on in opposing countries. For instance, they flood Spain and other neutral nations with false reports that immediately minimize any statements made by the Allies, and contradict such statements with a celerity that is amazing. He asked Commendatore Marconi if it were possible that the Germans might have a wireless plant concealed somewhere in England. The Italian inventor replied that it would be quite possible, and that he himself would be able to erect a wireless plant in England that the authorities would have great trouble in discovering.

Like other far-seeing public men, Lord Northcliffe has always opposed an inconclusive peace, realizing that the German people, who have given strong support to the Kaiser's iniquitous war policy, cannot be induced to change their views until they are effectually defeated. It would, moreover, be impossible to trust a government that holds no word sacred, and that has been constantly busy concocting lies, fomenting conspiracies, and poisoning the thought of the world.

In answer to the question, "How long will the war last?" Lord Northcliffe replied: "I see no reason to expect a short war. Of course, we could have peace tomorrow, but it would be a short peace, and would mean a more terrible war than we are having, for you can rest assured that the Germans would not make the mistake they made in this instance of having so many nations against them. As a great Scandinavian said: 'Beat Germany this time, for if you do not she will beat you.' We are fighting for the permanent peace of the world and freedom for each nation. President Wilson is the inspired prophet of this dispensation."

In spite of what has been said to the contrary, Lord Northcliffe does not believe that any army raised and trained in a time of emergency can at once compete on equal terms with troops that have been equipped, organized, and drilled in the course of years. For that reason he has never underrated German military strength. "The Germans," he says, "have been educated for war and trained in military tactics for more than a generation; they have given their lives to this cause. There is nothing wrong about their war machine. Therefore, to suppose that people who are untrained and unprepared for war can conquer the Germans in a short time is the height of folly."

In a speech before the House of Commons Sir Auckland Geddes, who is at the head of the department of national service, declared that armies in these days are something more than men in the field. An army, as he explained, is now a body of experts handling the most wonderful machines, guns, mortars, aeroplanes, telephones, electric lights, gas, and a myriad of other things. All this equipment must be transported to the front, with hundreds of tons of shells, bombs, and high explosives. There is also a vast area of rearwards services, extending from the mines through the factories along the lines of communication right to the hands of the men who use the weapons.

Lord Northcliffe repeatedly emphasized this fact in his articles and speeches. In addressing the Western editors he pointed out that war to-day is entirely different from what it was in the past. "Formerly it was showy, dramatic, emotional; now it is none of these things. The present war is a very different proceeding from old-time warfare, when men enlisted, shouldered their rifles, and marched to battle. In this war the farmer, the miller, the butcher, and the men in the munition factory are just as important as the soldier. War, in fact, has become in part a vast business enterprise. In preparing a new army to fight the Germans it is just as if a party of amateur journalists should go to a big American city with a few presses to run a newspaper in competition with an old established daily. You are amateurs in the game of war, more so than we are, because we have had three years of practice. We began this war with almost no army at all. Great Britain underestimated the job at the beginning and went to war unprepared, as the United States has done. England, however, paid dearly for the mistake."

As the result of Britain's experience, Lord Northcliffe is convinced that conscription is the only democratic method of raising an effective army. "The draft system," he says, "is the only one for a democratic nation. We thought the only democratic system was to take those who by their enthusiasm volunteered and went to war, but we soon discovered that was a mistake. We found that while the patriot went to war, the unpatriotic man stayed behind and stole the patriot's living. We had an absurd slogan, 'One volunteer is worth three pressed men.' It sounded well, but it was not true. When we adopted the draft we found that the drafted men fought just as well as the volunteers. There is the same spirit of brotherhood among soldiers. The drafted men are received in the same spirit as those who enlisted of their own free will."

By means of conscription, as Lord Northcliffe pointed out, the United States will eventually have a formidable army, and although the Kaiser sneered at "the contemptible British army," and has scoffed at the idea of American participation in the war, he will find that, when the decisive struggle comes, the armies of democracy are more than a match for the German machine.

In explaining why he had been impelled to speak frankly when addressing American

audiences in regard to the war, Lord Northcliffe said: "I have spoken in this way because I have been talking to friends. We
are banded together by a feeling of brotherhood, and we should plan and work together
in order to win this war. No one has a
better or clearer idea of the infinitely difficult task before us than I have. I know,
moreover, how difficult it is to deal with
prosperous people—they are so optimistic.
At the beginning of the war it was much
the same in England.

" The British race is like the American,
anti-militaristic. It is even anti-authority.
It is therefore the antipode of the German,
whose government embodies authority more
completely than any other in the world.
The British idea is solid opposition to the
principle of unrestricted authority. The
American Revolution, like Magna Charta,
forms a milestone in its development. I
am impressed by this fact as I travel in the
United States. I find that your country
is very similar to our country, that your
people are very similar to our own people.
Here the people rule, and it is the same in
Britain. You hated an army, and so did

we. Being opposed to war, we did not have an army, and it was the same in your case. I hope and pray, however, that we shall never have another war, and I believe that if we keep together when the soldiers come back and conditions are adjusted, we shall have a continued peace; for the people will see to it that nothing like this shall happen again as long as they live."

One of the greatest statesmen in England has declared that the destiny of the world depends to a great extent upon how the United States and Great Britain act toward each other when the war is over. They can be keen trade rivals and compete to the limit, as they probably will. But between the two great English-speaking peoples, he says, there should be coördination and understanding. It should be their duty to police the world and make it free not only for democracy but for trade. Lord Northcliffe takes the same view. "As the result of the war," he says, "the United States and Great Britain have been brought very close together. If we two peoples keep together we can, I am sure, see that there is never another war."

That there is a silver lining to the war cloud Lord Northcliffe has perceived. In an impressive address, in which he dealt with this aspect of the war, he said: " After all the harm that Germany has done to the world by forcing it into this war, we may gain a grain of comfort if we glance at the other side of the account. The war has brought the Allied nations together as never before; mistrust and animosities have been swept away and forgotten, and we stand together as a band of brothers and sisters.

" Unintentionally, Germany has taught us a higher meaning of duty, of patriotism, and the sacrifices they entail. Having to face peril, suffering, death itself, we have reacted from superficial things, feelings, thoughts even, and live our lives among the realities, sterner, harsher, more primitive perhaps, but infinitely more important in the right conduct of existence. We are living in a great age. Romance has been restored to us. Men die ' for Belgium,' ' for Italy,' ' for France,' ' for England,' ' for America,' literally day by day, these heroes, these paladins of ours. May we not believe that this

kinship of the battle line, where men of
widely different races have stood shoulder
to shoulder in the cause of Liberty, is destined to endure?"

XIV

WHAT THE FUTURE HOLDS

In judging a man, it has been said, the only right course is to ask: "What effect has his life, taken as a whole, had on the world?" To pick out samples here and there and hold them up does not show us the man any more than a block of stone would give an idea of the Capitol at Washington. So in viewing the career of Viscount Northcliffe, from his youthful days when he started his first paper, to the man as we behold him now, the net results must be considered. If that be done, we are compelled to acknowledge his genius, originality, usefulness, and power.

That Northcliffe has more than an average proportion of enemies and detractors, that he has been misunderstood and misrepresented, is admitted. Even his remarkable success and swift rise to eminence and influence have served to create enmity. Success in others is apt to sour those who have failed to achieve success themselves, and frequently it begets opposition that is cruel and unjust.

Northcliffe's fault, if fault it be, is that he has succeeded too well. Success is a hard thing for some people to forgive; personality repels as well as attracts. It is enough for a man to have distinction and brains for every malicious tongue to wag against him. Northcliffe has been a trail-maker, and for that reason he is not understood by many conservative people in England who shudder at every startling result of social progress and sigh for the good old times.

In the career of Lord Northcliffe, however, the maxim, " To foresee is to rule," has been illustrated repeatedly. It is because of his ability to sense coming events —the highest expression of journalistic genius—and his skill in meeting new conditions that have placed him in the front rank of British public life, and have gained for him such a vast following that in comparison with those who accept his views and believe in him, his opponents sink into insignificance.

In attempting to forecast what the future may hold for Lord Northcliffe it is essential to bear these facts in mind, and to consider what scope he is likely to find, in coming years, for his originality, his energy, and his ability to deal with new problems. As we look to the future it is easy to foresee that such talents as his will have unprecedented opportunities for their exercise in the stupendous work that lies ahead. Strong men who can wisely direct the efforts of others are always needed. They were needed in 1915 when Great Britain was struggling against muddling inefficiency. They will be needed still more when the war comes to an end and the gigantic work of reconstruction begins.

When that time comes Great Britain will need the services of the business statesman of Lord Northcliffe's caliber. His thorough knowledge of British social questions and his progressive views regarding capital and labor and the upbuilding of foreign trade, through his intimate knowledge of foreign countries,—their resources, industries, and business conditions,—fit him to become a prominent figure in the momentous delibera-

tions which must follow the return of peace.
What Great Britain will need then is
not professional politicians, but hard-headed,
sophisticated business experts, familiar with
the whole world.

That Lord Northcliffe, more than any
other man in England, has the power to
bring about important reforms and accomplish speedily what would otherwise require
much time to effect has been admitted by no
less an authority than Lloyd George, the
prime minister. For many years Northcliffe was Lloyd George's most bitter critic.
He has now become his ally in the government of the British Empire. In commenting on this fact, a recent English writer
pointed out that despite the differences in
their outlook on life there are wonderful
resemblances between the two men. There
are sympathies too. "Northcliffe," the
writer observed, "early recognized that
Lloyd George was a person to be watched,
not because of his speeches, but because he
was a man of action. On one occasion
Lloyd George, in speaking of Northcliffe,
remarked: 'What a power this man can be
whenever he chooses! He can carry through

a political project while we are thinking
about it. We talk of tackling the question
of housing the poor people of this country,
for instance. He could do it single
handed.' "

When the stress of war time has ended,
Lord Northcliffe will have an immense field
of endeavor in which to exert his energies.
He has been of immeasurable service to his
country during the war, but great as his
past deeds have been they may become
of secondary importance to that which
he is likely to accomplish in coming
years.

Whatever happens, one thing is certain,
that when the war ends, as it must some
day, there is bound to be a staggering
amount of political and industrial disloca-
tion in which Great Britain, among other
countries, will have to share. The war has
destroyed wealth beyond precedent, trade
has become disorganized, and each of the
combatant powers has added stupendous
burdens to its national debt. In Britain,
when peace returns, great questions will
crowd upon each other for attention, questions of domestic and foreign policy, of

social and industrial reconstruction. To
meet the difficulties imposed by the war
some revolutionary experiments have been
made. These innovations will have to be
carefully and dispassionately surveyed with
a view to deciding whether they shall be
retained or discarded.

To deal successfully with this colossal
work of reconstruction new methods will be
required. It will also demand administrative ability of the highest order. For the
old school of English politicians to attempt
to grapple with it would be a hopeless proceeding. Here it is that Lord Northcliffe
seems predestined to take a foremost part.
His genius in foreseeing the approach of
new conditions, and his skill in solving new
problems, which have made him the greatest
force in British public life and placed him
at the head of the popular current of
thought, will assuredly enable him to assist
in the giant task of restoring prosperity to
his war-worn country.

It has been predicted that when the dust
and din of war time have cleared away a
new era will dawn, and that its approach
will be heralded by political and social

changes of a radical nature. In England
such an inspired prophet as H. G. Wells
foresees the advent of a new economic system in which private capitalism will eventually disappear and government ownership
will emerge. In his recent work, " What Is
Coming," he has given the reason in a few
words—" Whereas we were individualists,"
he says, " now we are socialists."

Radical leaders of the people in Great
Britain are bent on effecting far more drastic changes than even Mr. Wells foresees.
They declare that not only must every trace
of capitalism be obliterated, but the whole
social fabric must be reconstructed. Class
distinctions must be abolished, the government must be remodeled, and the working
people must rule. Opposed to these radicals and their followers are the conservative
middle and upper classes, who would undoubtedly prefer to see " Business resumed
as before" when the war is over.

Always closely in touch with public feeling, and glimpsing future events by present indications, Lord Northcliffe has already
perceived that a great change is certain to
be wrought in British national life. Writ-

ing on this subject recently, he expressed some startling views.

"I have talked with our soldiers at the front," he said, "and have discovered that they have strong ideas regarding capital and labor, government, education, and other questions which are paramount in the public mind to-day. After the war two million young men who have been through rough hell for their country will require better working conditions as the price of their sacrifice. Just as Grant's soldiers, the Grand Army of the Republic, dominated elections in the United States for a quarter of a century after the Civil War, so will the men I have seen in the trenches go home and demand by their votes the reward of a changed England, an England that is likely to be as much of a surprise to the present owners of capital as it may be to the owners of land. As the result of this change there is certain to be a great social development in Britain. Eventually there will be a change in the wage system. The rich will become poorer and the poor richer. A species of state socialism seems inevitable. The socialism of the soldiers is not of that irresponsible type which is nothing but anarchism, but they have made their sacrifices to the uttermost, and when they return they will see to it that they control the government."

The extent to which British industries and labor have been dislocated by the war can be understood when it is explained that four million men from all ranks of life are now serving in the British army, while several millions of men and women are employed in the government munition factories or in industries subserving war purposes. A large proportion of the latter must be got back to employment of a different character within a year after the return of peace. Places must also be found for the millions of soldiers who will return to civil life.

In the meantime trade has been crippled and transportation disorganized, so that any attempt to resume business on a normal basis would result in chaos. The men returning from the trenches, as Lord Northcliffe remarks, will feel that they have deserved well of their country and will not be inclined to stand any nonsense from the governing classes. Many of them will have been infected with radical ideas regarding capital-

ism and the rights of labor. Clear-headed
statesmanship, therefore, will be needed to
avert disaster.

All these possibilities have been plainly
foreseen by Lord Northcliffe, and in his
practical manner of dealing with serious
problems he has urged that in time of war
preparations should be made for the readjustments of peace. Influenced by the
arguments of his newspapers, which had
repeatedly called attention to this important
subject, the British government was led to
appoint a Ministry of Reconstruction under
the direction of the Right Honorable Chris-
topher Addison, M.D. This board is now
working out an orderly and scientific system
of rehabilitation. Its principal object is to
prevent confusion and suffering when the
war has ended, by readjusting the army and
war machinery to peace conditions.

Dr. Addison, it may be added, is one of
the miracles wrought by the war. Ten years
ago he was professor of anatomy at University College, Sheffield. Entering Parliament, he sided with Lloyd George in the
great reform campaign which made the famous Welshman's career as Chancellor of

the Exchequer one continuous storm. At
that time Dr. Addison wrote the Health Insurance Act which was passed by Parliament. He showed such marked ability in
other directions that in 1915 he became one
of the co-workers with Lloyd George, who
was then Minister of Munitions. When his
associate ultimately became prime minister,
Dr. Addison succeeded him as head of the
munitions department.

Such have been the experiences of the
former doctor. It has been equaled only by
the career of Sir Auckland Geddes, brother
of Sir Eric Geddes, who was for several
years professor of anatomy at McGill
University, Montreal, and afterwards became Britain's minister for national service. With the same degree of skill that
he displayed as a professor of anatomy Dr.
Addison has taken up the gigantic task of
business reconstruction. At his office near
Queen Anne's Gate in London a visitor will
find the whole vast scheme of readjusting
finance, labor, and demobilizing men and industry mapped out on charts with every task
outlined, each department having a staff of
statisticians and expert investigators.

One of the first problems that will have to be dealt with by the government experts is the employment of a large proportion of the four million British soldiers who will be disbanded. According to present plans, men belonging to the essential industries will be rushed home immediately, regard being taken as to whether they are married or single. Soldiers whose places have been reserved for them will also return. There will be about one million of this class. Then the other classes will be gradually returned to civil life and set at work.

Here it is that a serious difficulty arises. It will be impossible for most of these workers to return to their former occupations. Thousands of private firms which were flourishing in 1914 exist to-day only as names or empty shells. Their staffs have been dispersed, their machinery exchanged, rebuilt, or modified, their buildings enlarged or taken over by the government. As the result of the government having embarked in the business of munition making on a gigantic scale, there are more than four thousand government-owned factories in Britain.

It has been proposed by various social-

istic writers that these factories shall remain
under government control and produce commodities urgently needed. The same plan,
it is urged, might be followed to some extent
with shipbuilding. Such an arrangement
would provide immediate employment for
disbanded soldiers and also for large numbers of workers now engaged in manufacturing war supplies. The war has done much
to increase British efficiency. Thousands of
hitherto untrained men are able to use lathe,
drill, and engine. An equally large number
of women have been trained in various
crafts. What more obvious course, it is
asked, than to keep the government plants
in operation, manufacturing such things as
standardized automobiles, railway equipment,
electrical supplies, and food products?

The government, it is argued, must continue as an employer on a vast scale, for if
the national factory system were suddenly
abandoned the risk of social convulsion would
be enormous. On the other hand, by keeping them in operation England would be
equipped with standardized and intensified
machinery capable of bringing about a new
era of trade supremacy.

When peace returns England will need labor-saving devices to an almost incredible extent if a new and scientific England is to arise out of the ruins of warfare. The arsenals that have made shells can make typewriters, adding machines, cash registers, and other time-savers, and they may possibly do so. In the production of raw materials, in industrial research, in the promotion of efficiency and the upbuilding of foreign trade, the men of the reconstruction ministry are determined that England shall take the lead.

Arrangements are being made for an all-British production of sugar, rubber, metals, chemicals, cereals, cotton, wool, jute, etc. Great Britain and her Allies, including the United States, control four fifths of the raw materials of the world. This important asset will be one of the strongest arguments in the readjustments of peace. To a great extent it will offset the bargaining value of the land the Germans have seized and ravaged. It also guarantees a new economic freedom.

Among other proposals for making over Britain is a scheme for supplying British factories with electric power from sixteen stations, and thus saving fifty-five million tons of coal yearly. This, in turn, would release a host of men employed in the mines and enable them to take up other work. It is realized that if England is to compete industrially with the rest of the world, she must have efficient tools, and more power is one of them.

In spite of the government's efforts to readjust after-war conditions, the British radicals are not satisfied and are clamoring for a complete sweeping away of the capitalistic system. These revolutionary ideas have permeated the working classes to some extent. They were much in evidence at a recent important labor meeting. On that occasion resolutions were presented, demanding the abolition of the wage system and a general conscription of wealth, one proposal being that all private funds amounting to over a thousand pounds should be seized.

While it is true that these resolutions were rejected, and that the leaders of the British Labor party have been moderate in their views, still this aspect of the situation is disquieting because in these unsettled times revolutionary doctrines are apt to spread. The Labor party, it may be added, has forty members in the House of Commons and is likely to get a still larger representation. Some English writers predict that before long the party will control Parliament, and once in control its power is not likely to be relinquished.

The British Labor party, it should be explained, consists of trade-unions, labor organizations of various kinds, and several socialistic groups. Membership is by groups, not by individuals. At the present time the party is in process of reconstruction to admit individuals and also to admit " brain workers." The " brain and hand movement," as it is termed, is intended to enroll professional men and other intellectual workers in the labor movement, and men of this class are entering the labor organizations in large numbers. With these acquisitions, it begins to look as if the British Labor party will soon be what the American Federation of Labor would be if it included practically all the labor organizations of the country and in addition the medical societies, law associations, engineering societies, and the Authors' League. In other words, the Labor party seeks to enroll all radicals and to form a new British party of democracy which will gain control of the government.

The Socialist groups of the British Labor party are extremists and ardent pacifists. They have expressed warm admiration for the Bolsheviki and the criminal fanatics who caused the collapse of Russia. Fortunately this section is far in the minority, numbering only some thousands, while the saner membership runs into millions. But whenever the party as a whole has a special grievance it seems to give the extremists the lead, and they lose no opportunity to indulge in revolutionary sentiments. It is quite probable, however, that as the result of the upheavals caused by the war a new democracy will emerge in England, recognizing no privileged class, not even a labor or even a male class.

Some idea of the aims of the Labor party can be gathered from its programme for reconstruction, which was recently drawn up by a sub-committee. It visualizes, as no American party platform hitherto constructed has done, the vital subjects of political and economic unrest which are gripping the world to-day. Some of the things

which this remarkable document contains are
not pertinent to the American political situation, but nevertheless it is worth the attention of everyone, not only because of its
clearness of expression, but also because
there is every prospect that in the near future
the Labor party will become the dominant
power in the British Parliament, and therefore in the government.

In this document the leaders of the party
have described, with remarkable warmth, the
struggles and sufferings of the laboring
classes in Great Britain. They outline the
failures and successes of the labor movement,
and point with remarkable penetration to
the future aspirations of the masses of mod-
erately circumstanced people in the United
Kingdom.

In the opinion of the Labor party, what
has to be reconstructed after the war is not
this or that government department, or this
or that piece of social machinery, but so far
as Britain is concerned, society itself. On
this point the statement is made: " We recognize in the present catastrophe in Europe
the culmination and collapse of a distinctive
industrial civilization which the workers will

not seek to reconstruct." Briefly summarized, the main points of the Labor party's ambitious programme are as follows:

Government responsibility for obtaining employment at a minimum wage, and government maintenance of " willing workers " for whom employment cannot be found.

The progressive elimination from the control of industry of the private capitalist; eventual common ownership of the means of production, including land, and immediate nationalization of mines, railroads, steamship lines, and the production of electric power.

Meeting of national expenses mainly by direct taxation of incomes and inheritances.

Devotion of surplus profits above the " standard of life " to the common use of the people.

Devolution of the British Empire into an alliance of autonomous States, with increasing self-government for India and other dependencies as rapidly as the peoples are fitted for it.

To carry out the general details of this programme would practically lead to the establishment of the Socialist State. The plan, however, does not contemplate the introduction of everything at once, and there is no evidence that anything but political action is to be employed to bring about these changes.

According to the present plans of the British Labor party, capital is to remain for the present, the wage system will also remain, and the new order is to be rooted in and based on the old order. The document shows, in a striking way, that the British labor movement, like our own, is evolutionary, and has little of the revolutionary spirit of the wage-earning classes of the European continent. British and American workers have a longer tradition of liberty behind them, are more sophisticated, and have analyzed more deeply and experimented more thoroughly. As a rule, they prefer a smooth transition to a new order along constitutional lines. Formula-loving continental proletarianism is more naïve, immature, and deductive than the more grown-up proletarianism of Great Britain and America, where capitalism directly rests on the public will.

But the British programme, rich in provisions to make capitalism declare greater dividends to workers, does not clearly show how the industrial product is to be increased sufficiently to meet new distribution demands. The leaders of the British Labor party are, of course, clear enough thinkers to recognize that goods can be divided only after their creation. Yet they have little to say on this essential phase of the industrial problem.

In the United States few of the advocates of class war are taken seriously, but there are undoubtedly many Americans who agree with the views of Charles M. Schwab, the head of the Bethlehem Steel Company, who is not likely to be suspected of Bolshevik sympathies. In discussing the modern labor movement recently, he said: "Call it Socialism, social revolution, Bolshevism, what you will, it is a leveling process, and means that the workman without property who labors with his hands is going to be the man who will dominate the world. It is going to be a great hardship to the owners of private property, but like all revolutions it will probably work for good."

It is a significant fact that apart from the declarations of the Labor party and the utterances of prominent radicals, the phrase " Conscription of wealth " has been much employed by British statesmen and econo-

mists in recent times. Although many people suppose the principle suggested to be
entirely new, the United States has a property tax, Germany, for military purposes,
levied heavily on capital just before the war,
and "conscription of wealth" is already
practiced in England through the higher
rate of income tax imposed on "unearned
income."

As a means of paying off Britain's gigantic war debt, "conscription of wealth" is
said to be favored, to some extent, by the
Chancellor of the Exchequer, Bonar Law,
and by Lloyd George, the prime minister.
Stated concisely, the argument is as follows:
The total wealth of the nation is estimated at
a hundred billion dollars; say the net amount
of the war debt is twenty billions; a tax of
twenty per cent on all property would pay
it; appraise everyone's estate just as if an
inheritance tax were levied against it; assess
it twenty per cent. As very few people
have one-fifth of their property in cash,
however, it has been proposed that the tax
should be levied in installments spread over
a number of years. It has also been proposed that small property owners should be

exempt from taxation, that fortunes of ten
thousand dollars should pay about five per
cent, while on larger amounts of capital the
rates should be proportionately increased.

These drastic plans for obtaining increased
revenue have been much opposed by British financial experts and others. Hartley
Withers, editor of the *Economist*, who is
regarded as one of the most brilliant stu-
dents of finance in England, has taken
this position. In a recent article he said:
"There is the very serious economic objection that taxation which is aimed at accumulated savings may have far-reaching effects
in checking the desire to save, on which the
nation's industrial progress depends. For it
is only out of savings that we can provide
the capital which is essential to the extension of industry and the full employment of
all the labor that will be set free when the
war is over."

With labor gaining in power, the attitude
of the British trade-unions is likely to cause
much concern when peace readjustments begin. To avoid trouble with the unions, the
British government induced capital and
labor to waive their differences temporarily.

There were to be no strikes or lockouts during the war. Penalties were prescribed for employers or laborers who broke the agreement. When peace returns these restrictions will be removed. Predictions are made that the unions will then put forth strenuous efforts to regain their former power.

During the war the ranks of skilled labor have been invaded by thousands of men and women unconnected with the unions, while large numbers of soldiers retired from the ranks have been set at work in various industries. The unions, it is asserted, will probably refuse to allow these newcomers to compete with union labor, and any opposition to union demands will precipitate strikes which may have serious results.

The subject of non-union workers has, however, been taken up by the Labor party, whose declaration in regard to the minimum wage reads as follows:

" In view of the fact that many millions of wage earners, notably women and the less-skilled workmen in various occupations, are unable by combination to obtain wages adequate for decent maintenance in health, the Labor party intends to see to it that the Trade Boards act is suitably amended

and made to apply to all industrial employments in
which any considerable number of those employed
obtain less than 30 shillings per week. This
minimum of not less than 30 shillings per week
(which will need revision according to the level of
prices) ought to be the very lowest statutory base
line for the least-skilled adult workers, men or
women, in any occupation in all parts of the United
Kingdom."

The spirit of discontent in the ranks of
union labor, which also exists among other
classes of workers, has caused much unrest.   It is significant that Lord Northcliffe's great daily, *The Times*, recently
treated this subject frankly in a series of
articles entitled "The Ferment of Revolution," which contained misty presages of evil
and declared that there is a rank and file
movement in British labor, with its subservi-
ence to the official hierarchy of trade-union-
ism, that deserves the watchful attention of
the public.   Sidney Webb, the well-known
English writer, asserts that industrial unrest
in England has become so acute as to create
a possibility of spontaneous industrial dis-
turbance.
    In a recent pastoral letter, Cardinal

Bourne, Archbishop of Westminster, dwelt upon the grave changes in English social conditions caused by the war. " During the war," he said, " the minds of the people have been profoundly altered. Dull acquiescence in social injustice has given way to active discontent. The very foundations of political and social life, of our economic system, of morals and religion, are being sharply scrutinized, and this not only by a few writers and speakers, but by a very large number of people in every class of life, especially among the workers. Our institutions, it is felt, must justify themselves at the bar of reason. They can no longer be taken for granted. The army, for instance, is not only fighting, it is also thinking.

" The munition workers, hard working, but overstrained by long hours and heavy work, alternately flattered and censured, subjected sometimes to irritating mismanagement and anxious about the future, tend to be resentful and suspicious of the public authorities and political leaders. They, too, are questioning the whole system of society."

Conservative Englishmen, unperturbed by these alarmist views, are convinced that when the war ends British national life will continue in much the same way as before. Men who are conversant with affairs, however, take an entirely different view. H. G. Wells, as already explained, insists that Britain is on the eve of a complete social change. The old capitalistic system, he declares, has gone forever, and it would be just as easy to restore the Carthaginian Empire as to put back British industrialism into the factories and farms of the pre-war era. "There is," he says, "a new economic Britain to-day, emergency made, flimsily built, no doubt, a gawky, weedy giant, but a giant who may fill out to such dimensions as the German national system has never attained. Behind it is an *idea,* a new idea, the idea of the nation as one great economic system working together, an idea which could not possibly have got into the sluggish, conservative British intelligence in half a century by any other means than the stark necessities of this war."

Mr. Wells has been called a dreamer and idealist, but strangely enough, one of the greatest financial authorities in the United States has taken practically the same view of the future. In writing on after-war conditions recently he said: " In the State of the future, particularly in Europe after the war, the most efficient government promotion of industries in many lines will be held to exist in actual government ownership and operation. More than ever before will States become solid industrial and financial unions organized for world competition, driven by the necessity of perfecting a system of the greatest efficiency, economy, and thrift in order to be able to meet the incredible burdens created by the war."

When all the confusion and wrangling of the reconstruction period have ended, England's prophets foresee the advent of improved conditions. Two evils of the capitalistic system, poverty and unemployment, are likely to be mitigated. The war has shown that under a system of government ownership every capable worker can be profitably employed. Under the old system men have been scrapped in the prime of life to make way for younger and cheaper workers, with the result that our large cities have been filled with efficient unemployed men whose services have been lost to the

community. During the war the number of
these victims of a wasteful and pernicious
system has been materially reduced. In
Britain the Labor party is determined to
make it possible for every willing worker to
earn a decent livelihood and to have no fear
of a poverty-stricken old age.

In the matter of profit sharing Lord
Northcliffe has set a notable example for
the world. In his opinion, even the large-
wage system of Henry Ford is not satisfactory. Employees, he believes, should
receive a percentage of the profits. "That
principle," he says, "must eventually be introduced in all businesses. When the men
get back from the trenches, that is the sort
of thing they are going to demand."

As the result of the labor movement there
has been a widespread demand in England
for improvement in the education of the
masses. At the present time the "board
schools" are much inferior to the American
public schools. They teach the working-class
child very little and make no effort to inspire
him to rise above his station. Class preju-
dices have been largely responsible for this,
but in the new order of things the depress-

ing influence of caste, which has been called "the curse of England," may possibly be modified.

Even the education of the higher classes is likely to undergo some important changes. In his recent work Mr. Wells predicts that in the future it will be modernized and made more practical. "Our boys," he says, "will be studying science in their colleges more thoroughly than they do now, and they will in many cases be learning Russian instead of Greek or German. More of them will be going into the public service as engineers, technical chemists, state agriculturists, and the like, instead of entering private business. The public service will be less a service of clerks and more a service of practical men."

Through his newspapers Lord Northcliffe has done much to arouse the British people to the importance of increasing their industrial efficiency by an improvement in technical education. He has also taken a foremost part in what is known as the "Back to the land" movement. Among other things he has advocated a system of intensive farming by small land holders. It is probable that some of these ideas will be put into practical effect. Thousands of men who have been drawn into the army from shops, factories, and offices, and have been hardened and stimulated by out-of-door life, will have no inclination to return to their former conditions. The government has been urged to acquire large tracts of farming land for settlers of this description, and to put up cottages and farm buildings for them. Such a plan, if carried out, would, it is argued, greatly increase the food supplies of the nation.

In talking with the men at the front, Lord Northcliffe found that the question of land nationalization formed a popular topic of their discussions. "The British soldier," he said, "has seen enough in France to know that a man and his family can manage a bit of land for themselves and live on it. A young sergeant told me that the men in the trenches discuss a great many subjects, and while there is the usual difference of opinion, there is one subject on which all are agreed, and that is the land question. They are not going back as laborers or tenants, but as owners. Most of them have used their eyes to good advantage. I wonder if the people and politicians in England understand that the bravery and camaraderie of officers and men in the field have broken down all class feeling, and that the millions of men abroad are changed communities of whose thoughts and aims little is known."

Among the subjects likely to receive attention when peace returns is the question of women's suffrage. That some system of votes for women will be introduced in Britain seems practically certain. A new type of woman is emerging from the war, and the demand for political rights and freedom from social restrictions will probably be more insistent than ever. It is also probable that one of its results will be some reform of the English laws of marriage and divorce, more particularly in the latter. A few years ago a parliamentary commission reported in favor of modernizing the present barbarous divorce law of England.

In his predictions of the future, H. G. Wells has expressed the belief that eventually marriage will be based upon compatibility, and therefore be more amenable to divorce than the old unions which were based upon the kitchen and nursery. Marriage, he says, will not only be lighter but more durable. " Women will be much more definitely independent of their sexual status, much less hampered in self-development, and much more nearly equal to men than has ever been known before in the whole history of mankind."

During the war many English industries formerly considered the exclusive province of men have been invaded by women. There is scarcely a point where, given a chance, women have not made good. As stated in the first chapter, hundreds of thousands of women and girls, when the war began, were turned out of such feminine trades as dressmaking, millinery, and confectionery, as well as the so-called luxury trades, such as jewelry. These women, with thousands of office workers and domestic workers, were drafted into the munition factories. The number of women included in the engineering trades alone has reached 800,000, many filling places formerly held by men.

The government also gathered in workers from the women's universities and higher schools, the suffrage societies and women's organizations. Women of superior intelligence from business and the professions were called upon to help in organizing the munition factories on a basis of health, safety, and efficiency.

Working together, the women in charge have performed a feat which has been described as an industrial revolution. They have set standards of humanity in factories which it would be criminal to lower. They have established an efficiency system such as England never dreamed of before, and they have created a working class which will never consent to be placed on a basis much lower than it now occupies.

Although women have proved their worth to the greatest extent in the munition plants and in farming work, the variety of other occupations in which they are usefully employed is enormous. They have served in the fire brigades, in the subways, on the street cars, in warehouses, on railroads, in banks, in the government service, behind the army, and in reconstruction work. In fact, it is difficult to mention an occupation in which they have not engaged.

It is realized that women are likely to continue in many of these employments after the war, although it is not easy to foresee what will result from their competition with men, or what the attitude of the trade-unions will be. Leaders of the women's movement assert, however, that owing to the losses of the war there will be fewer men to fill positions. There will be a greater necessity for women to work than there was before, because a smaller number of them will be able to marry. Thus for a generation at least they will be free to do a large amount of the world's work.

In discussing this subject recently, Lord Northcliffe observed that while throughout the English-speaking world the sheltering of women had been a matter of pride with men, and they had not cared to see women at work in the fields or engaging in other manual labor, there had been a great deal of self-deception about this matter. In most of the indoor and many of the outdoor occupations there were still wide fields of opportunity for women, although there was an objection to women entering employments for which they were not physically adapted. On the other hand, no self-respecting male should engage in occupations for which

women are peculiarly adapted, such as type-
writing, matching ribbons behind a counter,
or piano playing. That problem, however,
would probably settle itself, for large numbers of young men who have been hardened
in the trenches will have no desire to re-
enter gentle and essentially feminine pursuits in which they had formerly made their
living.

As his story has shown, Lord Northcliffe
was the first public man in Great Britain
to grasp the fact that modern warfare is
primarily a stupendous business undertaking, and that battles in these days are won
chiefly through organization and efficiency in
matters of transportation and supplies. He
took the lead in securing the abolition of
the time-honored administrative system and
replacing it with a compact war cabinet of
practical business men.

A business administration supplied Great
Britain with an excellent system of war
taxation. By a simple procedure, a tax of
eighty per cent is levied on the excess profits
of a business, which means, for example,
the amount by which 1917 earnings exceeded
the average earnings in pre-war years.

Carefully worked out and modified by experience, this system has proved thoroughly successful.

The new system of government has proved so satisfactory that a demand has arisen for the continuance of a business administration when peace returns. Those opposed to the idea assert that the term " business government," if analyzed, is meaningless; that an ordinary expert is an official without experience; that statesmen of the old school, trained in the science of government, are still needed to rule the destinies of the nation.

Conservatism is strong in England, and even Mr. Wells is not quite sure that the nation will at once take the right course by adopting state socialism. " There is," he says, " no spirit of coöperation between labor and the directing classes." It is also idle to ignore the forces still entrenched in the established church, in the universities and great schools, and the influence of class prejudice. He argues, however, that if masses of unemployed and unfed people are released clumsily into a world of risen prices and rising rents, of greedy speculators and hampered enterprises, there will be insurrection

and revolution, bloodshed in the streets and
chasing of rulers.

In devising means to avert these threatened social upheavals, and in helping to solve
the stupendous problems which will be presented when the war is over, it is certain
that Lord Northcliffe will be one of the
chief instruments. It is still true that the
man who knows, who can think, and who
can write holds a sword of Damocles over the
head of every politician. The older parties
in England may be disintegrated, new ones
may be formed, and many ideas once considered dangerously radical may be adopted.
History has shown, however, that the radical
ideas of one generation oftentimes become
the conservative ideas of the succeeding age,
and that which was considered radical was
radical only because it was new and untried.
Old party ideas are swept away, traditional
notions are dethroned, and the nation's leaders deal with facts.

In the great battle which is certain to be
fought between conservatism and radicalism
in Great Britain, with various factions inter-
posed, it is safe to predict that Lord Northcliffe will be found on whatever side repre-

sents progress, stability, and common sense. Although he believes in the cause of democracy and has opposed the retention of old ideas that have prevented advancement, he has been keen visioned enough to realize that a spurious brand of democracy has arisen in recent times which means simply the bludgeoning of the people by the people for the people. There is also a brand of socialism which aims to bring humanity to a dead level of mediocrity, and to crush out individuality as effectually as it has been crushed in Germany.

Such were the views expressed by Colonel George Harvey, editor of the *North American Review,* in the course of an eloquent address delivered at a gathering of the Pilgrims' Society, in New York, when Lord Northcliffe was the guest of honor. In hailing the distinguished Briton as a product of free institutions and a free social system, Colonel Harvey said: " History has proved that the only hope of the human race is in the development of able individuals. Withdraw ten thousand of the best minds of any country, and you would atrophy the nation to mediocrity. At the present time the whole future of the human race is in the balance. Great Britain stands upon the brink of economic heresy. Even America, the great republic, dedicated to promote the consciousness and liberty of the individual, has paused in her marvelous career under the pandering influences of political aspirants regardless of anything but their own selfish ends.

"For that reason Lord Northcliffe interests us as a living indicator of the fundamental truth whose recognition has made great every Anglo-Saxon people. It is the triumph of individualism, and the exemplification of the wisdom of conferring upon the maximum of capacity the maximum of reward. Lord Northcliffe is a Briton in every fiber of his being, but he has grown as an American grows. He inherited brains, and discovered how to use them in order to gain wealth, power, distinction, and honor at home and abroad. He has won by his own endeavors. Such a career as his could never have been possible in a state held in communal bondage."

This magnificent tribute to the great journalist, patriot, and public man forms an

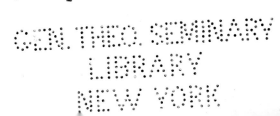

appropriate ending to the story of his rise from obscurity to eminence, his brilliant achievements, and his services for his country. The embodiment of manifold attainments, forcefulness, and real worth, Viscount Northcliffe assuredly represents the individualistic triumph of a man of genius. Providence apparently has ordained that whoever serves most shall reap most, a fact that has stood forth conspicuously in his career. Success in his case has come to mean service, a revelation of organized efficiency adapted to the national cause which, amidst the perplexities of war time, conveys to Americans an impressively significant lesson.

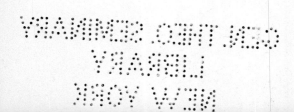